Women Awakened

Swati Chopra is a New Delhi-based writer. She is the author of a travelogue of the spirit, *Dharamsala Diaries*, and has written a modern introduction to Buddhism, *Buddhism: On the Path to Nirvana*. Her writing explores spirituality and its relevance to modern lives, and has appeared in several publications in India and abroad. www.swatichopra.com

Women Awakened

Stories of Contemporary Spirituality in India

Swati Chopra

HarperCollins *Publishers* India

First published in India by
HarperCollins *Publishers* in 2011

HarperCollins Publishers India, Cyber City, Building 10-A, Gurugram,
Haryana-122002, India
www.harpercollins.co.in

2 4 6 8 10 9 7 5 3

The publishers acknowledge the use of the photographs of Anandamayi Ma by fotokannan/Wikimedia Commons and Khandro Rinpoche by Birrell Walsh/Wikimedia Commons as used on the back cover.

ISBN: 978-93-5029-050-7

Typeset in Sabon 11/13.5
InoSoft Systems

Printed and bound at
MicroPrints India, New Delhi

This product is made of FSC®-certified and other controlled material.

HarperCollins Publishers, Macken House, 39/40 Mayor Street
Upper, Dublin 1, D01 C9W8, Ireland

For Amma, who inspired me to write, seek, question.

For Shakti, who walks with me on the path,
and from whom I learn every day.

Contents

Part Three: When Women Go Forth

Foreword

It was a memorable evening when Swati Chopra, a well-known writer on wisdom traditions, walked into my office and started talking about her new, yet to be published book, *Women Awakened: Stories of Contemporary Spirituality in India*. As we started talking, I was surprised to find myself asking her some of my own questions about this whole tradition of gurus and disciples that I have been lately questioning. Little did I know that Swati's own book was not far from my own quest and we were deliciously amused that unknowingly we had already started a discussion on it.

Swati has explored a relatively less researched subject, living women gurus and renunciates. An independent, spiritually awakened woman, breaking the bonds of matrimony and domesticity, is a revolt; it is the declaration of autonomy in a patriarchal society that regards women as subservient, duty bound to serve their husbands, children and extended families while being kept on the margins of religious instruction and sadhana, if allowed into that realm at all.

Extensive interviews, readings and conversations unfold the lives of several women—Anandamayi Ma, Nani Ma, Sadhvi Bhagwati, Mata Nirmala Devi, Mata Amritanandamayi, Sarada Ma and Pravrajika Vivekaprana, Jetsunma Tenzin Palmo and Khandro Rinpoche—and also raise questions about several of the assumptions made not only about them but also by them. At least two strands run through the lives of all: the universal mother love that they shower on all and the insistence that wisdom and enlightenment are gender neutral. Even the river Ganga, by which some of them live, is a mother, which flows soothing her children and purifying all their sins with her unconditional love.

However, it also means that these courageous women have to evolve strategies on how to transcend the patriarchal norms that form a part of the collective ashram or sangha life and places them in a secondary position to their male counterparts or deprives them of learning or relegates them to the very tasks from which they had escaped. It is fascinating to see how the prejudices of caste and foreignness too oppressively play themselves out in these so-called religious collectives that have to be overcome without overt confrontation.

Their lives are sagas of courage, determination and the subversion of patriarchal norms through the subordination of their egos, only to reach higher points of spiritual evolution than everyone else. It is to walk with pinpointed concentration on the razor's edge, cutting out all that appears irrelevant on the way to the aspired goal. But the journey is not without its many moments of bonding, love, humour and playfulness that relieve it of unmitigated arduousness.

Throughout the book, I heard echoes and could not but feel a sisterhood as I too go about negotiating my way in a man's world as do many other women in different spheres, however humdrum they may appear in comparison. The book is written in lyrical prose that mesmerizes. Swati's own love, compassion and understanding are to be found on every page as she makes her own journey together with them. What makes the book so valuable is Swati's honesty. She does not shy away from raising questions pertaining to the women's vulnerabilities, insecurities and even exploitation as they renounce everything to enter a world that demands unquestioning surrender, unswerving faith and absolute obedience.

Dr Kavita A. Sharma
Director, India International Centre
New Delhi

Introduction

Over the centuries, countless women have walked the inner paths of spiritual realization despite the thorns placed in their way by patriarchy, discrimination and unequal opportunities. Their journeys have been characterized by courage, determination, ingenuity and creativity. Where they couldn't get past the gender roles assigned to them, they found ways to lead spiritually rich lives under the skin of their worldly selves, amidst the babble of babies and bread, home and family. When they did manage to step outside the spaces designated for them by patriarchy, and found fulfilment as wanderers and mystics, as god-intoxicated, wise madwomen, they remained largely anonymous, their heroism unsung, in sharp contrast to their celebrated male counterparts.

This hiddenness, and the anonymity that stems from a 'second-class spiritual citizenship', persist till this day, at the dawn of the second decade of the twenty-first century when few male bastions remain untouched by feminine presence. At a time when women gurus have become far more visible than ever before, via new age media like television and the internet, there is still little understanding of a spirituality that could be qualitatively, even uniquely, feminine. For even when women gurus are written about and their voices heard, it is either in uncritical hagiographies or in discourses that tend to be gender-neutral and rarely address the issue of an empowered femininity. Because most spiritual paths lay such an emphasis on material and physical detachment, even 'dis-embodiment', that they tend to render the body, the personality attached to it, and consequently its gender, irrelevant, the possibility of a 'women's spirituality' rarely gets scrutinized or acknowledged.

In my view, while the aspirant might ultimately reach a stage that is beyond gender, it is worth exploring how gender impacts the experience of the spiritual path. For instance, a 'spiritual glass ceiling' comes into play every time women are denied certain teachings because they are women, are not given as free an access to knowledge, cannot touch or teach certain scriptures, are told they are inferior and cannot reach the acme of perfection (nirvana, moksha, kaivalya, in different traditions) in their current bodies. Also, women's emotionality and psychology might differ from men's and, accordingly, their needs, priorities and values, what is precious to them, might also be dissimilar. All these factors must be taken into account when we think about the process of negotiating the spiritual path as a woman. Because, simply, it may not be quite the same as it is for a man.

These are some of the ideas that form the core of this enquiry into contemporary feminine spirituality, which has taken the form of extensive interviews with women across the spectrum of spiritual traditions, lineages and hierarchies, and includes gurus and teachers, nuns and novices, lay practitioners and householders, movements led by women, for women. A lens kept purposely wide-angled captures women within wisdom traditions as well as free spirits who shake off any attempts at classifying them like they would pins and combs from their wild, unruly hair.

You might well ask—how did this book come into being?

As a spiritual seeker, and as a woman, I suppose *Women*

Awakened has much to do with my own quest and questions. In its making I have drawn extensively from the well of my experiences and observations, gathered and examined over the years, illumined in different degrees by various sources of knowing.

One of the key inspirers of this book is my mother. Not just because she is my mother, but because in her life I have had the chance to observe a 'woman awakened'. Her spiritual journey began when I was an early adolescent, and continues till today. In these two-odd decades, through sustained and diligent effort, she is a woman wonderfully transformed. A woman whose heart and mind and being are in balance. Who can let go of corrosive emotions and love almost without discrimination. A woman who is, quite simply, happy.

Watching her do this while balancing a career, single parenthood and the demands of living with ageing in-laws planted the thought—could there be a 'feminine spirituality'? A variant path that is unique to the business of being a woman, that fills the interstices of her day and plays out in her space which could, in equal parts, be messy, emotional, stressed, worldly-wise, practical, efficient, nurturing? Just as my mother worked her spiritual practice into the commas of her day—in between teaching high school history, lugging provisions home, cooking and cleaning, ministering to her family (which included a tumultuous teenager!)—and used the inevitable frustrations and irritations as opportunities to make theoretical knowledge practical, and function more mindfully, perhaps other women did too. Surely, this has been going on for a long time, perhaps ever since the first man opted out of home, work and family to pursue his inner call? The woman he left behind might have heard that call too. But there were babies to raise and feed, fields to tend, animals to rear. And so she practised through it all, her inner life deepening under the surface of her daily self, a phenomenon I have called 'iceberg seeking' in this book.

What has emerged from this quest to investigate the ground of feminine spirituality is a cluster of extraordinary experiences in women's voices that pertain directly to the mysterious and little-explored realm of spiritual adventuring. Their stories, which take place in real life and real time, as in they are contemporary to us, gleam with the fireflies of insights that came to them on the path, and which they hand to us as credible ways of understanding our selves, our identities, our place in the world. They are examples of the kind of liberation that is meaningful and enduring because it is based upon a profound, inner transformation. This understanding of liberation, as a fruit of spiritual endeavouring, is a radical addition to the aggregate of social, political, economic, cultural and linguistic freedoms that women's movements have sought, are still seeking, around the world.

In sharing their stories, in describing their lives, in articulating their choices, in alternating between the shadows and penumbrae of light that have splintered their lives, these women of spirit hold back little. In sewing these conversations together into a cloak of a book that will be beautiful and warm, inspire and heal, I have tried to retain the original flavour of the conversations as much as possible. So that the book reads like an intimate conversation in the inner courtyard, where women have taken off their veils and slipped into an idiom that is familiar and frank, honest and unhesitating, marked by a deep seeing that often delves into undercurrents and nuances to emerge with a jewel of fresh perspective. The writing is not tightly wound around individual subjects alone—it moves back and forth, and spirally, to weave a fabric that includes elements from folklore, ancestresses' herstory, literature and poetry, philosophy, gender politics, and many such assorted threads that add to the richness and colour of the narrative.

I must also mention here something about the process of sculpting this book into the form you hold in your hands. The women who are at the centre of each of the eight chapters are as much representative of an idea or issue as they are individuals with incredible stories to share. So if Mata Amritanandamayi and Nirmala Devi are emblematic of the phenomenon of woman gurus who came to be regarded as embodiments of the Great

Goddess, Devi, they are also women navigating their way through the thorny circumstances of caste and class, scorn and apathy, the burdens of familial expectations and universal adoration. If Nani Ma and Tenzin Palmo are renunciates who speak of the relevance of *sannyasa* and a woman's right to it, they are also women who have spent a lifetime on an odyssey as much physical as emotional, travelling out of the land of their birth, shepherded by charismatic gurus, into their present forms where they evince a diamond-like clarity that cuts each thought, word and action into perfect, exquisite shape.

A crucial factor that determined the inclusion of women in this book was their accessibility and willingness to be interviewed. Some voices that could have contributed much unfortunately could not be included because they were not available for interviews, or were located in places I found difficult to travel to. While email exchanges were useful in making initial contact and setting up visits and meetings, I was unwilling to use these as substitutes for one-on-one conversations where I had the chance to question, counter-question, and probe where necessary.

In the cases of Anandamayi Ma and Sarada Ma, who are central to contemporary feminine spirituality but are no longer 'in form', I spoke with close students and long-time followers. When it turned out that Mata Nirmala Devi was too indisposed to meet me at her home in Pune, I asked to be introduced to her husband, C.P. Srivastava, instead. Unprepared though I was, that conversation turned up a windfall, revealing unexpectedly the view from the 'other side', what it meant to be a 'universal mother's' spouse, to be seated at the left hand of the Goddess, so to speak.

When I initially began casting my net for ideas and subjects, I decided to be open to as many conversations as came my way. In all, I have spoken to more than double the number of women who eventually came to inhabit these pages, travelling to their homes and hermitages, meeting them in conferences and coffee shops, sharing their space and food, participating in their rituals and daily regimen, chatting with their children, co-seekers, their gurus. When I actually started writing, I realized the problem of plenty I had, and eventually needed to accept that not all could be accommodated within a single book. It was a decision difficult to make, and execute, to leave out some and include others, though I do believe that the ones who do not turn up as actual voices are present as whispers of wisdom that lingered in my mind and informed my writing. Absence, then, is certainly not non-presence.

Most of the women I interviewed generously gave of their time and energy in speaking about issues that required them to introspect, analyse, explain their positions and thoughts and, at times, grapple with ideas that were new and contrary to their own. On my part, because my motivation was to enable a frank exchange, as opposed to putting them in a spot and extricating information, I tried to conduct the conversations in a 'safe space'. I questioned respectfully and without scepticism. I certainly did not shirk from asking difficult questions, or criticize foibles where I found them obfuscating and obstructive to the spiritual process. Overall, I have chosen to focus on what would be of use to many in their spiritual quests, and what would help unravel the mystery of feminine seeking, rather than what would merely be enjoyable, or make for a good read. In this sense, I have hoped that this book might become a friend to my co-seekers on the path, one that takes them by the hand and walks with them a few steps, and perhaps shines a light on something that lay in the dark till a few moments ago.

The idea of the spiritual friend is a beloved and abiding one in spirituality, finding favour in traditions as diverse as the Sufi and the Buddhist. The Sufi Friend points out the path to the Beloved, to reach whom is the goal of spiritual endeavour, indeed of human life. And the Buddhist *kalyana mitra*, 'auspicious friend', encourages one to avoid what is harmful and practise what is wholesome. This book, and the women whose voices ensue from its pages, are friends of the spirit, sisters of our collective soul. If we are willing to listen, they will sing to us of possibilities and potentialities, of germinating seeds and budding shoots, of what we are and what we can become. Women *and* men will find something of value, heart-lessons shimmering in the heat of honest enquiry, discovered in the crucible of the awakened, aware self.

Come then, let's walk together awhile. Let's talk of the truth of this moment, in which we can... awaken.

My feet walk
with the Friend.
My hand
touches hers often
We talk
We smile
We float on
falling leaves,
and settle
on the red-brown earth.

Part One

By the Mother-River, I Heard...

1

Mystic, Mother

SRI ANANDAMAYI MA

Ganga is mother, goddess. She births, sustains, transforms. She is one and many. She is the majestic river that journeys from the Himalayas to the Bay of Bengal, and she echoes in the many tributaries that also carry her name.

She has nourished cities and civilizations into being, watched their decline, wandered across their remains, sown new seeds, revived old ones. In her womb are interred stories of old cultures, murmurs of lost tongues, silences of sages, an entire history of human effort. She hums a seamless song in which Vedic mantras composed beside her merge with the rustic ditties of boatmen who ferried generations across her expanse, with the lullabies village mothers sing to their babies along her course.

She cleanses bodies of dirt, hearts of their burdens, souls of their sins. She is a portal between worlds, a bridge that simultaneously connects and divides the divine and the mundane. By immersing oneself in her heaving waters, one could attempt to touch the edge of eternality.

She is sustainer of knowledges, weaving her way through time to bring the old to the new. She is ancient and contemporary;

she was then, she is now. Somewhat like the land she roams, on whose earth she deposits jewels from the past—ideas and icons, thoughts and texts—that challenge its lethargy and impel it to think these anew, in the context of today.

Custodian and witness, she has observed the narrative of humanity unfold in suffering and hope, chaos and order, life and death, in its eternal search for something more, something beyond. Those on the inner path of truth have often found themselves in her presence, walking her shores, setting up their *dhuni*, sacred fire, before her. They are drawn perhaps not just by her holiness or her legendary divinity; they see her as the guru-mother who will nurture them towards a wholeness of realization, who will guide them on through her relentless flow, her eternal song.

This is where I begin. Sitting by her side, at a place somewhere between her birth and merger, where she evaporates only to return as snow and rain, to begin her flow again, and again.

—

Everywhere in India, even far away from her physical presence, Ganga is mother. Along with the great epics—Ramayana, Mahabharata—and the way of life termed 'Hindu', her veneration could well be one of the largest signifiers of the shared cultural identity of this vastly varied subcontinent. As a child of this culture—a deracinated, casteless, questioning one though I may be—it is difficult for me to be wholly dispassionate about the Ganga. To even refer to her as 'the' Ganga, without honouring her goddesshood, her motherhood, her womanhood by affixing 'ji' or 'Ma' is oddly discomfiting, as if I have called out to my own mother by first name.

Even if we never go to her, never call out to her grace, Ganga Ma is omnipresent in our psyches, our lives, our collective consciousness. We may receive her purifying benediction sprinkled over our heads if we wander into a ritual, or get married the Vedic way. Many of us have vials of her in our homes, forgotten in little-used cupboards, where she will reside, year upon year, never putrefying, the very 'waterliness' of water, its pure essence. When we die, hers will be the last taste upon our lips, just before the first flame licks at our flesh. And finally, she will claim the last traces of our corporeal selves and whirl us away, towards who knows what?

Some of the most densely populated human settlements in the world are located along Ganga Ma's banks. Yet they never seem to overwhelm her rhythm, her mantra-inspiring flow. To the receptive mind, she can appear as a moving, flowing scripture. If you sit long enough by her side, you will find the insight of inherent change, the fluidity of reality, the is-ness of being, reflected in her current. She may inspire a purging of the restlessness of the conditioned mind, which becomes a still point in her constant flow.

So my journey into the heart of feminine seeking must begin with her blessings, in her presence. Because she *is* feminine, she is goddess, she is guru, and she is everywoman too. Ganga Ma is as defiled and wronged in her everyday journey as she is venerated. Like the women whose lives are wound around her flow, who walk the ground of today swathed in the repressive mores of yesteryears, even as their femininity continues to be worshipped as Devi, Maximum Goddess, the grandest divinity ever to be assigned to the feminine.

Over the centuries, many feminine wanderers and spiritual adventurers have found their way to Ganga Ma. Perhaps secure in their co-femininity and motherhood, eager to glean the truth from her unheard song?

—

A grey pall lingers over Hardwar on a winter morning, veiling the rosy fingers of the goddess of dawn. Two women sit on the stone steps leading into Ganga Ma, their shawls drawn tightly around them, occasionally peering into the mist that rises from the flowing waters. Their white saris slide off their heads now and then, affording a glimpse of grizzled, close-cropped hair, before their vigilant hands pull the errant edges back up again.

At first glance, the pair appears to be old friends, now widows together, who meet at the ghat once in a while to discuss recalcitrant daughters-in-law and other knotty problems. But if you part the mist you will see their fingers rotating prayer beads, their beings immersed in mantras. And if you wander within earshot, you might discern a whispered invocation, a breath-warmed call... 'Om Ma!'

The two come here often, to this little canal that carries Ganga Ma through Kankhal, a smaller, quieter limb appended to the bustling pilgrimage town of Hardwar. From their austere living quarters they walk down the lane that runs through the suburb's centre, their feet drawn instinctively along a route memorized over years of walking it. They prefer the early morning quiet when there are no honking jeeps or tourist buses jamming these ancient paths that are really meant for the bare, dusty feet of pilgrims.

Exhaling deeply, the older woman opens her eyes. The cold has begun to bother her of late, causing aches and pains to bloom in her joints and down her spine. Whenever her knees become too stiff, as they are now, she smiles and remembers her beloved Ma's instruction—this is *rog roopi bhagavan*, the Lord in the form of disease, take care of it as you would any aspect of the divine. Practise where you are, right here, sickness and all. And you will be transformed.

She folds her hands, her breath rising and falling to the rhythm of the Ganga that flows before her.

Her companion, younger by a couple of decades, rolls a plump sandalwood bead between her fingers, feels its fragrant smoothness before dropping it and pulling in the next, its identical twin. Her mantra, given by Ma when initiating her into a life of renunciation, is never far from her attention. It turns up on its own, wound around the rosary of her inbreath–outbreath whenever there is a blank space in her day, whenever the mind is at rest. Lately, it has even happened during chores, while cooking, washing clothes. Is she *becoming* the mantra, dissolving into it, as Ma said she would if she could only practise it with her entire being?

Okay, you might say. They are not two old gossips but *sadhvis* of some sort. But aren't there many of them in Hardwar?

Yes, there are. But these two, they are special, even unique. Because they were among a small group that lived with Sri Anandamayi Ma, the great twentieth-century master, mystic, sage, seer, some of them from childhood, and were her constant companions, who cooked, cleaned, studied and sported with her, and for whom she was guru, mother, friend, everything.

There may be nothing visibly girlish about them any more, yet they are still 'Ma's girls', their lives shaped by her powerful influence, living reminders of the revolution she wrought in legitimizing women's presence in a domain from which they had by and large been excluded—that of spiritual adventurism. Ma's appearance on the horizon, radiant as a rising sun that couldn't be ignored, signalled the end of a long night of slumber and seclusion for women and created conditions for them to join the mainstream of spiritual seeking. Which is why I turn to her first, to pick up the thread of contemporary women in spirituality. Even though she passed away in 1981, I hope to be able to glimpse her being, feel my way into her area of influence, through her 'girls'. Who are, at this instant, sitting on the banks of the other great mother in their lives, Ganga Ma, contemplating her omnipresent flow.

In the first decade of the twentieth century, in a small town in unpartitioned Bengal, a young man returns home from work. His young wife fixes him dinner, and when he's finished, brings him a hookah to puff on while he relaxes. Then she lights some incense, sits on the floor and begins chanting a sacred syllable. She is soon absorbed in deep meditation.

Gradually, her breathing slows down and seems to come to a standstill. Her eyes become transfixed at a point in the centre of her forehead. Her limbs loosen and at times spontaneously flow into intricate gestures and movements. Her husband watches in awe, unable to comprehend this change in his wife who sits before him in *samadhi*, mind stilled and consciousness withdrawn.

And so the night passes, as does another, and another...

She who would come to be known as Sri Anandamayi Ma was born Nirmala Sundari, 'pure beauty', in 1896 in Kheora, a small village now in Bangladesh. Her life constantly travelled upriver, in a sense. Her birth placed her at the end of Ganga Ma's earthly sojourn, where she releases her identity into an oceanic bosom. Anandamayi's wandering as a spiritual nomad took her by turn to the ancient city of inner illumination, Varanasi, where the Ganga is a middle-aged matron, wide of waist and heart, and then to Kankhal, where she is younger, just about blossoming into a lively, giggling adolescent. It was here, close to the site of Ganga Ma's birth, that Anandamayi dissolved her own self into the ocean of life. In life and in death, river and mystic were profoundly entwined, each the chronicler of the other, each the keeper of the other's faith. For Anandamayi found a facility for connecting with the Ganga Ma's sacred essence, and would establish two of her beloved ashrams on her banks, in Kankhal and in Varanasi, which would perform vanguard service under her guidance towards the temporal and spiritual education of women.

Nirmala's own schooling was minimal, her childhood unremarkable except for the extraordinary religiosity of her parents. In keeping with the convention among Brahmins at the time, she was married at the age of thirteen to Ramani Mohan Chakravarty, though it would be a few years before she would go to live with him.

Nirmala was born in interesting times. Change was in the air. The decades following the failed attempt to wrest independence from foreign rule in 1857 saw the gradual emergence of a national consciousness in the Indian subcontinent. For the first time in her ancient history, India was beginning to think of herself as one nation, one that was destined to be much more than a slave colony servicing overseas masters. An idea of India had begun to crystallize that would soon envision her as a modern democracy, governed by her own people, ready to take her rightful place at the global high table.

The period until 1947, when India would begin her journey as a modern nation, and after, saw not only a struggle against external domination but an equally important one with her inborn social and religious conflicts, feudal repression and cruel inequalities that had shackled her people far longer than any foreign ruler ever did. There could be no political movement without a corresponding social and spiritual one, which rooted out old prejudices and turbid traditions and replaced them with a healing, humane and humanistic spirituality. Mahatma Gandhi, the leading voice of the freedom movement and also its conscience, was to insist on inner change and introspection as being crucial to the task of building an 'India free from exploitation from within and without'.

The Mahatma, and indeed most national and grassroots leaders of this period, advocated social reform as a necessary prerequisite for the foundation of modern India. And there was much to reform. The heinousness of untouchability, the oppression built into the caste hierarchy, the emotional Hindu–Muslim divide, the inequalities within the feudal economy, the physical, intellectual and social confinement of women and their lack of freedom to explore their potential, were only some of the issues that required attention.

At the outset, these may not seem to be 'spiritual' issues. In essence they were, and are, so. The sacred and the mundane have for long been intertwined in the subcontinent's social, religious, economic and political life, knotted together in the all-encompassing tapestry of dharma—natural law, cosmic order, 'that which is established'. The interpretations of dharma are so numerous and varied that they have bred and allowed to coexist such obvious contradictions as lofty notions of universal oneness on the one hand and the pernicious prejudices of casteism, a complex doctrine of difference, on the other.

Such paradoxes may be seen as an inevitable result of the movement of time, which led to the birth and proliferation of so many disparate, and at times exploitative, interpretations of what started out as a way of making sense of the world. With each bend in the river of time, as rulers and socio-religious law-givers added their patina to dharma, proponents of Brahmanical exclusivity added theirs. And from time to time, spiritual stalwarts, of which there arose many, if one takes into account the entire swell of history, attempted to scrape off all patinas, divest dharma of unnecessary accoutrements, wash away the gloss and goop, and understand it afresh.

In this sense, the first half of the twentieth century witnessed an attempt to revitalize dharma in accordance with the need of the time, last seen on a similar scale during the Bhakti and Sufi movements of the middle ages. This new spiritual impulse expressed itself through the compelling example of Mahatma Gandhi—his very title a reference to the spiritual and moral force his thinking carried for the people of India; his emphasis on ethics, truth, pure motivation and righteousness reminiscent of ancient core dharmic values.

During this time, in close chronological proximity, there emerged several men and women who powered modern India's spiritual renaissance. With the perspective of history one can look at their individual efforts as part of a collective movement, a pan-Indian blossoming of wisdom that paralleled the movement for political–social–economic freedom and attempted to nourish the spirit of India to a robustness that was vital for the journey she was setting out on as a modern nation.

If we consider roughly a span of a hundred years, from the mid-nineteenth to the latter half of the twentieth century, we come upon Sri Ramakrishna Paramahansa and Sarada Devi, Ramana Maharshi, Sri Aurobindo and the Mother, Swami Vivekananda, Jiddu Krishnamurti and Paramahansa Yogananda, among many others. Anandamayi Ma is a crucial link in this golden chain—she enabled a resurgence of the dharma that crucially widened its scope, steering it away from bland ritualism and blind faith towards a dynamic, experiential and transformative spirituality. She modified convention, demolished rigid boundaries and stereotypes and brought those whom it had traditionally barred within its ambit. All this she achieved not by doing so much as *being*. By embodying and becoming the change, she subtly and irrevocably altered the socio-spiritual landscape of a nascent modern India.

From a simple village girl prone to strange silences to a beautiful young bride who would slip into trances, glossolalia and yogic sadhana, the radiant, bliss-imbued mother, Anandamayi, emerged from the cocoon of the housewife Nirmala Sundari.

The story of Nirmala's transformation is as fascinating as it is inspiring. Fascinating because it provides a glimpse into the path and process of spiritual realization, the rigours of sadhana that accompany it, and their effect on the psycho-spiritual being at various levels. And inspiring because Nirmala, a 'regular' woman—a daughter, daughter-in-law, wife and later widow—could, through the force of her practice, moult into a realized being, a universal mother, an ideal guru for her times.

Gossip about the young bride who sat in samadhi all day reached her family. Her uncle arrived to investigate matters. 'What is going on here?' he demanded, as Nirmala sat in one-pointed concentration. 'She is not initiated into sadhana. Why don't you do something?' He turned to her husband in exasperation.

Suddenly, the young woman's manner changed. Her eyes alight with an inner fire, her being suffused with a surge of energy, she looked up and demanded, 'What do you mean by that?' Her uncle was taken aback. 'Who are you?' he managed to blurt out, possibly thinking that his docile niece had been possessed by an evil spirit.

'Purna Brahma Narayani,' she responded. Absolute Unconditioned Being.

Her husband, who had humoured his wife's yogic efforts as some sort of exalted religiosity, was stunned. 'Who are you?' he repeated. 'Mahadevi,' she responded with the same sureness. The Great Goddess.

'Who are you?' was a question Anandamayi would be asked throughout her life. Anyone who came in contact with her could not but experience her innate bliss, her unwavering stillness, her wide-as-the-world state of being. In this, she was a living example of the unconditioned oneness described in Advaita Vedanta, the school of philosophy that advocates complete non-duality as the state of supreme realization, in which Anandamayi's experiences and teachings were rooted. Even so, many were eager to place her on a pedestal, to ascribe to her an inherent divinity, rather than allow for the possibility of attainment as a result of rigorous self-effort and practice.

Placing extraordinary achievements on a pedestal is easy, emulating them much more difficult. Hence the predilection towards divinizing, which effectively removes the achiever from the realm of the human, and therefore the possible. We would rather worship than follow. In thinking of Anandamayi as divine and godly, a psychological distance is created between the perfect, represented by her, and everybody else who could perhaps hope for her grace but that was all. They couldn't *become* like her because she was special, born already enlightened, an avatar.

People came to her for guidance, teachings, solace. Some came simply for her darshan, to seek her blessings, request her benediction. Others came to observe her as they would a phenomenon of nature, like a volcanic eruption or a trailblazing meteor. Regardless of their motivation, each visitor carried this question in his or her heart: 'Who are you?'

Once a journalist from Ireland asked her, 'Am I right to believe you are God?' She answered, 'There is nothing save He alone;

everyone and everything is but a form of God. In your person also He has come here to give darshan.' The journalist persisted, 'Why are you in this world?' She responded, 'I am not anywhere. I am myself reposing within myself.'

—

So, who was Ma?

I place this question before Ma's girls at the mist-drenched ghat by Ganga Ma, the river whose sacred essence drew Anandamayi during her travels through India. Ashrams came up on spots along the banks of the mother-river where she felt a special benediction.

'I never tried to think, who is she? I lost my mother in childhood. Ma took my mother's place. I came to the ashram only so I could call somebody "Ma". And Ma loved me like a mother loves her child. That was my relationship with her. I don't know the higher stages.'

Vishuddha's eyes glisten as she remembers how she 'came' to Ma at age twelve. A memory floats up and her tears, and years, dissolve into a mass of giggles. 'You know, when I was young, around four or five years old, I thought Ma was made of butter! She was so soft and delicate. I used to look at her and she would smile at me. I never went to have a private talk with her. I never asked her anything. I thought, she knows everything, what can I ask?'

As she grew up, her relationship with Ma continued in the mother–child paradigm. 'Once Ma had a headache,' says Vishuddha. 'I peeped into the room where she was resting and thought, when we do something wrong it hurts Ma. She looked at me and said, "When a child is held in her mother's bosom, she sometimes hurts the mother by kicking her breasts. Does the mother take offence?" She was like a mother to everybody, not just me.'

Indeed, Anandamayi *was* Ma to everybody who came to her. A statuesque young woman, honey-complexioned, almond-eyed and wild-haired, as she appears in her earliest photographs, she conveys no undercurrent of sensuality, no hint of sexuality. Even in her mid-twenties, when some of these photographs were taken, she was mother to all, and her beauty, warmth and blissfulness evoke the goddess in the sanctum, who one can relate to as a mother, not as a sexual counterpart.

Her role as spiritual mother mirrors that of many other women gurus, guides and teachers who have come to be regarded as birth-givers and nurturers of their followers' spiritual lives, their refuge in trying times, strict in matters of inner discipline and practice, healing wounded psyches with care and comforting companionship. Anandamayi formed such a relationship with her spiritual children, often quieting the tumult of an anxious, insecure mind with a simple maternal entreaty: 'Ma is here. Why do you worry?'

Vishuddha waves her arm, taking the ghat, the road beyond, the temples, everything in its sweep. 'These days there are so many ashrams, so many gurus, you can see there are so many in Hardwar alone, that I think even the government doesn't know how many there are! In this jungle of gurus, we are so lucky to have come to Ma. Oh, I suppose everybody thinks my guru is the highest.'

Vishuddha realizes she is veering from the topic. She clears her throat and continues, 'Well, once a learned scholar of the Bhagavad came from Vrindavan, and he was asked, "We cannot fully comprehend Ma. We only see her outer body. But who is Ma? We want to know. She is not normal like you and me." That mahatma said, "You and I, we are climbing a hill. We cannot see who is on the other side. We can just see our own path. Ma is at the peak of that hill from where she is observing everybody." That is a good way of describing her.'

The question feels unanswered, lost in a devotee's sense of her guru's brilliance. It is not surprising, for Anandamayi inspired a great awe in those around her. I wonder if it was like being too close to the sun, its radiance making it impossible to see it in its entirety. Perhaps one does need to draw back a little, look from the vantage point afforded by the passing of time, to discern the truth about something, or somebody.

The mist thickens around the two women, challenging them to respond with as much clarity as Anandamayi herself would have brought to the query.

Aruna, who came to Ma after finishing college, echoes the idea of Anandamayi as universal mother. 'Bengal is basically Shakta. They are worshippers of Shakti (the dynamic, feminine aspect of divinity). The call of every Bengali is for Ma. There are so many saints who have worshipped the divine in the form of Ma. I feel it was a heartfelt cry of Bengal. That is why she came in this particular form. Ma said she reacted to the different *bhava,* emotions, of people. She would say that the action is a reaction to the bhava of each individual; *jaisa bhava waisa labh*. So if she has come in the form of a mother, it is because the call of the devotees has been for a mother.'

Rather like the Mahayana Buddhist ideal of the *bodhisattva*, who chooses to be born in response to the call of suffering sentient beings?

One of the first to accept Anandamayi as his guru was Jyotish Chandra Ray, a high-ranking government official in Bengal, fondly referred to among her devotees as Bhaiji. It was he who, upon experiencing Nirmala's state of profound bliss, exclaimed, 'We will call Ma "Anandamayi"!'

He too asked her the same question: 'Who are you?'

What Anandamayi said in response is reminiscent of the bodhisattva's vow of compassionate embodiment: 'This body is present in whatever form the devotees would like to see. Why don't you think that this body is the outcome of your prayers? You people wanted and got this body. Only this much knowledge is essential...'

Finally, to one particular questioner, Anandamayi gave her most comprehensive answer. 'I am conditioned as well as unconditioned; I am neither infinite nor confined within limits; I am both at the same time.'

From these instances it seems that Anandamayi would try and use the questioner's curiosity about her as an opportunity to turn his or her awareness inwards—to a direct experience of cosmic oneness, or unconditioned being, or perhaps the possibility of the bodhisattva in all of us.

Ramana Maharshi's key self-question—'Who am I?'—that could take the questioner to the heart of the mystery of the non-dual, non-self, perception of reality, was inverted in the case of Anandamayi. The seeker would ask her—'Who are you?'—and through her response, she pointed to the moon, the core truth. As in Ramana's case, here too the question and its response held the possibility of insight. But only if the seeker was able to actually look at the moon—reality as undifferentiated, unconditioned, whole and integrated, as Anandamayi herself experienced it—and not become mesmerized by the finger, the form, that pointed towards it.

—

When she was twenty-six-years old, in 1922, Nirmala underwent what has been described as a 'self-initiation' into spiritual life. It seemed inconsequential to her that she was a woman, not traditionally accepted into *sannyas*, and a married Brahmin woman at that, for whom the rules and taboos were even stricter. Her understanding of the nature of reality did not recognize any kind of duality. She had outgrown this *duniya*, the Hindi word for the world which she played upon to reveal another meaning—*du-niya*, 'that which is two'—a fragmented worldview. If everything was one, and if everything was The One, how could she honestly accept or validate any difference, whether of gender or caste or religion?

As in her self-sadhana, Nirmala pre-empted possible collision with prevailing gender prejudices by performing her own initiation. The guidance came from within. She was both guru and *shishya*, the initiator and the initiated. Four full moons later, she initiated her husband, whom she fondly called Bholanath, and gave him his first spiritual instruction. She became his guru, at the same time maintaining their relationship as a married couple.

If we examine Anandamayi's life, we find a strange, almost paradoxical penchant for inner transcendence and outer conformism. Throughout her life, she retained great personal freedom to follow her inner guide (or *kheyal*, as she referred to it, literally meaning 'thought'), even taking off in the middle of the night to board a train if she felt she needed to be somewhere urgently. And yet, to all outward appearances, she was an obedient housewife for the duration of her married life, deferring to her husband in all matters, seeking his permission even to speak.

It would seem that every spiritual teacher and practitioner must operate in the social context in which she lives, as did Anandamayi. She was a pathfinder who, in her relentless quest for truth, chose to circumvent obstacles instead of taking them head on; who found ways of going around rather than crashing into, of moulding and reshaping rather than breaking and destroying. It is a quality that to me is essentially feminine, to flow like water into crevices of seemingly insurmountable impediments, like Ganga Ma who gently but firmly makes her way from mountains to plains, through rock and stone, coaxing and cajoling change instead of forcing it through aggressive posturing and violent insistence.

In reality, Anandamayi was free. In practice, she followed convention. Perhaps it would be more accurate to say that she followed convention as much as possible, discarding it when she felt it to be unnecessary or when it interfered with the direction of her sadhana or teaching or going to the aid of anyone who needed her.

Vishuddha explains, 'Ma was very keen to observe traditional rules. At the same time, out of affection and love, she could change everything.' She recounts an incident when Ma went to a hospital in Mumbai to visit Gopinath Kaviraj, an eminent scholar with whom she often discussed matters of philosophy, metaphysics and theology. As she rose to leave, her attention was drawn to cries of pain. She found a patient in distress, a Muslim man who was suffering from leprosy, and she ministered to his needs, soothing him with her words and touch. Her companions, seized by the fear of contamination that for centuries has led to the inhuman segregation of people with leprosy, entreated her to bathe immediately and discard the clothes she was wearing. Perhaps there was another layer to this fear, of having become 'unclean' by touching somebody who was outside the caste system which was, for all practical purposes, followed quite rigidly among Anandamayi's devotees and in her ashrams.

Anandamayi did nothing to cleanse herself. 'As a mother, she didn't think it was necessary,' says Vishuddha. 'Though she was very strict about observing ritual purity in the temple or while fasting and so on, when it came to serving her children, she didn't think it was necessary to bathe or change because of contact with them.'

The caste system's repressive nature, its exclusivist interpretation of truth and reality, its ability to thwart human hope and imagination, its breeding of a trans-generational hopelessness among a large section of society, ensured that every social, political or spiritual mass movement in the subcontinent had to address it and find ways of either reforming it or rooting it out completely. Since the Buddha and Mahavira denounced caste as meaningless and of no consequence on the spiritual path in the sixth century BCE, successive 'transformers' and reformers have attempted to erase its particular conditioning, which is deeply entrenched in the Indian mind.

One can ask, then, why Anandamayi shirked this question. For her, personally, there was no other. There was no differentiation of any sort, even the most basic ones of 'I' and 'you', 'mine' and 'yours'. And as we see in the incident recounted by Vishuddha, Anandamayi was supremely unconcerned about caste purity when it came to performing an act of *seva* for one in need. Yet she never took a stand against it, always choosing to defer to its diktats, allowing her followers to practise segregation in her ashrams on the basis of caste. Why did she never point out that this might be detrimental to spiritual progress, that it was antithetical to the very experience of supreme oneness that they sought?

Once more, I am reminded of the feminine fluidity of the Ganga as she subdues barriers with gentle, insistent friction. Anandamayi too subverted and bypassed caste but was non-confrontational about it. She deferred to social diktats and simultaneously found a way of rendering them irrelevant by actually co-opting them into the cache of tools she used to shape her students' spiritual lives. For instance, Atmananda, an Austrian woman who spent several years with Anandamayi, and whose account of spiritual discipleship was published posthumously in the book *Death Must Die*, recounts the horrendous caste-based discrimination she faced as a Western woman in what was, for all purposes, a strict Hindu ashram. Each time she is not allowed to eat with the others or is forbidden from touching anything, Atmananda feels the sting of humiliation. She tells Ma of her suffering on this account; Ma comforts her but also makes it clear that things will remain as they are. It is she, Atmananda, who must change. She must use this opportunity and allow her ego-self to be worn down, reaching a state of equilibrium unaffected by what happens to her or around her.

Over the years, Atmananda does develop an inner stability and comes to appreciate the way Ma has used seemingly negative circumstances to help her let go of her emotional reactivity and craving for material comfort. It is not just caste-based discrimination that she has to get used to in her life with Ma, there is also physical discomfort, noise when she needs silence and, for the longest time, an insecurity regarding money that prevents her from completely embracing a life of renunciation.

By refusing to cater to her ego-self's demands, by taking away its sustenance, Ma enables a gradual erosion of the constructs of personality that keep one away from one's true nature.

This provides a glimpse into the way Anandamayi worked, using her ashram as a laboratory, constantly turning circumstances in her disciples' lives into opportunities for learning and practice. Clearly, her way was not the reformer's or the activist's, nor was it the Buddha's or Mahavira's, who combined social action with inner transformation.

Reading Atmananda's book, which is an excellent day-to-day account of the spiritual quest, I wonder if it is possible for a seeker to find a balance between the work of eradicating the ego and one's sense of fairness and justice. A balance which is jolted each time one is at the receiving end of injustice, or when one witnesses somebody else being discriminated against. How does one live by the dharma in a world that is blatantly unjust, and not even try to change it? Is it possible for a seeker to turn away from injustice, believing that the discomfort and hurt one feels is just a figment of the ego one is attempting to erase in any case?

Some sense of self might actually be necessary to negotiate our path in samsara, acting as a membrane between the inner and the outer. Perhaps the work of the seeker is to keep this membrane moist and flexible, and sufficiently porous to allow for dynamism and openness in one's responses to the world. If it ossifies and hardens, it loses its sensitivity to the interconnections that form the context of our lives. The membrane of the self, as opposed to the hardened shell of the ego-personality, is what will protect us from the vagaries of samsara while allowing us to respond to its call upon our conscience, which forms an integral part of our being and cannot be wiped away in the interest of 'ego-effacing'.

To me, Anandamayi's approach seems to have been to encourage people to change from within, to help them sweep away layers of ignorance and misperception, and move towards an unconditioned awareness of everything. One can say that she was completely involved in and committed to positive change; only, her theatre of action was the mind, the very ground of being. And, as we see in her own case, once *that* was transformed, everything else—points of view, attitudes, stances—changed automatically. When change occurs within, it cannot help but influence every aspect of one's being. If one inwardly comprehends the profound truth of oneness, how can one continue to discriminate at any level?

As Anandamayi has said, 'If after coming down from the state of contemplation you are capable of behaving as before, you have not been transformed.' Those who came to her, who followed her instructions, who walked the path shown by her, certainly were transformed, the level and intensity of their transformation determined by the degree of their own effort and perseverance.

In Anandamayi, India's ancient dharma encountered a woman who was comfortable with her femininity, who often disregarded its ritual taboos, who had never studied its scriptures, who followed no particular lineage or guru but claimed 'self-initiation', who went beyond punditry and towards an inner engagement, and who became its leading light through the undeniable nature of her personal attainment.

You could say she made history, reformed and re-formed contemporary Hinduism, and orchestrated a renaissance of its best practices while ignoring its worst.

In 1928, for the first time at a public forum, Anandamayi faced a barrage of questions from erudite pandits, scholars, philosophers and teachers of the dharma. The fact that it took place in Varanasi, the heart of sacred India, made the event especially significant.

It was a moment of truth for the establishment, so to speak, for the top brass of established Hinduism. A barely literate village woman stood in an open assembly and responded to queries on the finer points of philosophy, metaphysics and theology. She wasn't thrown by their clever metaphors and scholarly Sanskrit. Her slender back erect, her being ablaze with irrefutable truth, Anandamayi spoke with an incisive clarity that came from a sense of knowing, an incandescence that was not reflected or borrowed light but came directly from the source.

She wasn't parroting the scriptures, she was expressing their innate essence.

That day, Anandamayi picked up where Gargi had left off. That Vedic woman seer, luminously articulate and possessed of a sharp intelligence and an even sharper tongue, had been silenced by the proud sage Yajnavalkya in a debate of epic proportions. When he could no longer stand the swift onslaught of her queries regarding the nature of the created world and its core reality, Brahman, Yajnavalkya snapped at her, 'Do not question too much, Gargi, lest your head fall off.' And it is recorded that Gargi 'held her peace'.

It would seem that all women fell silent from that moment, and by and large 'held their peace' in matters of philosophy and interpretations of dharma over successive centuries (barring a few exceptions), until Anandamayi arrived in the pandits' assembly and called off the truce.

It was time for women to find their spiritual voices again.

Anandamayi established a school for women, now known as the Shree Shree Anandamayee Kanyapeeth, in Varanasi, where girls are educated in both worldly and sacred knowledge, a modern education is imparted along with an ancient one. It was a time of social churning and women's emancipation was being called for, through education and the ending of regressive and cruel practices such as *sati* and child marriage. Anandamayi extended the process of empowerment to the spiritual domain and, through her own life and that of her 'girls', was able to present a credible role model to women for an alternative way of life and liberation.

The going wasn't always smooth. To demonstrate the equality of genders, and to instil confidence among her girls, Anandamayi decided that they should be able to wear the *janeu* (a sacred thread worn as a rite of passage into adulthood), traditionally only given to post-pubescent, 'upper-caste' boys.

Aruna recounts the brouhaha that ensued. 'There was a lot of opposition. Ma told the pandits of Varanasi to look through their scriptures and let her know where this (that women couldn't wear the sacred thread) had been mentioned. For when she was undergoing her sadhana, Ma experienced a stage where there was no bar to women wearing the janeu. So she knew it must be in the scriptures otherwise this wouldn't have taken place in her. The pandits did check the scriptures and actually found mention of women, both married and unmarried, who had taken the janeu. So Ma revived the tradition.'

Another tradition Anandamayi revived for women was that of receiving *deeksha*, formal ordination into sannyas. Despite the presence of spiritually adept women through the ages, the tradition of formally inducting them into a life of renunciation had been lost. Because a *sannyasin's* life is essentially one of wandering, of living outside society and its norms, it was not an option readily available to women, who were expected to nurture the home and family and desist from doing anything that would disturb the social order. Moreover, because there were no orders or communities for initiated women among the Hindu wisdom traditions (as there were for Buddhist and Jain nuns), women also faced practical issues related to personal safety, sustenance and access to guidance and teaching. Anandamayi organized such a community for women and encouraged them to enter the sannyasin's life, using her own experience of self-initiation as a guide. And perhaps she did it more willingly, and gracefully, than the delayed and reluctant acceptance of women into his *sangha* (community of seekers) by the Buddha. One of the first women to be formally ordained among Anandamayi's followers was her own mother, fondly called 'Didima' by all, who had gradually veered towards her daughter's path.

If we were to examine Anandamayi as a feminist icon, which could be one interesting way of calibrating her impact, she'd fare rather badly by the currently popular yardsticks. She never rebelled in an outright, aggressive way and she conformed to established gender roles, yet she exerted a curious, alchemical influence such that these too were transformed. She attempted to change and subvert, rather than break or destroy. As far as her 'worldly' relationships were concerned, she did not get out of them or leave them behind. Rather, she integrated them into her spiritual life, fusing them into her path as mystic and teacher. In this, she marks a departure from the time-honoured convention of spiritual seeking, where the one (usually a man) who was seized of an existential longing would take off, forcing a break from all existing relationships and familial responsibilities.

Anandamayi brought her relationships along with her when she embarked upon her quest. For instance, both her parents became her followers, her father calling her 'Ma' as he lay on his deathbed. Something similar happened with her husband, though that seems far more remarkable, if only because of the drama that seems inbuilt in marriage and the gender roles that prop up traditional notions of it.

Through what she says of her early life, one gets a sense of Anandamayi's own attitude towards the gender roles she was expected to enact. 'This body has lived with father, mother, husband, and all. This body has served the husband, so you may call it a wife. It has prepared dishes for all, so you may call it a cook. It has done all sorts of scrubbing and menial work, so you may call it a servant. But if you look at it from another standpoint, you will realize that this body has served none but God. For when I served my father, mother, husband and others, I simply considered them different manifestations of the Almighty and served them as such.'

As mentioned previously, Anandamayi initiated her husband and gave him deeksha exactly as a guru would, four full moons after her self-initiation in 1922, when she was twenty-six years old. Thereafter, their relationship, which had never been quite conventional, became even more unusual. To all appearances, Anandamayi was the dutiful wife, never meeting people or speaking in public without her husband's 'permission', even when her fame spread and a group of seekers formed around her. On his part, Bholanath kept a tender watch over Anandamayi when she entered states of samadhi, from which she needed to be roused after a while. He provided valuable support to Anandamayi and her fledgling sangha in the early years, before his untimely demise in 1938.

Beneath the veneer of their traditional marriage was unfolding a unique story of spiritual apprenticeship. Anandamayi would play the wife's role, but when seized with a kheyal, a spontaneous thought to an end that would be of benefit to others, she would happily drop all pretence and exert a strong freedom of choice that could not be overruled. At these times, as also when she instructed him in his sadhana, Anandamayi was guru.

Struck by Anandamayi's exhortation that all is One, a woman asked her, 'Are your husband and all others alike to you?' Anandamayi looked at Bholanath, smiled and said playfully, 'If I answer that truthfully, he will be angry with me.'

Then, she laughed and added, 'Everyone is alike, yet, wherever it is necessary for a particular mode of behaviour to be enacted, it happens. In childhood my parents were my gurus. Then they introduced my husband as the guru. At that time there was a strong feeling of *gurubhava* towards my husband. Today I see the entire universe as my guru. You also are my guru. Everything is but His form. There is nothing other than the One.'

Aruna too expresses this uncompromising non-duality, which was the basis of Anandamayi's teachings, and which ultimately acted as the alchemy that transformed all her relationships. 'Ma lived with her husband but not as husband and wife. Their life was very spiritual. It is interesting because she told us that it was she playing both parts; it was she herself in two forms. She has attained perfection, and Bholanath is a *sadhaka* trying to achieve perfection, but at the same time not like an ordinary sadhaka. So this was a *leela*. Ma eventually became his guru. She gave him deeksha. She changed him from an ordinary sadhaka—incidentally, he was not an ordinary sadhaka but was of high calibre—but whatever trace of the human was there, Ma transformed that into perfection.'

The truth about their relationship was revealed at the time of Bholanath's death. Like her father, Bholanath called her Ma in acknowledgement of her having 'mothered' his spiritual life. Anandamayi passed her hand over his body thrice as a final blessing, and he breathed his last with her hand on his head, whispering the word 'ananda'.

Afterwards, Anandamayi bore no trace of sorrow. During Bholanath's illness, she had constantly been at his side. After his death, she was quietly joyful, blissful as always. It was as if she was unmindful of the calamity that had befallen her—her husband's death and her new status as a widow, amongst the lowest of the low in orthodox Hindu hierarchy.

Long-time devotee Bithika Mukherjee says in her memoir that Anandamayi noticed her followers' concern and explained, 'Do you start to wail and cry if a person goes to another room in the house? This death is inevitably connected with this life. In the sphere of immortality, where is the question of death and loss? Nobody is lost to me.' And because she recognized no rules save that of irrevocable oneness, she remained unscathed by social conventions and taboos. Marriage and widowhood, sickness and health, whatever circumstances came to her were like waves in the ocean. They rose and fell away, ascended and subsided. Ma remained as she was, the unstruck note in the symphony of life, the still point at the centre of it all.

—

The rising sun has dispelled some of the morning's mist and a sliver of sunshine shivers under the peepul tree's reflection on the ghat steps. The two women fall silent for a while, their eyes closed and palms folded, offering their gratitude, I imagine, for the countless benedictions of life—this quiet ghat, the beginnings of warmth on a chilly day, the company of like-minded friends, the joys of a simple life, the growing absence of anger, the fine strand of bliss that threads their beings, the chance at walking the path with Ma...

Watching their cold-pinched faces radiate equanimity, I wonder how different their lives and their paths would have been had their guru been a man. Because Anandamayi was a woman, it became easier for women like Vishuddha and Aruna to receive the kind of spiritual instruction they wouldn't have been able to access otherwise, given the orthodox gender rules that remain at play even now, the fear of sexual exploitation and the mistrust of any form of 'other-worldliness' in women that could potentially disturb the existing status quo.

Anandamayi stood the status quo on its head; only, she did it with such grace and self-assurance that the opposition was either charmed or unable to overrule the truth that formed the basis of her position. Thus she was able to encourage women not only to begin their spiritual practice but take to it wholeheartedly and, if possible, enter a renunciate's life. As Aruna says candidly, 'We are very lucky to have found Ma, because our parents wouldn't want us to go around with male sadhus. They would rather we were with a woman.'

The morning is getting on—it is time for Ma's girls to depart, somewhat unsteadily, on legs benumbed by the cold stone, towards the temple across the road. That temple houses Ma's samadhi, where her body was interred at the end of her eighty-six years in a manner befitting the most exalted renunciates, an honour rarely bestowed on a woman.

But then, Anandamayi was a woman, and she was so much more and beyond. She not only widened the scope and meaning of womanhood, but revitalized the dharma, extricated the opportunity of spiritual fulfilment from the confines of dusty scriptures and arcane rituals, and introduced us to the possibilities inherent in the closed bud of potential we all carry within. The fragrance of her realization, of which she shared as freely as a flower in glorious bloom, holds out the promise of that bud blossoming, of the seed becoming a tree, of the tiny trickle of a mountain stream one day emerging as the greatest river of them all, Ganga Ma.

2

A Hut by the Ganga

NANI MA

In the beginning, walking the spiritual path might mean following in the footsteps of those that have gone before. Indic wisdom traditions, particularly, encourage apprenticeship through the guru–disciple relationship rather than freewheeling soul searches. Except in the case of the god-intoxicated, or freespirits that dance to their inner song, who will not, cannot be tamed, it is preferred that you set out with a map of the territory you are about to negotiate, in the company of a guide who will hopefully know enough not to let you fall into a ditch, or pull you out, should the need arise. Who will be the lamp that picks out the way ahead. The finger that points to the moon. And who will, when the time comes, know to let go of your hand and allow you to snap the safety catch and plunge into the unknown, on that part of the journey that only you can make, alone.

In Hardwar, I witnessed the intensely close discipleship that had formed between Anandamayi Ma and her girls. Her disciples' lives had intertwined with Ma, their very sense of self and the spiritual search was immersed in Ma. As I leave the misty ghats of Kankhal, I think about the ageing 'girls' and how their identity was subsumed in Ma. One way to get rid of sticky habit patterns of self-cherishing is to dissolve one's identification with a finite, body-related personality. The guru could be a medium in which this dissolution occurs, the all-accepting ocean in which the ego disappears like a lump of salt.

Yet, for the modern mind, there is something disturbing about complete surrender to another of one's faculties of discretion and discernment, one's entire self. Partly because there is enough evidence in the public realm of disciples who have felt exploited because they did everything an unscrupulous 'guru' asked them to do, which they felt compelled to go through with because they had been told that surrender is a prerequisite of the guru–disciple relationship. It is indeed, though I am not at all sure whether one must give away all control of oneself immediately, without properly checking the antecedents and abilities of the guru in question. For women, the issue of sexual exploitation is particularly relevant because of the damage it can wreak on their physical, emotional and psychological health.

It is a thorny conundrum that has besieged this sacred relationship in our times, and one that the seeker must deal with if he or she is to embark upon a truly transformational spiritual apprenticeship. Perhaps it is a relationship that is so fragile, so potentially fraught with the pitfalls of lust and greed and power, that it does require the guru to be a 'perfect master', one who has been able to wear away his or her own afflictive emotions, one who is beyond their grasp in a sense, and thus able to hold the trust of another human being and use it to effect his or her transformation.

Perhaps I will get some insight into this relationship in its purest form, in the hut by the Ganga, where I am now headed. For there lives a woman who has followed her guru, attached to him like a feather to a bird's wing. And who, in her guru's physical absence, floats like that feather detached, blown along by her own effort towards self-realization.

—

O boatman,
Take me to that
hut by the Ganga
you know
where
she flows swift and young
singing over stones
shaping them
into the potbelly of Ganesha here
the discus of Vishnu there
the locks, matted, of Shiva
yonder.

O boatman,
Do you know that hut?
Where a woman lives
swathed
in white and wisdom
her name simply
'mother's mother'.

O boatman,
take me to her
daughter of Ganga
mother of my soul.

I am travelling upriver from Hardwar, following Ganga Ma back to her sacred source, the place of her birth on earth which, like everything ancient and revered in India, has a tapestry of legends woven around it. Sometimes it feels that nothing happens in this country without a reason, quite appropriate, I suppose, for the land that invented the doctrine of karma. Everything seems either predetermined by individual and collective actions, thoughts and intentions, or is divinely engineered. So a river isn't just a river, it doesn't form out of a snowy glacier for any natural, geographical reasons. She is a goddess, divine quencher of thirst, giver of life, mother of all.

The little car, in which I am, climbs higher into the Himalayas with every bend of the river. Lush fields and congested towns gradually give way to occasional huts perched precariously on outcrops and goats scrabbling on mountainsides that rise sharp and sheer. The river valley narrows with ascent, as if the young Ganga did not wish to disturb the mountains too much, and made just enough space to pass through. The road swerves into a bend that takes me right above the riverbed, which is studded with smooth water-rounded stones, clearly visible through the swift, clear flow.

It is like a journey back in time—the Ganga grows younger with each kilometre I travel, each foot I ascend. Her pulse appears to quicken, her girth diminishes to a stream in parts. For those of us who have seen her matronly embrace and her slow plodding pace in the latter parts of her journey through the alluvial plains of north and east India, she is a veritable adolescent here. Like the goddess as Shodashi, the sixteen-year-old virgin, Ganga seems at the cusp of womanhood—moody and giggly, a little unsure, brimming with playful energy. It's the maternal instinct of a little girl that I am reminded of, who hugs her dolls to her heart and mothers them fiercely.

At the last town before the ashram, I eat greasy cabbage and chapattis dusty with flour in a dirty hovel of a restaurant, soothed by the lilt of the Ganga close by. Alas, the boatman of my poem fails to materialize, and I must find the hut by the river on my own.

The somewhat tentative address I have tells me to get onto the road that leads to Gangotri, where the famous temple of the Arising Ganga is located. At some point on that road, a few kilometres before the temple, a path will lead down the hill. To get to that point, I must ask passers-by the way to 'Nani Ma's ashram'.

The ashram's location has no name except for that of its most famous inhabitant, Nani Ma. 'Nani Ma' too is not a name, not really. It is a signifier of a relationship, a respectful and loving honorific for one's maternal grandmother. How intriguing that this woman, who has spent most of her life as a celibate sadhvi, should be known only by this name, I think, as yet another person on the road responds to my query of 'Nani Ma?' with a nod and directs me to the village closest to the ashram.

I first heard of Nani Ma as 'an English sadhvi who is trying to get a cancer hospice going'. My curiosity was piqued not only by the possibility of documenting an exciting spiritual quest, but also by her engagement in a service project, for spirituality without a socially concerned, 'in-the-world' component, in my view, runs the risk of becoming divorced from daily life. Spirituality that is self-involved, or simply not concerned with the suffering of others, feels synthetic and unreal.

Because she doesn't travel out of her hut by the Ganga if she can help it, Nani Ma agreed to meet me provided I was willing to make the journey to her. So here I am, wending my way to her rather inaccessible hermitage, at more than 10,000 feet above sea level, in the dead of winter. Pilgrimages are meant to be arduous, I assure myself as an icy Himalayan wind slices through my several layers of clothing while stepping out of the car to ask for directions one more time. Pilgrimages are supposed to be as much about facilitating experience and inner growth as they are about going somewhere; as much about receiving benediction as unearthing it in the ground of one's own being where it has lain, dormant, until the waters of insight and knowing sweep away the layers of ignorance and make it shine forth, anew.

'Nani Ma? There!' A finger points down, towards the valley of the Ganga, and I see dilapidated steps overgrown with moss. I have arrived at the end of this pilgrimage.

Or is it just the beginning?

—

I slip on the wet slime on the steps a few times, thankfully not hard enough to break any bones. A tiny temple appears; I peep in. It feels nothing like a sadhvi's quiet hermitage. I continue my descent until I am almost at level with the Ganga. I step into a doorway, and it is like stepping through the looking glass into an alternative reality, removed from the noise and dust that cloak mine, literally and figuratively. Everything is radiant in the afternoon sun—the tiny wooden cottages, the stone-lined pathways, the moist grass, the blue-green leaves. A playful Ganga right in front. A frail woman in white, under a lemon tree, luminous with love. She comes towards me, arms outstretched, her eyes aglow with the penultimate rays of the winter sun. 'Welcome!'

Though we had exchanged emails, I didn't quite know what to expect of Nani Ma. Her spontaneous warmth right from the moment we met set the tone for our interaction over the next few days. She held nothing back, and tried to answer my questions and curiosities with honesty and openness. There was none of the pomposity that often accompanies punditry minus the lived experience—like roti without a sliver of ghee, dry and difficult to swallow.

That first evening, I am invited to join the ashram residents for aarti. I brace myself against the rising chill with my thickest shawl and set out on the path that winds from my 'guest hut' towards the small shrine. A saffron-robed swami, also a disciple of Nani Ma's guru, conducts the aarti and leads the rest, all women, in chanting mantras. Along with Nani Ma, there are two other women who are permanent, all-weather residents. Many others come and go, this tiny ashram the nerve centre of their spiritual journeys, where they find seclusion to recuperate from the noise of the world, and guidance to move ahead on the path.

The little shrine, warmed by the glow of clay lamps and our collective chanting, is infused with Nani Ma's guru's presence. His photographs adorn the minimalist altar, where he appears still and silent, his gaze penetrating the camera lens as if plumbing the depths of the photographer's being. I notice that none of the photographs is posed, nor do they have rays shooting out of raised palms, special effects which many disciples seem keen to inflict on their gurus' images. A cave appears in one of them, which Nani Ma tells me was Babaji's home by the Ganga in Rishikesh. His life as a wandering yogi ended when he entered that cave. It was here that she met him the first time.

I look at Babaji's photograph and try and imagine his sadhana, his journey, his shepherding of spiritual quests, his life by Ganga Ma. His presence conveys a sky-like quality—unbound by conventions or contexts, untethered to I-ness, wakeful and watchful. In the sky, clouds form and reform, chafe and rain, and pass away. In the sky-like yogi, thoughts and emotions follow a similar pattern, with the mind ever present in its consciousness, never clinging or pushing away. Everything is.

Nani Ma reads the questions in my eyes and smiles. 'You've had a long day. There will be plenty of time to talk tomorrow.'

—

Dawn at Nani Ma's ashram is a garden full of icicled grass, waiting for the first rays of sun to shiver to life. Dawn is Nani Ma walking down the path to Ganga Ma in the bitter cold, for her mother's embrace before she begins her day.

Dawn is cold and hard, a diamond of a day in the rough.

Dawn comes astride the ceaseless roar of the Ganga.

Dawn is also a hot cup of ginger tea for Delhi-dwellers unaccustomed to the ways of the wild winter of the Himalayas.

We meet well past dawn, when the sun has warmed the earth of her nightly frost and there are patches where the grass is dry enough to sit on.

A pebble of a question stirs the stillness of Nani Ma's morning. How did it all begin?

Nani Ma is silent for a while, as if casting the net of her present far enough to catch memories of long-gone days.

'Well, I was going to say the search started when I was born, but perhaps it started in hospital when I was young. I had a very serious accident when I was three months old, and spent most of my childhood in hospital.' This early trauma was followed by what one could call an 'existential crisis' at age sixteen.

The injured child healed into a thoughtful adolescent who loved God very much but had some questions for Christianity, the religion she had been brought up in. She didn't always find answers to the 'whys' that arose within her, and matters came to a boil when she was due to be baptised.

'There were two big questions in my mind. In the Bible, the way we were taught in church, there was this concept that if you sin you are condemned to eternal hell. Otherwise you get eternal heaven. I couldn't see that if you did something wrong, you would be in hell for ever and ever. So I would ask, but after you've been in hell for a while, can't you come out? The answer was no, it's for ever. It didn't make sense to me that somebody could be condemned for ever.

'Also, I had been told that only those who believe in Jesus will be saved by Jesus and go to heaven, the rest will go to hell. I said, what about other religions? I was told they will go to hell. I said this was not really fair because I had heard about Jesus every day of my life but what about those who hadn't? So I was told that everybody in the world will have the chance to hear his name at least once. I felt it was not an equal chance.'

The adolescent was reprimanded by the church for challenging its moral authority with questions it deemed 'irrelevant'. Hers was the kind of honest enquiry it wasn't prepared to deal with. In this, the church displayed an ossification that tends to afflict the bones of religions that have lost their suppleness in the long process of becoming religious establishments. Though their roots lie in the transformative spiritual journey of one or more individuals, over time these are overlaid by interpretations and reinterpretations, dogma and ritual.

This is not to say that the original wisdom is lost, it just becomes harder to find. Sincere practitioners might still unearth the jewels but their efforts may not always be welcomed by an establishment that has begun to take things—belief, faith, truth—for granted, rather than striving for it relentlessly. Like Jesus did, or Mohammad, or Krishna, because they understood the essentially dynamic nature of reality that can never be bound by dos and don'ts, that can never be truthfully represented by any doctrine that does not also reflect this fluidity. Like osteoporotic bones, religions that do not retain this flexibility at their core become brittle. To protect their structures and beliefs, they require their adherents to take their word as law, such that there remains no active space for creative questioning.

What must the seeker do then? Shut off the voice within that asks thorny questions? Or set off on a new journey, away from established religions and relationships, careers and comforts, parents and friends, home and country?

Or, as so many young people from the West did in the 1960s and 1970s, come to India.

'When I finished college I came to India,' says Nani Ma, her eyes soft with memories. 'And here I read the Gita for the first time, in a little temple down by the Sarayu river in Bageshwar in Uttarakhand. An American woman read it to me, actually. She said, "Lie down and I will read you something," and started to read from chapter two, verse eleven. And those were the words I had been waiting to hear all my life—that the self is never born, never dies. Tears started to pour down my face and she said, "What is the matter with you?" I realized she was not as moved as I was, so I asked her if she could lend me the book. I sat by the Sarayu and read it from cover to cover.'

To unravel the essence of the profound philosophy that lay in her hands, that explained so vividly the human condition and the inextricable connection between human and divine, to make some attempt to live by this truth, the young Englishwoman needed a finger to point the path ahead. She needed a guru. Even though she didn't quite know what a guru was, yet.

Before she came to Bageshwar, she had been in Almora, another town in Uttarakhand, where she chanced upon a group of people doing kirtan, singing devotional songs. Intrigued, she approached a foreigner who was part of the procession.

'What are you doing?' she asked.

'My guru makes us sing the names of God,' he replied.

'Who is a guru?'

'A guru is a teacher.'

'Where do these gurus live?'

He just said, 'By the Ganga,' and went to rejoin the procession, irritated that he had got left behind.

'I immediately looked at a map to see where the Ganga was,' says Nani Ma. 'The next day I got into a bus to Badrinath, which was the nearest place to the Ganga.' Midway, she found herself staring at a sign that read 'No foreigners beyond this point'. Her great Gangetic journey aborted, she found a bus to take her wherever it went, which was to Bageshwar.

Her powerful, life-altering encounter with the Bhagavad Gita revived her resolve to go to the Ganga and find a guru.

'I became my own style sadhu,' she remembers. 'I started to walk towards the Ganga. I left most of my things in Bageshwar because the American lady I was staying with said a sadhu shouldn't have anything… It's a crazy story!'

'No, it's not! I think it's fascinating,' I say, moved by the naïve courage of that young woman who set off alone to find her guru with practically no information, having given away everything she had. No security blanket, no money, no contacts, no safe haven. No shoes, even. This was it. She had leapt out of her life, literally, into the unknown; fearless and trusting that she wouldn't crash and burn. Like an acrobat who soars off her trapeze without a safety net, confident of being caught before she hits the ground.

'In hindsight, I feel it was an extremely strong *samskara* that was awakened. I didn't want anything else, I only wanted to find my guru. Bhagwan doesn't look at anything but the heart, and my heart was really completely pure, like the innocence of a child.' But at the time, it seemed that she had bitten off more than she could chew. A couple of days of walking in cloth shoes ('I had been told that's what sadhus wore') left her limping with painful blisters on her feet. Exhausted, she stopped by the wayside. She didn't know how she would make the rest of the journey. The situation suddenly seemed bleak.

'I realized I didn't know what I was supposed to be doing. A man saw me crying and asked if there was something wrong. I told him I was going to the Ganga and that I had become a sadhu. He understood everything and, *Bhagwan ki kripa*, he was a really good man. He took me with him and the ladies in his home were very kind.' She had a chance to rest and recover. In a few days it was Janmashtami and a pandit from Hardwar arrived for the ritual telling of the magical story.

'The pandit was an educated gentleman and I told him I was looking for my guru and was sure that my guru lived by the Ganga. He told me about Babaji. "My guru lives by the Ganga, under a rock. He is fully realized." I knew at once that this was my guru and asked the pandit to take me to him. He said, "Babaji is very traditional and there are no foreigners with him. I'll take you somewhere else." But I insisted.'

In the mysterious way that life often has of bringing us what we need the most to learn and grow at a particular point, the young woman found her guru. 'Babaji had already told people a few days before I reached, "Now a foreign woman will come." As soon as I saw him, that was it! I stayed with him for the next sixteen years, until he left his body in 1987.'

Nani Ma grows quiet, her eyes are turned towards the Ganga, her being as if merging, flowing with the river. In the bright afternoon sun, she is a river of gold.

A gentle mountain breeze carries with it the moist fragrance of rice being cooked. 'Come, you must be hungry,' Nani Ma says as she brushes away blades of grass that have flecked her snowy white sari with emerald. She won't have lunch, just some khichri later in the day. It is one of the conventions of Babaji's ashram, tethered to the value of conscious living, where one takes only as much food and other things as one needs to survive, rather than consume greedily, which Nani Ma has attempted to replicate in this hermitage.

I eat my rice and dal, watching the intense blue sky punctuated by wandering clouds. It is difficult to take my eyes off the Ganga for too long, though, because she is right here, incessant, beautiful. I am suspended between river and sky; one, the flowing, ever moving mind, the other, a vast field of is-ness, a still pool of clear consciousness.

Sixteen years seems like a long enough time to have spent with a guru who purportedly taught with every arch of his eyebrow, every flick of his finger, even with his silence. Is it long enough, though, to have dissolved the salt lump of the ego in his ocean-like presence?

I watch Nani Ma move about the tiny hermitage, directing the preparation of meals she won't eat herself, ensuring her visitors' comfort, getting a room ready for a new resident who will stay for a month or maybe a year, trying to do what she can to kickstart a cancer hospice... Where is her sense of 'I' in all this, the 'I' we hold closer than our breath, whose solidity we are absolutely convinced of, that keeps us from recognizing the oneness of life, that veils our eyes from the truth of our interconnected existence?

Perhaps the lump of salt did dissolve, after all?

The interplay of shifting clouds veils the sun and the Ganga turns a rich copper. Nani Ma sits with me again.

Our conversation turns towards the years of her apprenticeship with Babaji. Though I often use the term 'apprenticeship' to connote the guru–student relationship, with Babaji and Nani Ma it seems to have been so in the true meaning of the word. Wikipedia defines 'apprenticeship' as 'a system of training a new generation of skilled crafts practitioners'. Only, this particular apprenticeship was a systematic, thorough, step-by-step training of a skilled *spiritual* practitioner.

'When I came to him, I was a clean book and didn't know anything,' Nani Ma says. 'So he taught me in the traditional way. First there was *seva,* service. I was already reading the Gita. He gave me a Tulsi Ramayana in English, and I loved it. He saw that I liked to read. I wanted to learn Hindi so he asked some devotees to give me books. After one or two years, I was asking him questions like, why does it say one thing in this book and something else in another, for instance in translations of Gita ji. He said, "Well, you'll have to learn Sanskrit. *Mool mein pata lagega*, only if you read the original will you know what has actually been said."'

Before long she was, rather miraculously, composing hymns in this rather complicated ancient language. Later, Nani Ma would hand me two slim booklets, each containing a garland of shlokas celebrating the two poles of her spiritual axis—Babaji and Ganga Ma. 'I had a samskara so it wasn't difficult for me,' she smiles in response to my amazement.

Samskara is a word that often crops up in our conversation. Like so many Sanskrit word-concepts, it is multi-layered. It could mean 'characteristic', and it might also denote an echo from a past life embedded in one's consciousness. According to the doctrine of karma, something learnt or practised in a past life, or a habit pattern, is expressed in this life in the form of latent characteristics. It requires the correct combination of circumstances to surface, as a seed does to germinate, and might lead to fruition of past karma—the continued drawing of arcs that will complete the circle of an action, thought or intention. Samskaras can also be inclinations or predispositions, somewhat like genetic hardwiring—we are inclined to do something because our particular genes, which carry the experiences of preceding generations, predispose us to do so.

Another samskara Babaji would discover in Nani Ma was her affiliation to *jnana marga*, the path of knowledge-based spiritual practice. But that didn't happen until a few years later, during which a rigorous schedule of study and practice was set up. 'At first, Babaji gave me primarily *bhakti,* the path of devotion and surrender to the Divine. He wanted me to have a deep understanding of *sanatana* dharma, the eternal Hindu dharma', which you can't have if you only read Vedanta. If an Indian reads Vedanta, he goes to it from an understanding that is already inbuilt in his life. But a foreigner doesn't have that background. Babaji encouraged me to read stories of saints and the Ramayana, Bhagavad, Krishna Purana, Shiv Purana and so on.

'Then he gave me Adhyatmik Ramayana, which is Ramayana but it is jnana-based. I really liked it. He said, "Yes, this is your samskara, but I wanted you to read the other books first." After that he took me into the Upanishads and Adi Shankaracharya. That was my *ruchi*, my interest. I studied these for quite some years.'

Babaji carefully nurtured the spark of seeking that had been ignited within Nani Ma, fuelling it with guidance when needed, protecting it from the winds of distraction and despondency, supporting and stoking the tiny flame until it became a roaring fire that would burn away layers of persistent, grimy ignorance. The yogi's extensive experience of the inner life—his own and of those who came to him—had shown him the value of individual instruction attuned to each student's specific needs and samskaras and predilections. There could never be a one-size-fits-all sort of syllabus for spiritual apprenticeship, something the modern education system questionably imposes on all learners, irrespective of their aptitude and interests. The process of spiritual training must remain sensitive and flexible to the seeker's needs which might fluctuate and change with each step, each insight, each pothole she encounters. This is precisely why the guidance of a living guru is invaluable, who intuits where one is on the path and, having walked it herself, can guide one accordingly.

This is perhaps why gurus' teachings sometimes seem to vary. They will talk of bhakti to one and jnana to another. It is important to see this not as a contradiction but as part of the dynamism of a guru who, in his or her sky-like stillness, watches the disciple's state of being clearly reflected in his own as if in a ripple-less mountain pool, and advises suitably.

After years of teaching her the basics of sanatana dharma, of guiding her through scriptures and texts, through the yogas of study and seva, what did Babaji find reflected in the still pool of his consciousness?

Something that made him tell Nani Ma, 'Close the books and meditate.'

She had reached the point where practice must gain primacy over theoretical learning. Scriptural punditry can only be the beginning, not the end, of the path that must chart the ground of experience, of actual doing and being, if one is to touch the core of reality for oneself, taste it upon one's tongue, allow it to transform one's being. Reading about it or listening to somebody else's experience of it can hardly instigate the kind of radical inner change that walking the path requires of us.

Meditation is one way in which one can directly watch oneself and the dance of the ego-self; it is the one avenue one has of connecting with a deeper level of consciousness. So one can let go of tight self-perceptions and self-identity and begin the journey towards super-consciousness—the cusp where the Ganga leaves behind her Ganga-ness, the sacredness and the dirt, goddesshood and garbage, stories and histories, the hopes of millions, and flows into the vast ocean.

'For the rest of my years I meditated a lot,' says Nani Ma. 'I would read a little. Gita ji continued to be my favourite. It's always been with me. But it was more meditation.'

What was the form of meditation she was asked to practise? At a time when there are myriad meditation techniques that have been brought into the public space through television and publicized workshops, I am keen to know the yogi's approach.

'Well, I wasn't taught!' exclaims Nani Ma. 'Babaji said, "Now you meditate." I asked him how. He said, "Go and sit in your cave and come back in the evening."' She laughs, like a little girl, I think, her neck arching, her eyes crinkled, moistening. 'By now I had spent years in *swadhyaya* (self-contemplation). That's where my mind was, in the self. So when he told me just to go and sit, I sat and closed my eyes. After a few days, he asked me to read the *Patanjali Yogasutra*. He asked me to concentrate on *samadhi paath,* and to ask him if I had any questions. But he didn't teach me any particular method. My ruchi was *atma-vichaar,* contemplation of atman, and so he left me to it, really.'

The guru is the finger that points. The disciple must look, and figure the moon out for herself.

'If you were worshipping God with form, Babaji would instruct you to worship that form in your heart. And if you wanted to worship the *nirguna,* formless aspect, he would ask you not to think of anything. In the sixth chapter of Gita ji, there are two shlokas which are the *hridaya* of *dhyana*, the heart of meditation. One of them says, "Put the mind in the self and think of nothing else." Once, somebody asked Babaji, what is the mind and what is the self? The mind is not a thing that we can pick up and put in the self. Babaji said, "Take the mind away from everything else. Then it will be in the self. You don't have to put it there." He said that the mind is just thoughts, so if one removes one's thoughts from everything else, the silence that follows is the self.

'Through the years that I was with him, if anything happened in meditation I would ask him. There is a shloka that says, Yoga teaches yoga. So there is not so much, in fact, to teach. If you start to go inside, it's a different place. The signposts are not the same. The guru can only do so much. I mean, if he is a realized guru he can do everything. But it's you, yourself, who has to go inside. One's inner experience is one's own. It's relative. Somebody will say, "Oh, I had such and such experience." The person who hears this might understand something completely different. This is a realm where we are alone. And we are also not alone, because it is the realm of God, the realm of the self. There is a way, and one can find it only by walking on it.'

Nani Ma has affirmed the sacred law of spiritual seeking. The path is implicit in the actual walking, which must follow from effort and concentrated intent. No guru, not even an enlightened one, can inject you with insights, or change you, or make you do anything you don't have the courage and determination to do. It is a path forged in the heat of one's own effort, in the depths of one's own understanding, in the silence of the quietened mind. The guru is the light that illumines the cave of the heart, the presence that resolves knotty questions, the mother that soothes doubts and fears and nourishes with her company and example.

Who knows when the sky darkened, when the Ganga turned indigo? And when the silver-skinned half-moon began to brighten the sky again? The clanging of bells from the shrine rends the gossamer of our quiet communion and signals the evening aarti. As we walk back together, Nani Ma says, perhaps reminded by the darkness that has enveloped us in a soft, pashmina embrace, 'Babaji used to say it is like walking on a dark night. You carry a lamp and the lamp lights enough only for the next step. And if you take that step, the light goes on ahead of you. In life and in meditation, this is how he taught you to find your own way.'

—

I have refrained from Ganga Ma's touch since I came, fearing her icy waters would send electric shocks coursing through my skin. She calls out to me at every moment, though, sending her pure mountain breath to ruffle my hair, sweetening her roar to lull me to sleep. This morning, I cannot stay away any longer, and hurry down the steep path still hard with night frost, to be by her side.

Her waters swirl past, eddying around the rocks embedded in her path, softening their surfaces. She has worn away their rough edges, subdued their size, moulded hard, unyielding stone into smooth surfaces that allow her waters to flow unimpeded. Like the moods and habits of reactivity and emotional turbulence that can be sandpapered by the incessant onslaught of rigorous inner practice, until we can allow life to flow through us without fight or struggle, suffering or frustration.

This small beach by the Ganga is strewn with stones and pebbles, some smoothened into perfect circles or ovals, others slender like well-sucked lozenges, battered to the point of flaking into sand. Indeed, the grainy white sand under my bare feet is the final stage in the disintegration of what were once mighty Himalayan rocks, reintegrating with the earth. Big egos lie here, those at Ganga Ma's feet completely decimated, and those in her lap, the bigger ones in the thick of her flow, she is still working on, smoothening here, polishing there.

I watch Nani Ma emerge from her hut and walk towards me, her frail body barely leaving a mark upon the sand, and I wonder—she *is* like this sand, isn't she? Like the white sand at the mouth of Babaji's legendary cave, her 'I-ness' chipped away with constant care and attention, until all that is left of the ego-self is a handful of sand which the guru flings outside his door, upon the beach that kisses Ganga Ma as she flows past.

Nani Ma and I return to our patch of grass overlooking the deep cerulean throb the river is at this time of the morning, before the brightening sun pours molten gold into her veins. We spread out a mat to sit on, and I draw my shawl over my legs and feet. For a few moments, we quietly watch the river laugh and sing. Something about us, and the river, reminds me of Siddhartha and the boatman in Hermann Hesse's *Siddhartha*. Like the boatman, Nani Ma seems to say, 'You've heard it laugh... But you haven't heard everything. Let's listen, you'll hear more.'

I look at Nani Ma. She is watching the flow of Ganga Ma, perhaps the flow of life?

Shall we begin? Nani Ma turns to me, and her eyes are the eyes of ancient knowing, that have seen everything there is to see, that know the falsity of separation and are at one with everything. Another moment passes, and she has shaken off the 'old-as-the-earth' mood and is smiling at me encouragingly, waiting for me to ask her something.

How has being a woman affected your spiritual journey?

'There have been difficulties, and there have been advantages,' she says. 'Tulsidas said that in Kaliyuga, it is women and *shudras*, the lowest caste in the hierarchy, who will become saints. Because we don't have to do the *karamkand*, the rules and rituals that the Brahmins have had to do, which are difficult, if not impossible, to keep in Kaliyuga. Women are *hridaya pradhan,* their heart qualities are dominant and love and compassion come more naturally to them. Whether you are on the path of Vedanta or bhakti, it doesn't matter. The spiritual path is about bhakti, it is about surrender, it is about love. This is part of a woman's nature. So we have a tremendous advantage in this yuga. Because it is a yuga of our dharma. It is a yuga of bhakti and surrender.

'I am myself a nirgun bhakta, a seeker of the formless divine. But I feel when it comes to bhakti and surrender, it doesn't matter if it is to God with form or God without form. It's the same. In this sense there is an advantage.'

I am somewhat taken aback by Nani Ma's perspective on feminine spirituality that emphasizes Kaliyuga, the era of distortions, and her unquestioning articulation of the supercilious prophecy that women and the so-called lower castes would become spiritually eminent in this era, as if this is the only era in which such a thing could happen. This is clearly a view that echoes the patronizing condescension of Brahmanical patriarchy, that this too is part of the distortion of Kaliyuga—'we', the pure, the true holders of everything spiritual, will find it difficult to sustain our purity in these mucky times, so those that are lower than us will gain spiritual eminence. Of course, Nani Ma probably does not quite mean it like this, and is only repeating accepted scriptural positions. But I am troubled by this argument and have to try very hard to concentrate on at least one positive aspect—the primacy of 'feminine' spiritual paths of bhakti and surrender in this yuga.

Was there any discrimination from Babaji because she was a woman?

'No, absolutely not. You see, there has been discrimination against women only because of women's physical weakness. There is no other weakness. In fact, this has been less in India than anywhere else. Women had a different role but there was never discrimination against them in spiritual life. We've always had women saints. Women may not have been able to chant the scriptures but they would certainly listen to them.'

But wouldn't she agree that there is a sense of a glass ceiling in spirituality too, where, for instance, women could be taught this much and no more? They could be followers but rarely gurus, at least not where the mantle and the learning were handed down as matters of lineage? They could chant some mantras but not others, do some practices only, and not the whole gamut?

'In the self, there is no male or female. So how can there be a ceiling?' Nani Ma responds. 'What is the spiritual life? It is simply the path to God. There is no gender in God, even though we say this is Durga or this is Krishna. In perfect non-duality, there is none of this. Before the division came about, it was simply Self. It was simply one. Also, we are not going to join our body to God. In the beginning, we are going to join our mind and emotions. But even our mind and emotions cannot join God. Nothing can join God except the spirit. The spirit will join the Spirit. And that is far, far beyond masculine and feminine. Gender only applies to the body, which is left so far behind on the spiritual path.'

That there comes a point in deep spirituality that is beyond body, beyond gender, is indubitable and has been observed in the lives and teachings of realized beings over centuries, where the harsh contours of gender and sexuality are smoothened away, along with the clinging to an individual identity. This remains one of the strongest contentions against gender-based discrimination on the path. And yet, gender-based discrimination exists. Those of us who walk the path every day, in our feminine selves, know from experience that when dealing with tradition or scripture or spiritual authority, gender blindness is rare. Simply put, it does matter if you are a man or a woman.

Nani Ma concurs, if only at a practical, physical level. 'If we have a female body, we have to do things in a slightly different way because of our body. But this doesn't have anything to do with what we can attain. It is *prarambhik*—it is just in the beginning that there might be some differences. We have a lot of disadvantages. For instance, *maasik dharma*, the menstrual cycle, during which we are not so comfortable. We do not feel too well for a few days. There are so many things, small things. So we have to adjust our way of life a little bit. This is nothing to do with the spiritual. When we sit down and meditate, are we a woman or a man?'

As far as feminine physicality, including sexuality, is concerned, spiritual literature written by men is replete with derogatory references, at times equating it with the devastating effects of wealth and materialism (*kanchan-kamini*, literally, 'gold and woman'). A woman's body is seen as a sure-fire route to distraction and consequent derailment from the path. Nani Ma articulates the feminine perspective—for women, their physicality is at most a weakness, an inconvenience which they have to learn to manage, just as they would in a 'worldly' life as a career woman, in family situations, while walking on the road, and so on.

These 'practical' issues, are these the reason why women were largely kept away from sannyas, the life of the wandering sadhu?

'*Yeh stree dharma hai*, this is the feminine condition,' Nani Ma responds. 'We always have to protect ourselves to a certain extent. We do not have the freedom that men have. Mainly because we always have to worry about our physical safety. So many girls on the path have had problems because they have the idealism, they want to go and live in caves and everything. And so many of them come to grief. Not all of them, because our karma and *prarabdha* (destiny) protect us. And God protects us. But it is not always so, and it isn't as though only the "bad" ones have bad experiences.'

Nani Ma tells me of a sadhvi from Bengal who led a life of solitary wandering in the upper Himalayas, and often meditated in caves near Gangotri and Gomukh. However, her spiritual prowess and the respect it had earned her did not deter a group of men from sexually assaulting her. The ugly and tragic incident, which an increasing number of women have to grapple with every year in India, perhaps not only scarred the sadhvi for life, it also brought her spiritual journey to a halt.

'She was such a *tapasvi* (meditator), such a great *sadhika* (practitioner), and so many people respected her. But she was a woman alone. On the whole, we are physically less strong. While this is not a spiritual aspect, it still is. If we don't have yogic powers and are not *jnani* (fully realized), then we are living in the body and the body is a problem for women.'

Why must a woman who has been assaulted be considered 'ruined', and not the perpetrator(s)? Though I do not know the whole story, it does seem the sadhvi gave up her spiritual practice and left. One can understand and empathize with her need to do so. And yet, I wish that she had been able to find her way forward again, with the inner strength to continue on the path and deal with her pain and scars. It could have been one way of refusing to become defined, stigmatized or limited by the experience, an issue all victims of rape confront as they try to pick up the pieces of their life once more. In any case, this is one of the core practices on the path—dealing with and overcoming one's suffering, however traumatizing it might be.

'Women are every bit as able to do *tapasya* as men,' Nani Ma continues. 'They are every bit able to study as men. They are more able sometimes for bhakti. So there is no field in which they cannot be equal, but the fear of being a woman alone. I always give this advice to girls—not to leave home, stay with other women or stay in an ashram. The thing is, *tyag* (renunciation) can be done anywhere. Even though we have all conveniences here, in the ashram, I tell them you don't have to take them. If you are feeling *vairagya* (detachment), you are not obliged to take the conveniences. Live like a lotus leaf. I feel, in this way girls can live in a more protected society, but not renounce the renunciation and the dispassion. This is my experience.'

For women, there are issues apart from personal safety when it comes to sannyas, checking out of the world, because that 'world' contains relationships, children, families that they tend to hold close to their hearts and which require their presence and attention. This is a primary reason why I feel sannyas has largely remained a masculine spiritual space. Not only have they been kept out by the powers-that-be, women seekers too have not taken it upon themselves to storm the bastions.

So, is it possible for a woman to live in the world and find her spiritual path in its dust and din? A moment after I ask this question I wonder whether a renunciate could really answer it without prejudice, but the die is cast and Nani Ma is contemplating a response.

'Sure she can. For men and women equally, the path that is taught in the scriptures is of tyag and vairagya. It is the path to God. My Guruji always used to say, for a sadhu it is complete renunciation. For householders it is mental renunciation so that they are not attached to these things. But you see, it is easier to become a sadhu. To live in the middle of things is not as easy as to live outside. It is very easy not to stuff yourself with cream cakes if there are no cream cakes!' Her laughter fills the crevices in our conversation.

'I would never advise a woman to leave home until her children are independent of her,' she continues. 'If we haven't fulfilled our duties in the world then we shouldn't leave. Unless we are completely God-intoxicated. Because then there is no duty in the world—at least it's not real. As long as you feel some love towards your own body, you have to keep up your duties. If a woman is attached to her family, then she should do her spiritual practice there. Spirituality does not pertain to outer actions. Outer actions are the beginning of spiritual life, to turn us inwards. Spiritual life is in the spirit. It starts off with physical actions, the outer actions. It goes then to mental actions. And then the spiritual life goes to the spirit, the joining of the spirit with the Divine. So if anybody loves God enough, they can do it in any circumstances because the yoga, the union is within. That's where the meeting is. You could be doing anything outside. The outer *kriyas* of becoming a sadhu are to train your mind inwards, towards God. When a connection is established, it doesn't really matter what you do outside.'

Nani Ma's words feel as real as the warmth of this golden discus of a sun that is fast spreading through my veins. She articulates what has been repeatedly described as being in this world though not of it, the state of the *jivanmukta* who is free in life, a veritable lotus in the muck of the world. But what, then, of the life of sacred wandering and asceticism? It *is* of value to the woman seeker, in terms of cutting out the noise—the cream cakes—and initiating the yoga of inner connection.

'Spiritual life is about knowing where you are and living there. Not necessarily changing or going somewhere. But it is easier, for instance, to learn tennis if you are in a tennis club. In the same way, if you live in a spiritual environment, in an ashram with spiritual people, it's going to be much easier. If somebody has an intense longing for God, I would advise them to leave home. There's nothing wrong with leaving home. But you should have an intense longing before. Some girls come here and say, "I am thinking of leaving home but I haven't found a nice base yet." So I say, what do you mean? "Oh, I need a room and this and that and the other." You see, becoming a sadhu means that you are choosing God instead of his things. If you want to have both God and his things, then stay at home, work and earn a living.'

I think of Nani Ma's own single-pointed quest for truth, the leap into the unknown as a young woman, without anything that could qualify as a security net. As an older wise-woman and teacher, she expects nothing less of the young women who come to her. Her voice is strong, impassioned, as she lists the guidelines for anybody—man or woman—who wishes to live a life of renunciation. It cannot be a 'checking out' of the world, a casual foray or an escape from one's responsibilities and suffering. There's nothing escapist about sannyas, it's not for the faint-hearted. Rather, it requires tremendous inner work, determination, courage and a clearly focused motivation prior to the decision.

Nani Ma clarifies the kind of commitment required of the renunciate. 'If you become a renunciate, then if God feeds you, it's okay, and if God doesn't feed you, that's okay too. It is like saying to God, if you keep me alive it's okay, if you don't keep me alive it's okay. If someone is prepared to live like that, then they should become a sadhu. If they first want *poora prabandh* then they should stay at home. We have no rights—even with God we have no rights. I have learnt all these things from Babaji and am strict about them.'

Babaji's own life, says Nani Ma, exemplified the way of the sadhu. Having adopted the path of renunciation as an adolescent, his long and arduous sadhana (about which he rarely spoke) had led to a state of being of the jivanmukta, open as the sky, non-grasping, non-wanting. During this time, he walked alone all over India, barefoot, clad in a single cloth, without even a vessel to drink from. 'He saw quickly that Bhagavan had given water everywhere, so why carry a pot around?' Nani Ma smiles. 'He lived in *akash vritti* (sky nature)—he never had any possessions and never asked for anything. It was always like that, even when I went there. When he was wandering, he never even approached a place where food was being given away. If it came to him, then he would eat.' She once asked Babaji, 'How long did you go without food because nobody asked you?' He said, 'Two weeks. Then, I was in a jungle and found a *bilva* tree. I ate a lot!'

That this attitude of renunciation, of inner surrender, of not hungering after anything, even the basic necessities of food and shelter, survives in our century of materialistic greed and consumerist frenzy and is not just a myth from a golden past, can be seen as a measure of its doability. It is possible to live with less, to calm one's senses and reactions, to not crave, not consume mindlessly, to be gentle and fully alive to the utility of each thing, the *rasa* in each experience. And to allow oneself to feel sated, and say, 'I have enough.' An attitude that takes on an urgent meaning in these times of ecological crisis, when the earth's resources are rapidly being expended to fuel our collective hunger for more, an enterprise whose 'use-and-throw' values are simultaneously generating mountains of garbage and pollutants which are poisoning the earth. I'm not advocating we all become sadhus, rather, that we adopt some part of this attitude of renunciation in our daily lives as a way of caring for the earth, for our environment and ecosystem, and for ourselves. Babaji's great, complete, roaring Ganga of a renunciation could certainly water our smaller, inspired tributaries.

Nani Ma picks up the thread of my question once more. 'Your question was about women. A woman has to be prepared to accept anything and everything if she wants to lead a sadhu's life. She shouldn't leave until she has that *nishtha* (determination). Women, by nature, like to have someone. So until they are sure that it is God that they want to have, they better stay at home.'

Women in patriarchy are conditioned to believe that a male presence is necessary for economic, social, emotional and psychological support and fulfilment, that they are incomplete in some way without a man, that they will stagger and fall apart like ragdolls if a male shoulder is not available to prop them up. To walk the path, women must confront this aspect of their psyches, which may be prominent or subtle, and find some way to resolve it. Nani Ma's suggestion is to substitute reliance on a male authority figure with reliance on God.

'There have been many great women saints and there still are many wonderful sadhvis. Women have tremendous tenacity—if they set about something, they really do it. And women can do it. God wants this. My Guruji also encouraged women to take to the spiritual path—he didn't give sannyas. But he wanted good behaviour, he wanted good *charitra* (character), he wanted sincerity. He used to tell all of us, men and women, "If you can't do twelve hours of sadhana every day, stay at home. Everybody works eight hours. (Lay) devotees, in addition, do sadhana for two hours in the morning and two hours in the evening. If you are going to take *madhyam* (support) from other people, you must do at least twelve hours.'

I hadn't realized how quickly time had passed, debating the intricacies of issues that are close to both our hearts. Nani Ma is called away to attend to a phone call, after which she says she must try and log on to the internet while her untrustworthy phone connection is still working. Which reminds me how her sadhana now includes attempts to network and gather funds and resources to set up north India's first spiritually-oriented cancer hospice, a lot of the work for which happens on the internet.

For now, I sit and watch the stars appear, a quiet moon rise.

—

A chilly morning tempered by sizzling hot pakoras and scalding ginger-tulsi tea, which I gulp down too quickly in an attempt to get warm. I still haven't worked up the nerve to bathe in Ganga Ma's waters, as Nani Ma does every morning, and use the coal-heated water in the bathroom instead. A sacred splash on the face with Ganga Ma is sufficient for the moment, I decide, and invigorating enough for the task at hand.

Nani Ma and I meet at 'our spot' once more, and sit in silence for a while. My mind drifts to a thought that hasn't occurred since I arrived here, that this is a woman foreign by birth to the land she has made her own. I guess Nani Ma is so Indian in speech and conduct, in her sadhana and in the terms of reference she employs, that it is easy to un-see the colour of her skin, the one distinguishing emblem of her 'outsiderness'.

I look at her now. Her forehead is marked with sandalwood paste, presumably post her Ganga Ma bath, morning meditation and puja, the edge of her white sari is drawn above her head as it always is. I look at myself, in a pair of jeans, too cowardly to dunk myself in the waters of this, the holiest river of my culture. Who is to say who or what is Indian? I am, and Nani Ma is, too. Jeans and skin colour notwithstanding.

I am reminded of the discrimination non-Indians faced at the hands of caste Hindus in Sri Anandamayi Ma's ashrams. Was this ever a problem for Nani Ma?

'Tremendously! It was much more of a problem than being a woman!' she exclaims, a rivulet of laughter tinkling in her voice. 'Being a white woman, a European woman, was a terrible problem. Babaji's ashram was traditional. Babaji himself was far beyond any of those things. But the ashram wasn't. Because I was from a foreign culture, I knew nothing, so I did everything wrong. I spent my first two years being shouted at. I didn't even understand Hindi in the beginning, so when people didn't want me to touch something the only method they had was to shout at me!'

Didn't this upset her?

'Yes, for sure,' she says. 'There was prejudice, and it's not such a bad thing to be on the other side of prejudice. You see, the spiritual path is about the ego. Thinking of ourselves as the body is what keeps us away from God. So any type of hatred, any type of prejudice towards your individuality is wonderful!'

That's a unique interpretation of discrimination, of racism, of casteism—the most positive I've ever heard, if there could be anything positive about these 'doctrines of difference', that is.

'We have to beat down this ego,' Nani Ma continues. 'So I was in this wonderful position of being an absolute pariah. I was the lowest of the low in many people's opinion. But Babaji held me through everything with a cord of love and understanding. Sometimes I would be sitting by him. There would be nobody there. And then his devotees would arrive and the first thing they would do is to throw me out to the farthest corner.' She laughs. I look for any traces of bitterness in her eyes, any shadows stalking the laughter lines that spread across her face. I find none. 'Babaji would just look. And I would know it doesn't really matter. The love of a realized being is indescribable. It doesn't have to have words, it doesn't have to have anything. It is support, it is just a oneness.'

Anandamayi Ma used the feeling of hurt at being discriminated against to wear down her disciples' egos. Did Babaji do something similar?

'Babaji was really kind. In the beginning, whenever there was anybody there who knew English, Babaji would teach me the rules. The first rule was the 'golden rule'—don't touch anything. Gradually he taught me other rules.'

So did he concur with the caste rules and their enforcement in his ashram? Surely such a being would not, could not, support divisiveness and discrimination?

In response, Nani Ma tells me a story. After a couple of years of learning the rules of caste and conduct, and perhaps thinking that they held huge wisdom, Nani Ma confesses she became 'more Brahmin than anyone else'. One day, she was walking along the riverbank with Babaji.

'Oh, Babaji, but that's jhootha, it is impure,' she exclaimed as he was about to eat something that he had been given.

'No, nothing is impure,' replied Babaji.

Nani Ma was stunned. 'What do you mean, Babaji? That's not pure!' she insisted.

'Nothing is impure,' Babaji repeated. 'There is nothing here but all-pervading Brahman. How can anything be impure?'

'But Babaji, you've been teaching me all the rules for two years!' Nani Ma protested. She might have added, if everything is pure and is Brahman, then why these rigid boundaries, these thorny fences around life's experiences?

In response, Babaji handed her the key that would help her unlock the play of dualities in what is essentially a non-dual reality. 'This—caste rules and regulations—is relative truth. Understand Absolute Truth, and understand relative truth. It is good to keep rules because it is good to have our minds and bodies under control. This helps purity—purity of the body, purity of the mind leads to purity of *antahakaran*, the inner being. It is necessary, but never believe in it. This is not the truth but the *upaya*, the method. *Sadhana hai*, *tattva nahin hai*. It is practice, not the essence. Follow rules but don't believe in them. Some people will never rise above them, which is better than not having them, as long as it is not used for discrimination.'

Taking Babaji's teaching to heart, Nani Ma continued to respect others' prejudices and boundaries, understanding their need to have these rules to order their universe, using unpleasant experiences that stemmed from these as practice opportunities to erode the ego. Babaji held her in his compassion through this process, supporting her practice, watching over her like a vigilant mother.

'I never did anything that anybody didn't want me to do. For instance, I wasn't allowed into the ashram kitchen. Babaji told me I was very lucky. Because I used to gather the gobar and fetch firewood, and that was much nicer than being in a hot kitchen! He said, "Look how kind God is to you in this life. He's kept you out of the kitchen." I thought, that's true. I can do all the jobs outside. So I never felt it, but other people did. Another girl in the ashram wasn't allowed into the kitchen. And she was pained all her life by that. You can see the same thing in two different ways.'

Sometimes it must have been difficult, though. We may learn to practise ego-lessening with it, but the hurt doesn't magically disappear, does it? 'It was difficult,' Nani Ma admits. 'I mean, now I know Hindi and I know the traditions, so it's not so difficult. When I go to a new place, people do look at me and there is discrimination. It is a fact. It is foolish human nature. If they see a different skin colour or a different way of acting, fools laugh. They laugh or they hate. It is normal, I'm used to it. I don't say anything. If I'm on a bus or in the bazaar, everybody talks about me. If I don't speak, they don't know I know Hindi. "Usko dekho!" they'll say, or comment on the fact that I'm wearing a sari. It is a lack of understanding. If people don't understand, there's nothing to be in pain about it.'

This clear-eyed view on discrimination and harassment is immensely valuable, I think, for many women who confront similar situations, irrespective of the colour of their skin. In India, sometimes being a woman in a public space is enough to invite stares, lewd remarks, crude gestures. I have often seethed with anger when faced with such behaviour. One response could be to think of it, as Nani Ma does, as 'foolish human nature', a result of profound ignorance.

Suddenly, a loud clanging of drums and the blowing of trumpets pierce our conversation. The silence of the mountains lies beside us on the grass, shattered. I twist my head towards the source of the noise, and find a procession descending the steps from the temple, towards the shore of the Ganga below us. 'It's a funeral procession,' Nani Ma explains. 'They are going to cremate a dead body here, on the beach. We better go in.' We roll up our mats as the men begin preparing a pyre beside Ganga Ma. The end of a long life, well lived, is often marked by celebration rather than mourning, Nani Ma says. 'Because of the music, I sometimes can't make out whether it's a wedding at the temple or a funeral!' Life never ends, according to the Hindu worldview. It continuously moves, flows, completing one karmic circle after another, until no more are left. Drawing the final arc, it merges back into itself, into its source, its particularity, personality and ego extinguished.

As the first syllables of the Vedic mantras for passing rise from the beach, Nani Ma and I offer our respects to the departed. We then leave the mourners to their rituals and walk away towards the huts. There is nothing more to say, or do, at the moment.

—

The pyre
smoulders
all day...
All day
we are reminded
that this too
shall pass
This body
this identity
this person
that I think
I am
Its remains
will smoulder
one day
like this...
I have just
this moment
this day
this second
to burst forth
like this sunrise
over the shoulder
of that mountain

for tomorrow
I will be
a body on the beach...

—

Smoke from the pyre lingers for a long time despite the restorative river breeze. The mourners, all male, bathe in the river after the rites are over, and spread out their wet clothes on large rocks to dry. Some stroll down the beach in their underwear in groups of twos and threes, some light bidis to while away the moments.

Their presence feels like an intrusion into the idyll I seem to have slipped in ever since I walked down the steps from the road a lifetime ago. And yet the ashram residents share their space without a murmur, silently including the mourners in their community that includes each other, Ganga Ma, the sacred shadow of Babaji, the mountains all around, the rocks on the beach, its sand, the lemon tree in the carefully tended garden, the grass, the flowers, the rising and setting sun...

Walking up the path to the shrine, I find Nani Ma trying to log on to the internet with her maddeningly slow dial-up connection. She laughs and tells me that people who have known her as a sadhvi who meditated all the time ('twelve to fourteen hours a day') are shocked when they see her like this, working at her computer intermittently through the day.

After some thirty-five years of single-pointed sadhana, Nani Ma is now engaging with the world again. Her involvement with the cancer hospice project, known as the Ganga Prem Cancer Hospice, is seva but in a creative way, the employment of her spiritual learning to actively ease others' pain, their emotional and psychological distress. How does she view this newest curve on the path, this twist in the tail of her spiritual career?

'I don't know if I can talk about it because I am not a hundred per cent sure myself,' Nani Ma says, and for the first time since we began talking, I sense a mild uncertainty creep into her voice. 'In scriptures, especially in Vedanta, and in sannyasi dharma, we say that one of the last and very strong *vighan* (obstruction) on the path is compassion.' I must look aghast for she bursts out laughing. 'This is what I am looking at, at the moment,' she continues, wiping her eyes. 'And I am not so sure it is a vighan. I see compassion now as being inevitable. Because on the spiritual path, the one thing you are trying to do is to destroy the ego, destroy the boundary between yourself and the all-pervading. If that boundary is either destroyed or becomes thin, your individuality becomes... not so strong. Then there is a closeness with God, but there is also a closeness with everybody else. When the boundary goes, individual striving can't exist either.'

Compassion can be an obstruction only if it is tied to one's ego, I think, and not when it arises in a natural way, as a *result* of the erosion of the ego, the self-cherishing that keeps us in bondage to the millstone of 'me' and 'mine'.

Has her sadhana changed as a result of the welling of compassion?

'As long as you are an individual, you can strive for an individual goal. But when one's individuality is completely destroyed, or is in the process of being destroyed, there will be less and less emphasis on any goal. The goal disappears. And if the goal of an individual, which is to realize God, disappears, then there is nothing really left to do. Then it seems irrelevant whether you are washing a pot or you are meditating. Then you are also going to be very, very open to other people's pain because you can't separate yourself from them any more.'

I am reminded of the ideal of the bodhisattva, central to Mahayana Buddhism, and particularly cherished in Tibet's Vajrayana. The bodhisattva is the Buddha-to-be, one step away from final extinguishment, nirvana. Yet, he or she deliberately defers that which is the goal of all spiritual practice because of an overwhelming compassion for all sentient beings that wells as a result of the dismantling of selfish individuality. In this interconnected reality, there can be no individual nirvana while millions of beings continue to suffer, the bodhisattva reasons, feeling their suffering as acutely as she would feel her own. And therefore vows to remain in this penultimate stage for as long as it takes to help all other beings out of their misery.

In this moment, Nani Ma *is* that bodhisattva, giving of herself to help whoever she can.

Clouds in the sky above us catch fire in a last burst of warmth from the late afternoon sun. A brilliant crimson seeps into the Ganga, into the crests of the mountains, into this earth we are sitting on. Nani Ma is quiet for a while, as if contemplating the core of compassion, turning it over in her heart, trying to cast in words what is a deeply felt reality for her.

'I don't feel that my work with the cancer hospice is more important than any other cause. This is the cause that life brought to me, and I am not able to say no to it. I am not sure yet whether this is a weakness or a strength. But there is a certain point in sadhana when one no longer cares. I don't know, perhaps this is a very personal thing to say in some ways. Whether I should speak in such a personal way about sadhana... but also, why not? When you come to understand that your attainment, any attainment, is in God's hands and not your own, the striving has no momentum any more. This is another way of saying what I was saying just now. There is no momentum any more to stick to your... whatever it was that you were doing. And then you find yourself open to whatever comes along.'

Nani Ma's words might be misconstrued for 'path-weariness', a sort of spiritual equivalent of its samsaric version, 'world-weariness'. Nothing could be further from the truth, I think. What Nani Ma seems to articulate is the mature practitioner's state of being. Having walked the path long and hard and with all the fire one's being can muster, one reaches a place where it is the walking that is important, rather than the goal. It has been said that ultimately, on the spiritual path, there is no *going* anywhere, and that attainment is in the experience. Once one realizes this, then the walking is bound to slacken because one is not rushing to get any place. One is still on the path, but with a balance and quietude and a non-grasping to this, the idea of result and goal attached to one's spiritual endeavour, as well.

Spiritual adepts rarely share this aspect of practice openly because it can be easily misunderstood by those who have not reached the same place, the same insight. Nani Ma too perhaps realizes this and clarifies, 'I very much encourage other people to do their sadhana because I think if sadhana stops by itself, only then should it be stopped. So I am not advising anybody to do what I have done. And it is not as if I have changed my mind now. It's just something that has happened. I find myself in a strange position and I am trying to explain it to you.

'There has been nothing in my life except the desire for God, and there still isn't. At some point, the goal and the path get muddled and you can't see what is where, nor do you care any more. I just think He knows best; if this is what He wants me to do now, it is fine. One doesn't have the emphasis on individuality, and you can't keep yourself to, okay, this is the path and this is the goal. It's hard actually to put it into words because it is quite subtle. I think it is a natural progression of my sadhana, or, let's say, of God's grace.'

The point where the path and the goal become one. There is no going anywhere but here, no future but that which is right now, nothing to strive towards but that action which has come before me in this moment. Isn't this the raison d'etre of the spiritual path, the wisdom one hopes to come to after all the striving and seeking?

I ask Nani Ma if she wonders whether it is really Babaji who is whispering in her ear, advising her to move into this phase of her sadhana, just as he told her to close her books and meditate at another turning point, all those years ago?

'I don't want to blame him for anything I might do!' Nani Ma says, laughter bubbling in her eyes. 'But I think so. Yet, he said, *karma* yoga, the path of action, is not for sadhus. Karma yoga is for householders, and for sadhus it is *atma-anusandhan* (self-contemplation) or *bhagavat-bhakti* (devotion to God). That is why I am even more confused! Because I am so intent on my Guruji's words. But it has happened, and it doesn't feel wrong. So I am just plodding along. Babaji sometimes said things that were general rules, and individual ones may be different... I don't know.'

Times change. Everything changes. Perhaps, at one time, sadhus needed to be solitary. Now, they might need to go forth and use their knowledge for the greater common good?

'This is it! This is the thing I am wondering about. You see, people do look to sadhus, to spiritual people. A big danger in our society right now is selfishness, and lack of understanding and compassion. So maybe sadhus have to show this, so that everybody will take care of that part of us which needs help. There has been a transition of understanding in myself over the last five years or so. Earlier, when people asked me questions, I spoke only of sadhana. And now I find myself talking about two things—personal sadhana and our debt, our duty in the world at the moment.'

Nani Ma's 'duty in the world' became clear to her when cancer entered her life through a cascade of events. Members of her immediate family, with whom she had lost contact in her initial years as a sadhu, succumbed to the disease. In 1999 she was suspected of cancer herself, but the tumour was found to be benign. Then a close friend with terminal cancer came to die in her ashram.

As she tried to ease his last days for him and his wife, and through her interactions with cancer patients and their caregivers at hospitals, Nani Ma realized the need for spiritual succour in their lives. 'We think of death as being somewhere in the future. But when death comes right in front of you, when you have one or two months to live, then everybody wants to know where they are going. So I think that is the time when there should be a spiritual atmosphere and the possibility of speaking with people. It may not pertain to any particular religion, but to spirituality, which is beyond religion.'

The darkening of earth, river and sky signals the end of my last day at the ashram. There is one more question to ask, as Nani Ma hurries to the shrine hut for the evening aarti, her white sari silver in the moonshine.

How did a celibate sadhvi become a nani?

Nani Ma laughs and says, 'Babaji called me Nani. They had given me the name Gomti Mai at Bageshwar. That name stayed with me for a couple of years when I was with Babaji. One day, I said to him, "Sometimes I feel very old." He said, "Are you a dadi or a nani?' A lady we called Dadi was sitting there. I said, "She is Dadi, so I suppose I must be Nani!" It was just a joke, but after that, Babaji always called me Nani. I felt it was an honour because he spoke a lot of his own nani who had brought him up since he was a baby. Sometimes he called me Vishwa Nani! Nani became my name. Sometimes if I sign my name as Nani, people say this is not a name. But in fact in Gujarat it is a name also. Narsi Mehta (the bhakti saint) had a daughter called Nani. The name stayed, and now it fits because I am old!'

This mystery is solved. As are some others, I think, as I join in the prayers. I look at the photograph of Babaji that had so intrigued me the first day, with his open-as-the-sky quality. Tiny points of light glimmer in the dark before him, like stars in the night outside. I bow my head like everybody else, and whisper a prayer that is all my own:

Like you walked
Quiet and carefree
On the path
May I too
leave behind
the noise of the world
—the whiplash of materiality
—the chatter and buzz
of these soulless bazaars
And find my way
to that stretch of sand
beside Ganga Ma
where she
and you
guide

stony, world-hardened selves
to their final dissolution
so I too
may become
the potbelly of Ganesha here
the discus of Vishnu there
the locks, matted, of Shiva
yonder.
Until I too dissolve
into the eternal flow
of this mother-river
A few grains of sand
and then they too
will be
no more...

3

Ganga, Guru and Grace

SADHVI BHAGWATI

This river
She carries
countless centuries
in her flow
the past made present
made futureal
as she weaves them all
into the matrix of
an eternal now...

Sometimes
Her stories
and histories
get entangled
in nets
intrepid storytellers cast
into her mother-mind
for a good kissa
an audacious afsana...

and a heartwarmer
a soul-whisperer
a seeker's adventure
of a story
leaps out
from her ancient waters
and finds new tongues
  new ears
   new minds
to enchant, enspark, inspire...

—

I haltingly ascend the slimy, steep steps from Nani Ma's ashram, clutching a bag of lemons—prasad—some ripe, others green, from that fragrant tree under which I met her the first time. I stop often to catch my breath, and wonder whether I am actually leaving at all. For a piece of me is buried forever in the white sand on the sacred Ganga beach, embedded in the mother-river's eternal matrix.

If coming to this secluded ashram, and the *satsang* conversations with Nani Ma sparked a journey to the centre of my being, the physical journey out feels like the exact opposite. On the narrow mountain road, the first blaring horn splinters the enchantment wrought by the silent emerald hills, the shifting play of clouds, the sky and the sun, the moods of the Ganga. And I am a traveller once more, a seeker on the move, my backpack filled with questions, my dusty feet drawn to places that might hold the possibility of answers. I head towards the pilgrim-town of Rishikesh where another sadhvi, another Gangetic story, awaits me.

If I were a crow or a glossy-backed mountain raven, the distance between Nani Ma's ashram and Rishikesh could probably have been bridged with a few hundred flaps of my wings. On the road, the distance between the two has increased considerably after the construction of the big, controversial dam at Tehri, Nani Ma had told me as she urged me to leave early if

I intended to reach Rishikesh before dark. Damming the swift waters of the young Ganga and her tributaries in this neck of the Himalayas has endangered the region's fragile and unique ecosystem, displaced settlements and populations, and interfered irrevocably with the being and flow of this, the singlemost revered river in the world.

Nani Ma had recalled Babaji's great sadness when the mother-river first began to be dammed and defiled. Her eyes brimming with tears, she said, 'You know, they are speaking of making two more dams near here. In a couple of years, she may not be here any more. When I first heard this, I thought my heart would break. Until Hardwar, Ganga ji may not be flowing in her natural form. They think they are making some bijli. But it's like cutting down the wish-fulfilling tree for firewood!'

The conversation left me feeling guilty—wasn't I also complicit in this ecological, cultural, spiritual travesty? Wasn't the bijli meant to feed the gargantuan needs of big cities like Delhi, where I live? To air-condition our malls, light up our homes, offices, bazaars and streets, power our television sets and computers? Hydroelectricity may be less polluting in its generation than thermal electricity, but is it really 'clean'? I murmur an apology to the young Ganga as I ruminate this heartbreaking intrusion in her sacred flow.

Since that time, the outcry against the proposed dams has led to two of the projects being temporarily halted. But questions remain that pertain to larger issues of culture and faith, and the age-old clash between forces of modernity and the pre-existing civilizational values of the places they intend to transform and reinvent.

Will there come a time when the goddesshood of the mother-river, like so much else in this civilization-in-a-crisis, becomes a half lived half-memory, a story from history that intrepid storytellers will pull out occasionally from their bags of multicoloured *afsaneh*?

From a sociological perspective, it is interesting to observe tensions between ancient traditions, values and faiths and the compulsions associated with them that may at times be untenable and out of touch, and the impulses of the new, which might harbour strains of materialism, greed, accumulation, exploitation. To use the ideal of the middle path, the best way forward could be to meld that from tradition which is meaningful to us and which connects us with a deeper understanding of life, with aspects of modernism that innovate new ways of thinking and living, such as science, technology, medicine, as also democracy and humanism. The goddesshood of rivers, for instance, could become a way of softening the harsh edge of materialistic, unsustainable progress, and protecting the ecosystems, populations and livelihoods associated with them. As could the wisdom that sees the entire universe as an interconnected web of life be a guiding spirit in the formulation of gentler, ecologically sustainable means of material development.

To make these connections, to contextualize and contemporize traditions and their values in the light of the present, requires a mind that is dynamic and unafraid of change and challenge. A mind modern and ancient in equal proportions, one that doesn't take sides but fosters dialogue between two seemingly irreconcilable extremes. A mind that isn't caught in conflicting dualities, but can see the multiple potentialities inherent in each moment and can manifest some of these in thought and action. A yogi's focused, incisive, compassionate mind, perhaps?

Modern democracies usually function on the principle of separation of religion and state, necessitated by the historical tensions between church and state in medieval Europe, and the power struggles between feudal landlords and priests in India. Also, spiritually enlightened individuals have preferred to keep away from popular politics, though there are examples in history of enlightened rulers who wielded power for the greater common good. Janak, the Ramayana-era ruler of Mithila, Ashoka in the third century BCE and the sixteenth-century Mughal emperor Akbar, stand out as examples of rulers who were seekers themselves, and attempted to infuse statecraft and governance with their spiritual values and insights.

In an increasingly amoral world that prioritizes self-love, greed and personal ambition, there is a clear need for spiritually empowered individuals to take on the challenge of bringing deeper, kinder, ethics-based perspectives into the way we live and think, the way nations are governed and politics conducted, the way businesses are run and corporate policies decided, the way the earth and its ecology are handled, the way science and technology are employed, the way economic progress and human growth are evaluated.

One recent example of such an individual is Tenzin Gyatso, the fourteenth Dalai Lama of Tibet who, despite having lost his country, has displayed a tremendous facility in bringing together ethics and politics, science and spirituality, ecological awareness and statecraft, and a great compassion as the bedrock of all actions and decisions. He has challenged popular perceptions of politicians as being self-serving and power hungry, of monks as being unreal and other worldly, and the spiritual life as being a taking off and going away. The Dalai Lama has often spoken about how his rigorous spiritual practice has equipped him to deal with the formidable circumstances he has had to face. And it is his spiritual practice, and the clarity of mind and compassion of heart that are a direct result of it, that inform his humanitarian work, his promotion of universal responsibility and inter-faith understanding, and his role as an interlocutor of scientific paradigms.

But he is one person. For the idea of spiritual leadership to achieve wider credibility and impact, more spiritual masters need to step up to this challenge. I think of the sadhvi I am on my way to meet, and her guru, who has attempted to expand the boundaries associated with a yogi and a sadhu. Through incessant, compassionate, topical seva, they are recasting the role of a renunciate yet again, just as Swami Vivekananda did in the last century, with his call to purposeful action through the use of the potent tool of nondualistic philosophy in the cause of social upliftment. And Nani Ma is attempting this in the present, as she negotiates the newest bend in her sadhana, towards compassionate action.

The car turns into Rishikesh and the sights, smells and sounds of this bustling pilgrimage centre burst forth instantly. This, I think, is the postcard picture of the popular understanding of Indian spirituality—a stereotype that is not unreal, but doesn't give the whole picture either. Perhaps just a point, a sliver of it. Ash-covered sadhus walk barefoot by the wayside, their dreadlocks massed atop their heads in huge knots. Devotees on their way to temples are laden with puja thalis, those on their way back are distinguishable by the smear of vermilion on their foreheads. Shacks along the sidewalk sell coconuts, sweets, incense and flowers to offer the many resident deities of this Himalayan holy town. And some Western tourists, ubiquitous nowadays at pilgrimage spots made famous by tourist guides, gape at this unabashed, colourful display of faith, their camera-eyes glutted with a surfeit of what must be for them exotic, picturesque subjects.

Like Nani Ma, the sadhvi in Rishikesh too is not Indian by birth. She is an American woman who had been here for more than a decade since 1996, at the time of our interview. Watching the foreign tourists clicking away at every cow, sadhu and street corner, I pause to think about the inner alchemy that transforms a 'regular' person into a seeker. Something happens, and you are not the same again. You can't go back to closing your eyes to the truth of a reality deeper than this most immediate one. It is as if your being becomes attuned to a different *swar*, a different note and pitch, than the one it had previously hummed at. And so a tourist is transformed into a sadhu, a pleasure-tripper acquires the attitude of a pilgrim.

I find meaning, in a quirky way, in the fact that we must go through the bazaar, the noisy part of town, to reach the ashram that is on the other side, across the Ganga. It seems like a pointer to the fact that the spiritual path must traverse the noise of samsara, it cannot be separated from its heat and dust. The ease of equanimity arises once you have dealt with all the noise, inner and outer, once the Ganga of spiritual practice has been bridged.

Swargashram is the part of Rishikesh that is the hub of sadhus, wanderers, seekers. What today is overrun by concrete buildings that house ashrams of various gurus and sects was, not very long ago, when Babaji was alive, the stuff of spiritual lore. There weren't many buildings, except maybe some of the older ashrams, and the white, powdery rock-sand fanned out from the edge of the Ganga till... who knows where? Solitary sadhus lived in undisturbed caves along the narrow valley of the river, absorbed in sadhana. And those who lived in retreat in the higher reaches of the Himalayas would sometimes descend upon Swargashram to interact with seekers and disciples.

Though it is still a spiritual nerve centre, its stillness is compromised by the honking of taxis and cars, the influx of pilgrims and devotees, the familiar pressures of population. The noise of samsara is closer than we realize, I think, as the car lurches on narrow lanes that snake between the ashram walls; equanimity must be maintained in the face of it. It is only fitting that one arrives in a 'heavenly ashram' and here too there is the press of people, the occasional stench of automobile exhaust fumes. Samsara and its circumstances never miraculously disappear. It is how efficient we become in handling its irritants, the flies in the ointment, that determines the level and intensity of our suffering or its mirror opposite, equanimity.

I am finally at the gate of Parmarth Niketan Ashram which, with a thousand rooms, is the largest ashram in Rishikesh. I can hear Ganga Ma but cannot see her. From where I stand, huge cemented quadrangles ringed with gardens, corridors and rooms stretch out in every direction. Mesmerized by the scale of this ashram, such a contrast to Nani Ma's simple cluster of huts, I walk through verandas, past etchings and idols illustrating religious beliefs and stories, until I reach the very end.

There she is, the mother-river, again. Wider here and, somehow, more of a woman than the playful adolescent I have lived next to for the last few days. I descend the steps and immerse my hands in her flow.

Noise quietens... until there is only her...

—

My room faces Ganga Ma. When I arrive it is bathed in a gentle late afternoon light. There is no time to stand and stare—I must go to Sadhvi Bhagwati's office as soon as I've set my backpack down. Soon it will be time for the evening Ganga aarti, an experience she doesn't want me to miss.

We meet in a room that vaguely reminds me of my former workspace in a magazine office. There is a desk, a computer, books, chairs, telephones that ring sometimes. It could actually be an office anywhere, but for the woman sitting before me. Even she could be from anywhere—attractive, young (in her mid-thirties), curly-haired—but for the fact that she is wearing a white sari, an emblem of her renunciation of worldly ways of living and being, and of her commitment to the spiritual path.

'Let's talk as much as we can before the evening aarti,' she says briskly, her hands clasped around a steaming mug of tea. The river breeze has brought an icy chill in its wake, and even though we are ensconced in a closed room with hot tea, some of it gets into my bones, seeping in from the cracks under the doors, through the molecular interstices in the brick walls.

I begin with the assumption that she had some insight into the unsatisfactory nature of the 'good life', the overly stimulated, materialistic, greed- and ambition-driven life, that is fated to run aground in the silt of dissatisfaction and anxiety if one is sensitive enough to its limitations. Was that what prompted her to look for an alternative?

'It's an interesting question because it implies a lot more credit due to me than I actually deserve,' she says thoughtfully. 'My ego would love to say that I realized the inadequacy of Western life and I forsook it all and came here to India in search of a guru. But that's not what happened.'

So she was happy where she was?

'I was twenty-five, and in the West, if you haven't been exposed to Indian culture or to a deep spiritual tradition, you don't know these things exist. In retrospect, if I knew this life existed, I would have searched for it twenty-four hours a day. But you don't know that it exists. Nobody says to you there's something more. What they hand you instead is an equation. If you get a, b, c, d and e, it equals happiness. So you get a, b, c, d and e, and you are happy by default. I was not one of those disillusioned, jaded Westerners, prepared to leave everything in search of something higher. If you had asked me if I was happy, I would have said yes. It's only in retrospect that I look back and realize we were miserable.' She laughs, the corners of her eyes blossoming into happy crinkles.

She was in the middle of her PhD programme when, along with three friends, she decided to take a semester off from the hectic study schedule to travel. India turned up on their radar for entirely non-spiritual reasons—it was cheaper than Europe, they could live here more comfortably on less. And for Sadhvi Bhagwati, what tilted the balance in India's favour was vegetarianism!

'As funny as it is, the one thing at that point that drew me to India was that I was a strict vegetarian. When they decided on India, though I didn't have any particular pull to India, the one thing I thought was, for three and a half months, vegetarian means vegetarian and I don't have to worry. I can eat wherever I want, and if I simply say I am a vegetarian, that's enough. You don't have to add "and that means no eggs, no fish" and so on.'

I absolutely agree, I tell her. As somebody who became vegetarian because of not wishing to take sentient life for food, I often feel blessed to live in a country where vegetarianism is part of the cultural substratum, where ayurveda-inspired vegetarian cuisines have developed over centuries through some careful, some serendipitous experimentation, and where there is an abundance of seasonal vegetables and fruits and legumes and milk products that makes being vegetarian a delight.

Does she think this was a coincidence, or perhaps a pointer to what would turn out to be a life-changing journey?

'I can now point to things and characteristics in which this made sense. My mother was going through old photo albums and mailed me pictures where I was seven or eight, wearing bright yellow overalls, sitting in our backyard in *padmasana*! I have no recollection of being interested in yoga, but there I was. Now that I've made this choice, you can certainly go through the first twenty-five years of my life and say that these things were foreshadowing an event that would take place later. But it was something that was not in my consciousness at that time.'

Sadhvi Bhagwati's refusal to enforce a patina of foreknowledge or intuition upon anything is refreshing. Though she does believe it was all part of God's plan for her.

'When I was in the airplane coming to India, I made a vow to myself. I've got to keep my heart open because there is a plan, and I just don't know what it is. It wasn't me who had left looking for something. It was God who had for whatever reason decided that this was the moment in my life when the blindfold would come off. And that which had seemed to be reality would cease to be reality, and true reality would begin.'

Like the downhill rush of a mountain stream in spring, swollen with melting snow, the divine plan unspooled with an energy all its own. With no real plans and not much information about the country they had arrived in, the group of friends pored over guidebooks when they landed in Delhi. 'I flipped through the guidebook and said, "Rishikesh!"' says Sadhvi. 'I didn't know about the Himalayas or Ganga, but there were mountains and a river and it sounded very peaceful. I've always been an outdoorsy person, always loved nature. And it was close to Delhi. It seemed like a nice place to rest for a few days.'

Their choice of hotel—the only hotel at the time near Parmarth Niketan Ashram—apparently concurred with God's plan. The day she arrived, the moment she saw Ganga Ma, something shifted within the young American student.

'We get here, and I go down to the banks of the Ganga, and

I burst into tears. And that was it! I had come home. It was like twenty-five years of my life were on one hand, and that moment of being here was on the other hand. And nothing mattered. People talk about vairagya and detachment; for me, it was just God's grace. There was not an element of sadhana or tapasya that I had to undergo to pull myself away from that world. In that moment, it was like God came with a pair of scissors and just cut off anything that was not going to be conducive to the rest of my life. So there was no difficulty at all, again not due to any credit of my own, in making the decision to stay. It was all that mattered to me. I just cried, but not sad tears—tears of truth, tears of having come home.'

How can one describe an experience so profound, so unexpected? Here was this person, happy with the life she had, with no world-weariness, no existential crisis driving her inwards. There was no *seeking* whatsoever, no effort, no practice. And for no apparent reason, a cataclysmic upheaval occurs. Preconceived notions about self and other, life and death, home and work, pain and loss are detonated, as it were, and one's 'old' life caves in about one's ears. What *was*, no longer exists. What *is*, is new and unexplained.

Another recorded instance of an unstriven-for awakening comes to my mind, where there was no other conceivable agent except perhaps an inner urge that was not apparent to the everyday mind and, as Sadhvi Bhagwati contends, the mysterious working of divine grace. It is an awakening experience that is also indicative of the ecumenical and inclusive nature of the phenomenon—it doesn't always happen to saffron-clad renunciates, it may well happen to a holidaying American, or an adolescent Zoroastrian student. The year was 1913. In Pune, nineteen-year-old Merwan Sheriar Irani was cycling home from college. Something he did every day, except that on this day he encountered an old woman from Baluchistan, a mystic, Hazrat Babajan, who had come to Pune twenty years before and lived under a neem tree. They sat in silence for a while, and then Babajan kissed him on the forehead.

With that, Merwan's old personality seemed to dissolve. What he had been before he no longer was. A period of mystical madness followed, where the young man seemed to function at a plane of consciousness completely disconnected from ordinary reality. Gradually, through the guidance of such adepts of the time as Upasani Maharaj of Sakori and Sai Baba of Shirdi, Merwan's intense God-intoxication stabilized and became the bedrock on which he based his role as a silent, teaching presence in countless lives, in the form of Avatar Meher Baba.

I do not intend to completely equate Sadhvi Bhagwati's spontaneous and cathartic experience by the Ganga with the incident Meher Baba's followers refer to as his 'unveiling', when he began to become aware of his true purpose in life. But we may look at these as two examples in an extensive range of experiences that make up that mysterious inner phenomenon we refer to as 'awakening'. Spiritual literature has described the occurrence of inner awakening in different degrees and with varying qualities of insight. The full-blown awakening, the acme of human perfection and the Holy Grail of spiritual seeking, what is referred to as 'enlightenment' or 'nirvana' or 'moksha' or 'kaivalya' in different traditions, could be seen as its most complete form when no vestiges of a conditioned personality remain and individual consciousness is completely submerged in cosmic consciousness.

Obviously, 'fully awakened ones' are rare. A majority of documented instances of awakening belongs to a wide spectrum that ranges from dissatisfaction and ennui to an energic unwinding of the *kundalini* to a spontaneous recognition of one's guru—the list could be endless because of the sheer array of potentialities that exist in the ways in which realization can be triggered in the human mind. If there are as many paths as there are seekers, there could well be as many ways in which the quilt of darkness that covers true knowing comes off, bit by bit. Every spark of realization snips a corner off that heavy quilt and affords a peek into the true nature that lies hidden underneath. Zen, for instance, makes the distinction between *satori*, 'catching on', which implies a flash of sudden awareness that leads to greater knowing, and *kensho*, which refers to a momentary glimpse of one's true nature. Both are qualitatively different experiences of the same reality, and do not in themselves constitute enlightenment. A Zen parable compares kensho with preliminary baby steps, and satori with learning how to walk. Satori is also thought to be tentative and hesitant at first, and must be built upon with regular practice, comparable to wading into a lake—the further in one goes, the deeper it becomes.

Sadhvi Bhagwati's spontaneous experience by the Ganga could be seen as a first step towards a lifetime of walking towards Truth. Her outpouring of tears perhaps was an emptying out of her 'old' self, a catharsis that left her free and open to new possibilities when they presented themselves.

'I would walk through this ashram because it was a much cleaner and nicer way of getting to the Ganga from the hotel where I was staying. I was walking through the ashram one day and I heard a voice. It was loud and clear and it said, "You must stay here." I was not a mystic who heard voices. I was a scientist, and that too a neurologist. I had control of my brain. I knew how everything functioned. I didn't hear voices! I looked around and there was no one. I remembered my vow (*to remain open*); there was a message. I looked up and saw a sign that said "Office". I came in and that's how it all started.'

How did she meet her guru, Swami Chidananda Saraswati?

'I met Swamiji in a room, this room in fact, where he used to meet people earlier.' Both of us instinctively look around, and I imagine the self-assured woman sitting before me now walk in all those years ago, a little hesitant, unsure of herself. 'In the beginning I didn't understand Hindi and loved to just sit here,' she remembers. 'And what is amazing is the tone of voice he used and the attention and love that came from his eyes to the poorest of the poor and the dirtiest of the dirty was exactly the same as that which was given to high-ranking officials or distinguished guests from abroad. If you had been blind and could only hear the tone of his voice and his words, you'd never know who he was talking to. And it was a first-come-first-served thing. Those who came late had to wait for those who came first to finish.'

Swamiji's compassion does not differentiate on the basis of anything, she says, and focuses instead on the need each individual brings to him. To me, this is a refreshing departure from some eminent gurus who are known to confer special darshans and one-on-one meetings upon the rich and the powerful, while the ordinary follower must be content with a glimpse in a mass gathering. The playing field is rarely level in this, the world of spiritual endeavouring too, and a democratically organized ashram and guru may well indicate a better understanding of non-duality and oneness, which most gurus speak about but only a few seem to actually practise.

As she observed Swamiji, Sadhvi Bhagwati realized this was the person she would like to learn from, who could guide her on the path. But things weren't all that simple. Old conditioning, rooted in the culture and tradition she had grown up in, posed a challenge to all that she was feeling now, in the presence of Swamiji, in this ashram, by the river she was increasingly, inexplicably, coming to think of as her mother.

'I was raised in the Jewish tradition which, contrary to the Christian tradition, believes God absolutely cannot take form, does not take form, will not take form,' she says. 'To think of God in form is sacrilege. One of the ten commandments of Judaism is "Thou shalt not worship false idols". It is truly considered one of the worst sins you could commit to assume that God comes in form. Okay, we don't question these things. I wasn't one of those children who spend a lot of time thinking of religion's teachings and their validity. I mean, you accept it.'

Until now, that is, when the felt truth of her experiences in Rishikesh could not be denied and held up against the light of what she had been taught, led her to question some of those beliefs.

'I was sitting here and it was an amazing experience because I was in the presence of God. And it was as palpable and undeniable as anything I had ever experienced. Here is a core foundational belief of the religion in which I have been raised, that God cannot take form, and here I am having an experience that is totally contrary. Not that the religion is wrong. I am not going to say this is wrong or this is right. But for me, here I am having an experience that turns upside down literally everything I've been taught. There was no way I could tell myself this wasn't true and the religion was right because you couldn't deny it. It was palpable, it was there in that experience, like I'm hot or I'm cold, or this is a hot cup of tea. You can tell me as many times as you want and bring in as many people to tell me that actually this cup of tea is cold, but as it scalds my hand, I'm not going to believe you.'

With her scientist's mind, Sadhvi Bhagwati proceeded to question other aspects of the value system she had grown up with. 'Suddenly my whole world turned upside down because I started thinking, wow, if they're wrong about something as important as God, maybe they're wrong about other things. Maybe the whole value system in which I've been raised is wrong. This was the first thing that turned upside down. But couldn't everything else get turned upside down just as easily?'

Was that when she decided to enter into the spiritual life under Swamiji's guidance? 'Because I was not raised in this culture, the concept of guru never arose. It only arose much later when I realized that there was an official name for this connection I was experiencing. But it was a long time before I started using words like "guru" and "disciple"—they weren't part of my vocabulary. But I knew without a doubt that I was supposed to be here. That I was supposed to be near and in the service of this being. That I would learn where I needed to go in my life through his teachings, through being here, through his influence. Later, when you learn what a guru is, then you realize, oh yeah, he's my guru! But at the time I didn't have a word for it.'

The spiritual apprenticeship had begun without any fuss or formality, as the young PhD student found herself flowing into a way of life that prioritized inner growth above all else. Where the most palpable reality was precisely that which is the most ignored aspect of our everyday lives—the life of the spirit. As Sadhvi Bhagwati constantly emphasizes, the decision seemed to have been made for her, it was God's grace more than her own doing. An actual miracle, much more emphatic than the voice in her head, convinced her that this was indeed so.

She was still on her vacation and her friends, who thought she had 'gone completely nuts', planned to go up to the mountains for a few days. She could join them, or stay on at the ashram. Swamiji told her to do as she pleased—a room would be waiting for her at the ashram when she returned. 'I said okay, and walked out. I got to the hand pump in the middle of the ashram. Then I was going to turn right to go out of the ashram. And I froze. Literally. I was walking fine and it was as if I had stepped into a puddle of quick-bonding glue. I couldn't lift my feet from the ground.'

The bizarre situation threw her into a panic. 'Immediately I started thinking, all right, I've got some disease, tetanus or polio, something I was supposed to be vaccinated for and the vaccination hasn't worked. Then I calmed down and thought, tetanus and polio don't come on quite like this. There's no pain. I am not falling. Then I thought, well, I was sitting on the floor and I'm not used to it. Maybe my legs have fallen asleep. But there were no pins and needles and my feet were glued to the ground. Right there, in the middle of the day, eleven-thirty in the morning.'

Soon a crowd had gathered around this woman who was strangely and miraculously glued to the ground. 'The drama went on for about a minute. Then a group of kids came running towards me, and instinctively I moved back. And I thought, oh, I am free. Now I can go. And again I couldn't move. I couldn't lift my foot. Using my logic of deduction, I thought that perhaps I had got some weird disease and my legs don't move forwards now, they move backwards. So I flip around to walk myself out of the ashram backwards. And I couldn't move in that direction. Then I realized, all right, I get it, God. And I started walking forward back in this direction, into the ashram. And of course

I could walk fine! It was just that I couldn't walk away from the ashram.'

Only three minutes had passed since she had walked out. Swamiji didn't seem surprised to see her again so soon.

She said, 'I think I am supposed to stay *now*.'

He said, 'Welcome.'

—

The clanging of bells alerts us to the evening aarti. A mellifluous chanting of shlokas moves past the door as if borne by the swift Ganga breeze, before we have had time to wrap our shawls around us and step out. In the gathering dusk, I make out a group walking rapidly towards the Ganga. It is Swamiji surrounded by saffron-clad boys, *rishikumars*, young sages from the gurukul run by the ashram. Sadhvi Bhagwati signals me to run along, which I do, the cement floor cold under my bare feet.

The group has reached the steps that lead into the Ganga long before I make it. They are quickly surrounded by pilgrims, tourists, ashram guests and the omnipresent camera-toting Westerners. I find a quiet spot among the milling crowds, and orient myself towards the mother-river, her waters incandescent in the reflected light of the lamps flickering in her devotees' hands.

The aarti moves through shlokas and hymns dedicated to the Ganga and other deities, sung with a beauty that has more to do with heartfelt devotion than voice quality or musical training. Heavy brass receptacles that hold the leaping, sparkling flames to venerate the Ganga are passed around. At some moment, when I am lost in contemplation of the light-dappled water before and the darkening indigo sky above, I am handed the flaming receptacle.

Collective ritual to honour, please or placate deities of earth and sky is one of the oldest religious expressions of humanity. As I stand before Ganga Ma, weighted by the brass receptacle for my few moments as aarti performer, I feel the combined prayer of the congregation rise in my heart. I have never been attracted to ritual, preferring to delve into the spirit that inspired it, rather than its performance-oriented manifestation. Yet there is something magical about bending towards the eternal flow of this river goddess, my huge reverence for her crystallized in a cluster of light, my being articulating the ancient hymns that bespeak her power and beauty and love.

—

I leave Ganga Ma's side rather reluctantly, unmindful of the icy wind that has chafed my cheeks a brilliant red. The ashram's neon lights hurt my eyes after the soothing darkness illuminated by lamps glimmering unsteadily in the wind. I find my way back to Sadhvi Bhagwati's office where, as she had promised, she is waiting for me. As evening metamorphoses into night, we resume talking about her journey into the heart of spiritual life.

Did she just stay on after the 'glued to the ground' miracle? Did she never leave, then, the decision seemingly made for her by a divine extra-human power?

Not quite. At the end of the three-month vacation, she was certain she wanted to stay, that this was the direction her life would take from now on. 'I was getting my PhD in paediatric neurology to help children. But at the end of the day, the only thing that was benefiting was my own ego. Being here, even if you forget how much peace and joy you get, from a purely utilitarian standpoint, everything you do makes the world a better place. There is no correlation between the number of people with MDs and PhDs and the misery and despair and poverty in the world. I told Swamiji, "Every moment you live, everything you do, is making the world a better place. I want to be here and I want to be part of that, and I want to live in this paradise dream world! Please don't make me go back."'

But Swamiji asked her to go back. He could foresee implications of her actions that the young American woman, in the first flush of excitement about this new way of life, could not. Swamiji guided her through this phase of ecstasy, where she needed to ground her realization and turn it into a workable, practicable life-choice, like Merwan needed to relearn how to function in the mundane world after the doors of his consciousness had blasted open.

'When you are in those initial throes of ecstasy,' Sadhvi Bhagwati says, 'God cuts you off in such a way from the outside world that you don't wonder what people are thinking, what their reaction will be. All I kept thinking was, this is divine! This is God! Of course they're going to love it. So I was making calls home saying things like, "Mom, I found God and my guru," and you can't even imagine what my parents sitting in Hollywood were thinking about their twenty-five-year-old Jewish daughter in India who was calling home and talking about God and guru and Ganga!'

Her laughter carries an awareness of the fear such a dramatic transformation might invoke among those that have known and loved what one was before one's old life was torn asunder by the winds of spiritual realization. And who had no way of gauging the truth of her experiences first hand and were perhaps functioning from a wariness that comes from instances where people have been duped by con artists posing as gurus or been lured into exploitative cults.

She remembers Swamiji saying, 'Look, if this is going to be forever then you have to do this properly. For you to call home and simply say you're not coming back is not the right decision.' If she had done that, she says, 'My parents would have been on the next plane over with the police and the cult de-programmers and whoever else they needed in their army to get their daughter out of the clutches of whoever had brainwashed her!' What was a miraculously transformative experience for her could easily have been perceived as a threat, as an attempt to exploit or brainwash, and led to conflict, misunderstanding and sadness for everybody involved.

Swamiji had another reason to send her back to complete her PhD, and that was to ensure that her choice of a spiritual life *over* a worldly one was accorded respect, rather than being regarded as a running away, an escape. Sadhvi Bhagwati recounts what he said at the time, 'Nobody wants to accept the validity of a spiritual path. It's a mirror of their lives. They spend every day in the clutches of maya and running after possessions and sensory pleasures—they don't want a mirror of spirituality in their face.'

Is this also because of the herd mentality that breeds conformism to the status quo, which a spiritual life undermines by opting out of socially accepted norms? Not only does one begin to look and behave differently, the very goals of one's life are radically altered. One is no longer in the rat race for a bigger and better salary, one no longer covets the things of the world, or even its relationships. One finds a new way of being, which has nothing to do with what one has or is, but is based on a continual effort to perfect oneself inwardly, in one's thought, speech and action, and grow towards a union, a yoga, with one's true nature, the Original Self.

Sadhvi Bhagwati explains with an example of how peer pressure works. A group of friends goes to a pub. They order beer, except for one who wants to drink water. The others try and get her to drink beer too, not because they care what she drinks, but because the choice not to drink beer is a mirror of the decision they are making. If everybody drinks beer, there's no mirror. Hence the pressure to conform, which will make everyone comfortable with the choice he or she has made.

'People don't want that mirror in their lives,' Swamiji told her. 'They will always look to criticize or condemn or belittle the decision you've made. Nobody wants to accept that somebody could be thriving and succeeding in the Western world, to have the chance to be on the path to what they all want, and leave it for spirituality. Because that's a mirror of their own choices.'

Swamiji saw Sadhvi Bhagwati's potential to be a role model for the spiritual way of life. He said, 'If you're going to make this decision, you're going to stand as a model of somebody who has chosen this life over that life. And it's going to be a mirror because you are going to be someone they cannot write off. In order to do that, you must go back. You must show them that even having had this experience, you are able to succeed in their world. And then, if you still want to, you can make the decision to leave that world. If you just call and say I'm never coming back, you will be happy, but the message you are supposed to convey to the world will be lost because every person who hears the story will think something happened to her in India. She was brainwashed or she had a breakdown or she got scared to go back, whatever.'

'You go back and show them,' he said.

And show them she did. She had always been a straight-A student, and Swamiji urged her to complete her course with the same kind of high grades. Going back to college (Stanford University) was challenging because she didn't connect with the anxiety to achieve worldly or academic success any more. It was as if her spirit, the most vital part of her being, had been left behind at her guru's feet, by the mother-river. She felt disconnected with everything that had excited her in her old life—her studies, college, grades—and yet she knew she had to succeed to return to fulfil the spiritual yearning that gnawed at her and wouldn't let her be.

'It was quite a semester because graduate halls are small and I always sat in the front row. The teacher is doing probabilities and statistics on the board, and I am sobbing. Noiselessly, but tears are pouring down my eyes. I took my final exams a week early and was on a plane back here the Friday my exams finished. That was it! When the grades came, if mine were less than spectacular, I would have to go back. But I got straight As.'

What helped was that 'the nonsense that fills our brains 99 per cent of the time' wasn't there, so she could focus better. 'Even though I was no longer interested in the subject, it took me much less time to do things than it did previously. I was much clearer and focused. A lot of people think that when you get really deep in the spiritual path, it muddles your brain, you are not able to think clearly, that you are not able to be rational. What I have found is the opposite. It clears the brain in such a way... I mean, Swamiji's brain is like a computer. He doesn't forget anything.

The more I read and hear about the enlightened masters, they're not muddled. They're as crystal clear as it gets.'

Indeed, one of the functions of spiritual practice has been described as clearing the mind of its junk, its sticky thoughts and habit patterns, its clinging to notions of self and other, its own happiness and definitions of how things should be, and its insistent repulsing of that which is not agreeable to its narrow scheme of things. As the mud is sifted out, through repeated and strenuous effort, the true nature of the mind emerges, luminous and clear.

Hers is a clarity that will not be denied.

—

Sannyas cannot be selective leaving; all bonds to worldly existence must systematically be sundered, including the ones that have nurtured us into being and shadowed our lives, and the ones that are carved in our hearts, like the old man seems to be in the moon. Sannyas cannot be half-hearted, or half-minded. You must die, as it were, to be reborn into the spiritual path, into a childless, parentless, spouseless existence, where old relationships cease and all are perceived as manifestations of the one reality. For an only child like Sadhvi Bhagwati, the break with her parents, and their hopes for her, might have been more difficult than for most. For her parents would, in the language of the world, 'lose' her to an existence of complete dedication to her guru and her inner growth.

Their acceptance of her choice came as a relief, one that liberated her to walk the path without any guilt or residual sadness. 'They didn't understand the decision, yet they were very supportive of me,' she says. 'My dad was amazing, I'll never forget. He said, "In twenty-five years you've never taken a decision that I think is wrong. I don't understand this decision, but who am I to assume that just because I don't understand it, suddenly after twenty-five years you've started making wrong decisions?" I still get tears in my eyes when I think about it—for a father to have that kind of respect and faith was just wonderful.'

It has been more than a decade now. Has anything changed with them? 'Once they met Swamiji, they really, really understood completely. And once they came here they were completely sold. They love it. My dad says things to me like, "So, when you're talking to God, put in a good word for me. Tell Him I'm not as bad as I seem!" This kind of support for one's choices from loved ones, even when they don't necessarily comprehend what instigated those choices, empowers one in a manner that getting one's way with aggression and conflict doesn't.

Women in traditionally patriarchal societies rarely get this kind of unconditional support from their families who expect them to conform to predetermined gender roles. Sannyas, like education or a career or a self-chosen husband, or even planned pregnancies or same-sex affiliations—anything where the woman makes an empowered and informed choice for herself—are seen as threatening the gender status quo, and therefore are taboo. Even when women grow out of too tight a circle of conformity with education and jobs, they are still required to stay within certain 'inviolable' boundaries. For instance, they may be able to choose who to marry, as long as the caste, religion and in some cases sex, are acceptable. They must bargain with patriarchy for their freedom, for their right to wander outside the concentric circles drawn around them. I wonder in which circle the right to sannyas might fall?

This brings me to the question that Nani Ma and I had discussed—the importance of sannyas in leading a spiritually-oriented life. Though I think Nani Ma answered it conclusively, as somebody who has also grappled with the choice, I would like to know the inner journey that was required of Sadhvi Bhagwati before she was formally ordained, and the reasons that convinced her of its necessity and efficacy for her as a spiritual practitioner. The fact that she came to live at Parmarth Niketan Ashram in 1996 and her formal ordination took place only in June 2000 suggests she had some time to contemplate the issue.

'Prior to taking sannyas, I didn't think it was important at all,' she confesses. 'I was living this life and, from an external perspective, nothing in my life had changed. I was dressing the same and living the same. I went from being "Bhagwati" to "Sadhvi Bhagwati". That was it, really. I anticipated that it would be purely a semantic issue. And yet there is something indescribable and very powerful about the ritual itself.' She likens it to the difference between a live-in relationship and a marriage. 'On the outside, every aspect of a couple's lives prior to marriage and after it remains the same. And yet, going through that ritual of getting married—there's a reason people do it.'

This resonates with my epiphany about ritual earlier in the evening, during the collective aarti by the Ganga. It can exert a strong psychological impact, and lead to a deepening, a greater connecting.

'There is something powerful about ritual,' agrees Sadhvi Bhagwati, 'and I believe that this, the sannyas ritual, is particularly powerful. Simply having to do with the Vedic tradition in which it is done, there were some very powerful changes that took place internally, if not externally. Again, not in terms of decisions or actions, because the choices I was making were the same before as after. But there was a powerful shift that took place internally. A distillation and crystallization of that relationship with God, as though the remnants of anything else that were left floating around in my consciousness got stuck in the strainer and thrown out. And that which had been distilled was all that was left.'

Was there any particular aspect of the ritual that enabled this shift, this re-forming of her being in a purely spiritual context?

'It was a long ritual and there were many aspects, in terms of mantras that were chanted, baths in Ganga, taking of *sankalpa* (vow), yajna, all of it. It wasn't as if there was one moment in which I could say I felt the shift. And yet a very important shift took place. I remember right afterwards, when I came out from my last bath in Ganga and went to Swamiji to do my pranam to him, he put his hands on my head. And it was as though my entire mind just went into his hands. From that moment on, there's been this feeling that wherever he wants it to go, it goes. It doesn't have that aimless wandering that minds tend to have. It was like somehow stillness was imposed onto it.'

For a moment, I try and imagine how that would be. A falling away of un-needed baggage, a stilling of the ceaseless chatter that has earned the mind the well-deserved sobriquet of a restless monkey. Yet I am unable to fully come to terms with an inner experience being *given* by somebody, without self-striving, mainly because it is a dangerous assumption to carry on the path. Seekers sometimes tend to become completely dependent on external agents for spiritual attainment and forego the inner work required of them, such as cultivating mindfulness, watching afflictive emotions and their patterns of arising, substituting them with positive emotions, and so on. The guru, even an enlightened one, can only guide and direct. It is the seeker who must walk the path.

Sadhvi Bhagwati's journey, however, has had pivotal moments where her being was opened to the spiritual when she least expected it, her steps were guided (or glued!), her hand held, her mind stilled. This too, then, is part of the path. The acceptance of grace when it appears in one's life, along with the gifts of knowing and intuiting, requires one to give up the egoistic attitude of wilful doing. Sometimes, one needn't *do*. Only *being* might be sufficient. And allowing the Ganga of grace to flow through one's mind and life, flushing out that which is not required on the path, and purifying and watering that which is.

Does the quality of one's effort somehow improve with sannyas? And could some of those qualities be replicated by women who are unable to renounce home and family?

'Deeksha or official ordination is very important if this is the path you are choosing—the path of renunciation. But this does not mean that in order to walk the spiritual path, it is crucial to choose the path of renunciation. Those are two very different things. To officially walk a path of renunciation, to go through that ritual under the guidance of a guru, to be literally carried over the threshold from that world to this world, is very powerful. But there is certainly no need for women who want to walk the spiritual path to have to forsake everything and become renunciates.'

This is an important distinction—between renunciation and the spiritual path per se—because at times one is thought to be synonymous with the other. Spiritual practice should actually be as malleable as gold, capable of being compressed into thin sheets and spread over one's life, as foil over a bowl of rice kheer or wrapped around a delicate banarasi paan. Women, to circumvent their homebound existence and lack of avenues to train with gurus, have learnt the art of spiritual malleability well.

'I think women are inherently spiritual,' says Sadhvi Bhagwati. 'There are a lot of women I know, especially older ones, who have that light of realization glistening in their eyes, yet whose days are spent taking care of a family of who knows how many children and grandchildren. So there is certainly no need for them to renounce that family and run off to the mountains. One of my favourite quotes actually is from B.K.S. Iyengar, whose yoga I study. His is a type of yoga in which the practice is extensive. A lot of women complain that once they become mothers, their practice suffers. And his response always is, "Being a mother now *is* your practice." Don't consider yourself a yogi because you have perfected your *trikonasana* while your kid is drowning in the bathtub. That's not yoga. Yoga means the union of self with God. Whatever you are doing is uniting you with God.'

The inherence of the spiritual in women—a view expressed not infrequently—could be seen as a broad generalization, a particularization of the feminine into idealized, preconceived notions of what being a woman is. It would be helpful, at this point, to cast a question regarding the very nature of the feminine—is it bound to biology, or is there a deeper character to the feminine that is not physical alone, that is quite universal, like a value system or nature, if one has to look at it that way?

'I think a woman by her nature gives, whether it's her time, her love, her heart,' says Sadhvi. 'Society and culture, which have been recently trying to convince women that in order to succeed they have to be men, I think are stripping women of that. It's not that every woman today is a fountain of generosity, but I think by nature, their essence is giving. I believe that's why so many enlightened masters have that maternal aspect, because they don't want anything for themselves. They become this giving energy.'

She tells me how, when Swamiji travels, they make sure he carries enough food for five or six people because, inevitably, even on a flight, he will feed the people he finds around him during meal times. 'A stewardess will ask him, "Would you like a glass of water?" and he'll say, "No, but you should try this Indian roti." So if you pack for one, he eats nothing because he gives it all away. And he just becomes so happy doing this.'

Realized masters, and those who are matured in spiritual practice, seem to enter an extra-gendered space where 'masculine' and 'feminine' no longer carry the kind of harsh, divisive boundaries that they do otherwise. So, male masters acquire characteristics typically associated with mothers, while female masters shed some of the conditioning that comes with being a woman to embrace a fearless quality of being.

Having witnessed her own guru's motherliness and his capacity for nurture and giving, how would she describe the breaking or transcending of gender stereotypes on the path?

'So many people talk of Swamiji as their mother. I think what enables a mother to be a mother is not just giving, but because the child always comes first. It's sacrifice, which is more specific than giving. A mother will go hungry to feed her child with no resentment. She is not doing it because it is her duty, or because people will say she's a good mother. She does it instinctively. She would never dream of doing anything else. I think the same sacrificial nature is what you see in enlightened masters, men or women. They don't think of themselves but of others. That is a maternal quality.'

Our minds, operating from conditioned thought and perception, equate nurture with motherhood, which in turn we associate with femininity, because that is the way of the world—women become mothers, they care for their children, in a manner that is usually selfless. What if the kind of sacrifice and care that realized masters embody has nothing to do with gender, what if it is an essential quality of the pure compassion that comes with a freeing of self from ego personality, so that everything is experienced as one interconnected phenomenon, without otherness? Which is also perhaps what the mother feels with her infant who, for all practical purposes, seems like an extension of her, and with whom the ego has not come into play?

I ask Sadhvi Bhagwati about the genderlessness that comes with deep spiritual realization. About her guru, she says, 'He really is both—I wouldn't say he is neither, I'd say he's both. I would say he is gender-full, rather than gender-less, because he is feminine *and* masculine.' The ideal of *Ardhanarishwara* suggests itself in this context, where Shiva is half-feminine and half-masculine, the two halves conjoined to form a whole. Shiva, who is considered the supreme yogi, conveys in this form what Sadhvi articulates as a fullness of gender. He is this *and* that, as feminine as he is masculine, thereby a master of characteristics of both genders and an epitome of the balance and inclusiveness that forms the core of the nondualistic perspective.

In essence, as I see it, sannyas is a movement into genderlessness because the determinants and markers of gender and sexuality are deactivated in a sense, and one could assume they no longer play as crucial a role in determining one's identity as they would otherwise. Sannyas could also lead to gender-fullness, as the heart opens up and the practice matures.

What has been Sadhvi's own experience?

'I wouldn't say I am gender-full,' she says candidly. 'I would say I am more in the genderless part; I do feel genderless. The aspect that makes you feminine, I don't feel so much of it in terms of the things we normally associate with being feminine. I certainly feel the maternal aspect—all the rishikumars, I just love them. What I don't feel is that aspect of the feminine *with relation to* the masculine. Usually when you think of "feeling like a woman", the implication somewhere, even unspoken, has to do in relation to a man. And I don't feel that. If it ever comes up externally, I always find myself very surprised to be reminded of the fact that I am still a young female. Because it's not part of my consciousness to navigate the world from the framework of a female.'

The vow of celibacy, I think, is much more than not having sex—it is a widening of one's circumference of being, and one's capacity to love. As a woman, or a man, there are a finite number of relationships we can pour our love into. As a celibate sannyasi, however, if one can open one's heart to the immensity of life, one's ability to love could possibly become infinite. By leaving one's gendered identity, one's sexuality, behind, one gets out of a lot of compulsions and boundaries and straitjacketing that come with gender. For women, this genderlessness can be especially empowering because it affords an experience of dealing with each human being on an individual basis, and not as a woman, and having to tailor one's responses accordingly.

Sadhvi Bhagwati talks of her own un-gendering as a sannyasi. 'I have noticed that the aspect that makes us feminine in relation to men—that "I am half, you are half, let's become one"—it's not there in me. The difference in vibrational energy, the unspoken energy between a man and a woman—I don't feel it in the presence of men. On that level, I would not say that I am a full, total embodiment of the feminine and the masculine, the way I think Swamiji is. But my own feelings about femininity, in terms of being a woman in the world, that has gone away. Now it's much more "I am me in the world". And I may have the body of a female, and that may enable me to put a rishikumar on my lap with more love and tenderness than an *acharya* (male teacher) would, but I don't necessarily associate that in my consciousness with an aspect of being a woman.'

This is interesting, I tell her, the fact that she doesn't feel her motherliness to be automatically rooted in her femininity. Perhaps it *is* part of the spectrum of human emotions that can be accessed by anybody who attempts to open their heart and love unconditionally, as a mother does her child. What is also fascinating is the idea of sexual neutrality, of not navigating the world as a man or a woman. Just as a human being.

'Many times, women who come from abroad talk about the inappropriate comments men make on the streets. It makes me realize how much of a role the energy we exude plays in how the world treats us. Because it's not just that I don't navigate the world as a female. It's been years and years since anybody, and not just the people who know me in Rishikesh but anybody wherever I go, has made any sort of inappropriate comment or advance. And it's certainly not that I've become really old or hideously ugly. Somehow, the energy shift that took place in me has changed the whole unconscious, unspoken energy dynamic with others. And when I became unavailable, and not just in the sense of being married or in love with somebody else, but unavailable with the awareness that in this lifetime, this body is no longer available in that way to anyone, people stopped responding to it as though it were.'

What Sadhvi says about the shift in one's energy dynamic rings true. But there have been times when I have been the target of sexual remarks on the streets and in public transport, and I don't think it is because I have given off a particularly sexual vibe. Perhaps it is her white sari, this garb of a renunciate, that acts as a protective shield? People in this culture respect a sadhvi instinctively, young and beautiful though she may be, as Sadhvi Bhagwati is with her long, flowing hair, petite frame and gentle, smiling eyes.

'It's really been an interesting thing to watch,' she says, 'because as I said, it's been so long since anybody's hooted or winked or whistled. And it's true abroad also. Here, you can say you are in white and people know what that means. But it's also true in the streets of Manhattan. So I think the energy we give out plays a huge role in the energy we get back. The way my energy has shifted has played a really big role in the way people's energy is with me. It would never occur to me, for instance, to say that a woman could come and sit here but not a man because I'll be uncomfortable. That whole concept of woman–man has gone from my consciousness.'

What has changed, I suppose, is that as a sannyasi, she is relating directly with the core of the person before her, rather than their gender or any other aspect of their identity. 'Exactly!' she says. 'And what I have found is that people respond to me in the same way. I don't feel I get treated as an attractive female. I get treated as who I am. That's why it has been said, "Change yourself first".'

And that is why, perhaps, true seekers have always laid greater emphasis on an inner sannyas, a renunciation of the mind and heart, rather than sporting its external symbols. As Kabir says,

Tan ko jogi sab kare, man ko virla koye
Sahaj sab vidhi paiyye, jo man jogi hoye

It is easy to don the garb of a renunciate,
true renunciation is where one renounces from the heart.

For such a person, everything flows effortlessly.

I think of the issue of 'foreignness' that Nani Ma had to deal with while staying at Babaji's traditional Hindu ashram, and what Atmananda went through in the ashrams of Sri Anandamayi Ma. Did Sadhvi Bhagwati live through something similar? Was she ever a pariah in this community because of her race, the colour of her skin?

She thinks really hard, and the answer is no. She wasn't debarred from doing anything, or touching anything, or not given spiritual training because she was not a caste Hindu. This is a departure from accounts of so many other ashrams, and could be a sign of the cosmopolitan nature of the guru *and* his disciples, the latter perhaps more so, because the guru rarely effects prejudicial dos and don'ts. Rather, he or she defers to the norms followed by a majority of followers, and tends to use the feelings of hurt and discrimination to help the targeted disciple wear away the ego. Swami Chidananda Saraswati has ensured that his ashram is open to all castes, nationalities and genders, and he teaches and tours abroad where he attracts sizeable following. He is more of a twenty-first century master, in terms of his broad-based appeal and his emphasis on the essence of sanatana dharma than on the narrow-minded prejudices that came to afflict its practice, which are best left behind as relics of the past.

Sadhvi Bhagwati did have to undergo some cultural readjustment, though, and learn what was acceptable and what wasn't in her adopted culture. She tells me of an incident when she was new at the ashram and didn't speak any Hindi. One day, as she was getting her morning cup of tea, she asked a young man, who spoke English and visited the ashram with his family, if he would like to join her by the Ganga. 'Now, from the minute I got here, I was sannyasi in my mind. I didn't know what sannyas meant, but any thought of a physical relationship or romance was completely absent. It had all been sucked as though by a vacuum cleaner out of me. Nor was there any such thought in his mind, I'm sure. In less than an hour, the news that the new American girl was sitting on the banks of Ganga, having tea with the young boy, went back to Swamiji! And I got called in and was told what appropriate behaviour was and what inappropriate behaviour was. So things like that, you learn. Things that seem innocuous in Western culture might carry huge connotations in this culture.'

One's cultural conditioning can be altered through diligent learning but one's physicality cannot be changed. Though she wears the attire of a Hindu renunciate, has embraced India completely as her spiritual and cultural home and was never discriminated against in Swamiji's ashram, there are times when she is rudely reminded of the fact of physical embodiment.

'For years I'll completely forget that I am Western. It will only occur to me at moments, like when we were in Nepal recently, on our way to Mount Kailash. Everybody went for darshan at Pashupatinath mandir, and I wasn't allowed in because I was foreign, I was white. I could chant more mantras in Sanskrit than the man standing there. Everybody with me got into a huge fight with him about it. But it is on rare occasions like these that I even remember I am not Indian.'

The convention of the world is to judge the value of a human being on the basis of appearance, which might be the colour of one's skin, one's gender, the way one speaks, the quality (and these days, the brand) of one's clothes, and so on. Rarely is the superficial overcome, and the jewel within discovered. As Sadhvi tells me about being judged for the colour of her skin, I am reminded of a story from the life of the great Vedantin sage, Ashtavakra. His name implies one whose body is deformed in eight places. Already a knower of truth as a young boy, he visited a congregation of scholars in the court of the dharma-king, Janaka. Upon seeing him, the learned pandits stopped their knotty deliberations on the nature of Brahman and burst into laughter. Ashtavakra himself laughed the hardest. When the astonished Janaka asked him why, Ashtavakra responded with, 'I thought these were *jnanis*, but they know nothing about intelligence or intrinsic worth—they are little better than leather workers who can value only pelts and hides.'

Their Brahmin pride outraged at being likened to the lowest of the low in their society—those who skinned dead animals and worked with their hides—the pandits demanded an explanation. Ashtavakra said, 'Like cobblers who only know the skin, this gathering only sees my deformed body, not me. In the curve of the temple, is the sky curved? When a pot is smashed, is the sky that is contained in it also smashed? My body is twisted, not me, but you cannot see that.'

Prejudice and discrimination on whatever basis—caste, colour, race or gender—are usually based on the superficial shifting grounds of physicality, appearance, the accident of birth. The self, hidden beneath the veil of this body, this physicality and its egoic identity, is one's truth, and is connected with the vast ocean of interbeing that forms the core of reality, as understood by Advaita Vedanta.

Sadhvi Bhagwati seems to have glimpsed something of that reality, it is evident in the way she connects with her self, her gender, and the irritants that inevitably arise now and then. I ask about her learning curve with Swamiji, the rigours of apprenticing with a living guru. Has there been a particular accent to the path she has followed, of bhakti or jnana and so on? Or, like Nani Ma, has she been taken through the paces of all the different kinds of yoga, methods of union with the divine, so she could find one she was most attuned with?

'What makes Swamiji such a genius as a spiritual guide is that he's got it all,' she says. 'But he's going to give you what you need, not necessarily what you think you want. For me, it's been a mix, as I think it is for everybody. As the years evolve, the sadhana evolves, what you need at one point varies from what you need at another point. When I first came, if he had said to me, "I want you to spend three hours a day, an hour and a half in the morning and evening, sitting in meditation", I couldn't have done it. So what he said to me was, "Can you type?"' We smile at the incongruity, the anti-climax of a seeker turning up to learn from a guru, only to be put to the task of typing. This too became part of her practice, its humdrumness transformed into a means of caring for others, contributing to the ashram and developing her own mindfulness.

Today the banyan tree of her seva work covers a vast ground that includes the writing, layout and design of all of Swamiji's publications; his correspondence; teaching yoga and meditation; counselling people who come to the ashram; and giving lecture–demonstrations and responding to questions when they travel abroad. She is also the managing editor of the 'Encyclopaedia of Hinduism' project initiated by Swamiji, and oversees the functioning of the free schools and gurukul run by the ashram.

'Here it is, and it evolves, and Swamiji has great faith in the divine plan, so he never said to me at any point, "By the way, there is such a thing as a mantra, or meditation", or that these are really good things and I should try them. He waited for me to say to him, "I've heard of this thing called the mantra. I'd like to have one, what do I need to do?" or ask him, "Will you teach me meditation? What am I supposed to do?" He waits for the right time.' Like the patient gardener who knows the tree will bear fruit in its own time, it will not be forced.

As the years passed, and Sadhvi practised more and stepped further into the lake of knowing, Swamiji's guidance changed accordingly. 'As you change, meditation changes by itself, the practice changes, and even the work changes. The work he'll tell me to do today is very different from the work he would have had me do ten years ago. Similarly with study. It's possible that this has to do with my coming from the West. From his mouth, he would never have said to me in the beginning, "Chant this mantra" or "Read this scripture". And I don't know if he wouldn't say that to people in general. I know he tells people the importance of reading the scriptures. I think that has to do with my coming from a different background. Whereas now, somebody may raise a point about some scripture and he'll say to me later, "You should study this thing more" or "Instead of reading this you must read this" or "Add this to your scriptural study". It's an evolution.'

Rather than take her through the scriptures and train her systematically in the fundamentals of santana dharma, Swamiji allowed Sadhvi Bhagwati to mature in her own way, in her own time, in an organic, unprompted manner, before he began honing her understanding in a specific direction. The process has been one of constant challenge and transformation, yet done at a pace that came to her naturally.

Sadhvi tells me a story that exemplifies this kind of nurture, where the student is allowed to flow freely into the kind of sadhana best suited for her at a particular point in time. For a guru, a knower of truth, there are no boundaries that cannot be vaulted over, no rules that cannot be innovated with, no strictures that can barbwire the flow of the spirit. He or she, therefore, is able to watch the sadhana of a student as clearly as the stones in the bed of a mountain stream, and guide its course accordingly, rather than be stuck in a scripture or notions of how things are 'supposed to be done'.

While preparing for her sannyas deeksha, Sadhvi recounts how she was keen to know the ritual preparations required of her. Her guru, Swami Chidananda Saraswati, tended to guide her towards the essence, rather than prescribing adherence to a ritual, and would give directions like, 'The purity of your heart is much more important than the number of hours of *japa*. One mantra chanted with devotion is going to get you much further than five hours of japa done with your mind in the kitchen or in the office or somewhere else.'

Says Sadhvi, 'This was a very specific ritual I was going through. And I felt like I needed some regimen.' So two weeks before the event, she went to consult a swami from Vrindavan, a Mahamandaleshwar in the Udasi tradition, whom Sadhvi relates to as a 'divine mother'.

She asked him, 'What do I do?'

He said, 'First, for one week before your deeksha, you will fast. You will take only fruits and milk, and that too as little as possible. You will observe silence; you will work very little. Maybe you will stay in your room and chant your mantra.'

'Fine.'

'Repeat what I just said.'

'I will fast and have only fruits and milk.'

He interjected, 'Unless you become too weak to do what Swamiji needs you to do, at which point you will eat a full bhojan.'

'I will observe silence,' she continued.

He interrupted her again, 'Unless Swamiji needs you to speak for any reason, at which point you will speak.'

'I will stay in my room as much as possible and do japa,' she repeated his final instruction.

'Unless Swamiji needs you to do any work, at which point you will march right over to your office!'

This exchange, according to Sadhvi Bhagwati, is typical of the way a realized master will teach, with an open hand, where everything is open to interpretation and circumstance and there are no obstructions that cannot be circumvented in the interest of inner growth. 'It shows how really all of them, regardless of how traditional or modern they may seem, if they are really in touch with the higher truth, karma and bhakti and jnana all come together. What you realize, and I've seen, is that all three really are part and parcel of the same thing.' The by-lanes might be many and varied, their destination is the same.

—

One of the things that struck me about Swami Chidananda Saraswati, when I first heard of him some years ago, was his deep involvement in social activism. With the wide range of his activities he reached out wherever he perceived a need. Under his guidance, the India Heritage Research Foundation runs gurukuls that provide a home and a learning environment to orphans and underprivileged children, free healthcare facilities in Himalayan villages that don't otherwise receive much medical care, ecological programmes that cultivate sensitivity towards and an awareness of the preservation of Himalayan ecosystems, and self-help training for girls and young women.

In the wake of the devastating south Asian tsunami in December 2004, Swamiji travelled to south India with his followers, including Sadhvi Bhagwati, to see what could be done to ease the suffering of thousands who had lost their loved ones, homes, livelihoods. The scale of destruction prompted the group to devise a three-stage plan: first, they concentrated on providing immediate relief through community kitchens, shelters, medical centres, distribution of essentials and the repair of boats which were the lifeline of the coastal fishing communities that had suffered the maximum damage. In the second stage, three villages were reconstructed in Pondicherry. The third stage, which was completed in 2008, saw the opening of an orphanage for over 300 children where, in a unique synergy enabled by the sensitivity with which the project was conceived, a centre for women who had lost their families was built alongside, so that the children and the women could become each other's family and provide emotional, mental and physical succour to one another.

Through his seva initiatives, Swamiji seems to be constantly widening the circle of his being—a sadhu who quit the world, only to return to embrace it completely, as a mother, as a compassionate friend. As a soaring wave that returns to merge with the ocean of inter-being.

For long, the sadhu was one who wended a lonely path, away from the distractions of samsara that included compassion, as Nani Ma had said of the ancient belief system associated with sannyas. He set his face against any human suffering he encountered, looking upon it with the cool dispassion of one who realizes the constantly changing nature of reality. 'This too shall pass' were perhaps the only words of solace he had to offer at such times, before he hurried along his path, eager to be off to pursue his self-enlightenment.

The Buddha Sakyamuni attempted to dislodge this 'moksha for self' preoccupation of Indian spirituality through a vision that his sangha of monks and nuns would live close to their root communities and provide help and guidance when asked to do so. But within the pale of sanatana dharma, the shift began more recently, in the nineteenth and twentieth centuries, with Swami Vivekananda's strident activism and his appeal to sadhus to become active agents of positive social change. Inner empowerment through spiritual practice was to be the source of an equalizing, cleansing, suffering-alleviating, fair and free revolution in the outer world. No longer would sadhus be negaters of samsara—they were being called to enter it and put their wisdom to use where it was needed the most.

Swami Chidananda Saraswati's vision for the spiritual life seems to concur with Vivekananda's. 'Swamiji believes that the purpose of sadhana is not just to get yourself enlightened,' says Sadhvi Bhagwati. 'It is to make you a proper tool in God's hands. It's not about my practice, my evolution and my enlightenment.

In his book, *Peace*, his premise is, until you are at peace inside, you cannot bring peace in the world. Because if your own ego and your own desires and fears are prominent, you can't work successfully towards anything. His premise is, we must start with ourselves. But it doesn't end with ourselves. If you really want to be a force of change in the world, you must do the work on yourself. But regardless of what you want to be in the world, once the work on yourself is done, you have a responsibility. Now use that.'

Swamiji is suggesting a dual shift, a binding together of activism and spiritual seeking—the one must not proceed without the other. The activist must resolve her own issues and afflictive emotions, empower herself, before she steps out to change the world. And the seeker must step out into the world, return to samsara, once her inner work is well under way.

Sadhvi Bhagwati illustrates this with the analogy of a bowl—making a bowl is an art, and it is possible to fashion bowls of great beauty. But the real function of a bowl, the essence of its being, is to be a vessel to feed somebody. It can be made as beautiful as possible, but then it must fulfil its inherent purpose. 'That's really what Swamiji's sadhana philosophy is. Sadhana must be done. Those hours in the morning and evening cannot be avoided or bypassed. But you've also got the rest of the day. That should be used.'

One creates oneself with care and effort in sadhana, just as the potter turns the bowl out on his wheel, fires it in his kiln and glazes it at high temperatures. Beauty is born, perfection is glimpsed. And then what? Is there a purpose self-realization can serve? According to Swamiji, it can and must, by working, in an ever expanding circle of compassion, for the greater common good.

Sadhvi Bhagwati speaks of a conference organized by UNESCO in New Delhi in November 2005, to discuss female foeticide and infanticide in India. Swamiji was one of the participants, along with other spiritual leaders, politicians, social activists, journalists. During the open discussion, everybody began to blame somebody or the other for this problem. 'Some people said it's the religious leaders' fault because they are not telling the people properly "*yeh paap hai*". Some said it's the politicians' fault because they are letting the people who do illegal abortions off the hook, some said it's the media's fault because they are showing how great it is to have a son, and so on. They were all saying these things and then defending themselves.'

When it was Swamiji's turn to speak, he simply said, 'I'm going to go back and open a centre where women who don't want to have girls can bring them anonymously; no questions asked, no judgements passed. They can bring those babies and know that they'll be cared for. It doesn't matter whose fault this current situation is. What is relevant now are the hundreds of us in this room who are powerful in our particular spheres—what are we going to do about this? This is what I am going to do. Now I give you all the challenge to figure out what you are going to do.'

Swamiji's seva originates in the greatest need of the present, perhaps a characteristic of a mind that is fully engaged with the here and now. A mind that is not stuck in the dance of lamenting or reminiscing about the past, or in dreaming up scenarios for the future which can actually be created only through constructive action in the present. Mindful awareness of the present moment enables one to channel one's entire being in alleviating the causes of suffering *now*. It is a feature of spiritual leadership that can rid politics of its preoccupation with avenging historical wrongs, as well as emotional rhetoric that keeps us tied to impossible dreams of golden tomorrows.

A veiled moon shimmers in the sky as I leave Sadhvi Bhagwati's office, its brightness dimmed by an embrace of clouds. I walk one last time to the mother-river, to feel her cool fingers upon the heated excitement that comes from the burst of new ideas and thoughts in my heart. In the weakening moonlight, she is a dark song of lament and longing, a wanderer weighted by her own history, mother of millions, goddess of power and play, and also of death and the passing of time.

This is the end of my Gangetic journey for the moment. During which I have, in a way, traced her course from end to beginning—from the Bengal of Sri Anandamayi Ma, where Ganga Ma is an old crone preparing to dissolve herself in the ocean, to the Himalayas of Nani Ma and Sadhvi Bhagwati, where she is young and newly arisen. I have experienced her playfulness and beauty, her adolescence and motherhood, her ever changing being which is quintessentially feminine in the range of roles she enfolds.

Though the Ganga Sutra is drawing to a close, this quest for the lay of the land of contemporary feminine spirituality isn't. There are other women who will share their insights and quests, with whom I will converse and question, but none of those stories will be told with the lilt of this, the great mother, shadowing and nuancing each word. They will carry some of Ganga Ma's spirit, though, in their femininity and wisdom, their playfulness and abandon, their fearlessness and fortitude.

The answers that have come to me on the banks of Ganga Ma have sown the seeds for further conversations, other journeys through the land she criss-crosses and fertilizes, in search of mothers who, like her, are nurturers of the secret life of the spirit. Who are formidable gurus, perhaps even goddesses, guiding their spiritual children towards the vast ocean of knowing.

Part Two

Mothers of My Soul's Quest

4

Guru as Goddess, Guru as Mother

MATA NIRMALA DEVI

In the vexed darkness
of demonic night
arose
a being of light
a woman...

She harnessed
her powers
to create
a golden-maned lion
whom she mounted
in one fearsome leap
and rode into battle...

She roared
her challenge
to the cunning shape-shifter
overweening with pride
and bloodthirst nonpareil...

In an epic battle
She subdued
the subverter of
dharma, of
natural order…
and then disappeared
into ether
becoming the breath
of the universe…

Whenever the odds
are insurmountable
and ignorance
hardens hearts
She reappears
as guru, guide, mother
solver of problems
slayer of demons
ender of the dark night
of the soul…

—

It is said that the Goddess retreated from the world when a male god, buffed and buffered by the early Aryan and Abrahamic religions, ascended the throne of ultimate divinity. She was either cast out in the interest of establishing an uncomplicated, solo, masculine god in monotheistic religions, or she became relegated to spousal roles, as in the polytheistic religions of the Indian subcontinent. What is interesting is that though she never recovered her lost horizon in the rest of the world, she did manage a full-blown resurgence in India, where the worship of the Divine Feminine continues as a mainstream, living tradition till today.

Like all early agrarian societies, the Indus Valley Civilization (3000–1500 BCE) worshipped the Goddess as the life-giving earth mother, fertile and uncomplainingly benign. The early Aryans, who are believed to have supplanted the Indus Valley

Civilization, were nomads and not farmers yet, and so their connection with the earth and reliance upon her fecundity were understandably shallow and underdeveloped. They introduced a horde of male gods inspired by natural phenomena into the realm of the Goddess, and established a divine hierarchy of patriarchy. So while there are goddesses in the earliest Aryan sacred text, the Rig Veda, such as Ushas (dawn), Prithvi (earth), Aditi (mother of the gods) and Vac (speech), they have nowhere near the kind of clout wielded by primary gods like Indra (associated with lightning), Agni (fire), Soma (sacred potion), Surya (sun), Vayu (wind) and others. The central religious and cultural narratives of the early Aryans were associated with these male divinities, also referred to as 'male sky gods', who were given to macho displays of strength and anger, as opposed to the earlier, gentler earth goddesses.

It would be extreme to claim that the Goddess disappeared with the rise of the Aryans in the early Vedic age, placed between the sixth century and the second and first century BCE. Rather, she was driven underground, her adoration not part of Vedic 'mainstream'. But she was definitely present in parallel streams of faith and belief. She continued as a patron deity of rivers and villages, of farmers and women, her powers invoked while sowing and reaping, her divine motherhood petitioned during fertility rituals and childbirth. The Goddess had seeped into the everyday lives of the common people and become part of their eternal, on-the-margins culture, even as the Aryanization of large swathes of the subcontinent, their conversion into Aryavarta,the land of the Aryans, was changing and recreating every aspect of the social, economic, political and religious fabric of the land.

When the Goddess reappeared in the mainstream Vedic religion, it was in what can best be described as 'watered down' versions, splintered into many minor goddesses, each married off to a god, or a hero in the epics Ramayana and Mahabharata (400–450 CE). Historian Lynn Gatwood has termed this rather anaemic return of the Goddess as a spouse with little or no individual significance as 'epic spousification'. She analyses the appearance of major and minor spousal goddesses in the epics as a way of appropriating non-Aryan goddesses that flourished under the seams of the increasingly dominant Brahmanical religion. This was how the independent force of the Goddess was tamed and devitalized into a docile feminine role model that adhered to norms of established patriarchy and was whole only when conjoined with a male spouse or in familial roles. These epic goddess-heroines continue to be idealized in the present as yardsticks of desirable feminine behaviour, and women's lives are hemmed in by the patriarchal standards they embody.

The true resurgence of the Goddess as Devi, an uncoupled, divine, omnipresent force that almost caused the gender of God to change from an indeterminate, all-encompassing 'He' to a very decisive 'She', occurred with the rise of what is today known as 'Shaktism', circa 400 CE. The Shakta world-view essentially saw everything as permeated with and made of Shakti, the feminine energic principle. In an earlier stream of philosophy, Samkhya, reality was interpreted as an interplay of male and female energies, identified as Purusha and Prakriti, respectively. Purusha was the undifferentiated core of reality while Prakriti was the energy that created the universe and made it work, so to speak. Purusha was pure consciousness, Prakriti its content. The Shaktas went a step further in their adoration of the Divine Feminine and placed the entire onus of creation and destruction upon her, even as she continued to exist in conjunction with Shiva, the male principle, the two forming the twin poles of the axis of creation.

Religious literature of the period, comprising the inventive and imaginative Puranas that purported to be devotional chronicles of the doings of deities, married Devi to Shiva in a literal representation of the union of the two. The Shakta orientation specifically manifests in the Puranas in the figure of Devi, the one Great Goddess who harboured within her self all minor goddesses and heroines, thereby undoing some of the damage caused by epic spousification and the consequent 'taming' of powerful female deities. During this phase, goddesses like Lakshmi, Saraswati and others were acknowledged for powers that went beyond wifely duties to their divine husbands, and began to be invoked individually.

The greatest triumph of the Goddess, the definitive work where she was hailed as the supreme creatrix, second (and spouse) to none, and where the functions of creation, sustenance and destruction, till now the privilege of the male triad of Brahma, Vishnu and Shiva, were entrusted to her, occurred with the composition of the *Devi Mahatmayam* around the fifth century. One could say what the Bhagavad Gita did for Samkhya philosophy in terms of explication and popularization, the *Devi Mahatmayam* and the literature that followed in its wake (commentaries and supporting texts like the *Devi Bhagavata Purana*) achieved for Shaktism.

In the *Devi Mahatmayam*, for the first time, God became Goddess, He became She. It heralded the Goddess's own theology, embedded though it was in a larger text, the *Markandeya Purana*, but was considered an independent hymn for all practical purposes and combined many divergent and possibly pre-existing narratives from marginalized, non-Brahmanical wisdom traditions. As C. MacKenzie Brown says in *The Triumph of the Goddess*, 'The various mythic, cultic and theological elements relating to diverse female divinities were brought together in what has been called the "crystallisation of the Goddess tradition".'

With this integration of all goddesses in one Great Goddess, the *Devi Mahatmayam* provided the Goddess with a theology as well as a pantheon populated with her emanations. In it, Devi is said to proclaim, 'I am all alone in the world here. Who else is there besides me? See these goddesses who are but my own powers entering into my own self!' 'These goddesses' are the Mahavidyas—a group of ten that covers a whole spectrum of characteristics, a full circle of attributes from the mundane to the fantastic, from the creative to the destructive, from benevolence to bloodthirst, from life to death and back to life. It is said that the Great Goddess, the quintessential Devi, assumed these different forms to reveal to Shiva (her spouse/guru/partner-in-wisdom) the core truths of creation. Hence the term 'Mahavidya' or 'great knowledge'. (The entire range of Mahavidyas developed over time and only some, like Kali, actually appear in the *Devi Mahatmayam*).

The theology of the Mahavidyas is exceptional in world sacred traditions in terms of the range it imagines for the Divine Feminine. The Mahavidyas are Kali, Tara, Shodashi, Bhuvaneshvari, Chhinnamasta, Bhairavi, Dhumawati, Bagalamukhi, Matangi and Kamala. Kali embodies the fierce energy that destroys negativity; Tara is the compassionate guide; Shodashi, literally 'the sixteen-year-old', also known as Tripura Sundari, is the beauteous and virginal goddess petitioned by the gods to slay uncontrollable demons and who is thus an eternal refuge; as Bhuvaneshvari, she is creator and owner of the world; as Chhinnamasta, she embodies the play of life and death as she cuts off her own head to nourish her attendants with her life-blood; as Bhairavi, she symbolizes the decay and destruction inherent and inescapable in the created universe; as Dhumawati, she denotes the unsatisfactory nature of desire and material life and the need to discriminate truth from illusion; as Bagalamukhi, she wrenches the tongue of a demon who abuses his power of true speech (*vak-siddhi*), thereby ensuring balance; as Matangi, she subverts the norms of ritual purity and leads the mind out of conditioned spaces of 'right' and 'wrong'; and as Kamala, she is ever auspicious, the wise goddess who reigns over the material realm. I am amazed by their stories and struck by this motley group of unlikely goddesses who veer from one extreme of human experience to the other, covering everything in between.

The *Devi Mahatmayam*'s significance and impact are multi-layered. It could well be the first recorded instance where a scripture accords the Goddess supremacy and celebrates her independence, her power, her superior intelligence, her uncompromising protection of ethics and dharma, her essential femininity, her graceful compassion and her universal motherhood. Through stories of her valour and martial exploits to restore the balance of creation and her alacrity in responding to devotees in distress, the *Devi Mahatmayam* quite ingeniously introduces the Goddess as the Great Mother-Guru. She not only creates and gives birth like the earth goddess of old, she also goes to great lengths to blow away the sand of unknowing that blinds us to the truth. As the scholar of religion, Thomas P. Coburn, says in *Encountering the Goddess*, 'Her adversaries represent the all-too-human impulses arising from the pursuit of power, possessions and pleasure, and from illusions of self-importance. Like the battlefield of the Bhagavad Gita, the *Devi Mahatmayam's* killing grounds represent the field of human consciousness.'

To my mind, the Devi seems to be ever-expanding her role as the Supreme and Universal Mother. She brings the universe to birth and nourishes all in it, she goes to battle against her children's bugbears and slays them, and through her unconventional forms she tries her best to draw us out of ignorant self-love and narrow perspectives. Whether benevolent or aggressive, she constantly attempts to guide our attention away from that which is illusory and impermanent towards that which is true and real. If we think about our own human mothers, haven't they whacked us when we were naughty or stubborn, cajoled us out of dark moods, held us when we needed reassurance and, as our first gurus, did all they could to ensure we blossomed to fulfil our potential? Now one just needs to blow up that effort a million times to arrive at a role good enough for the Mother of the Universe. It is no wonder that she is so varied in her forms and activities!

We see this in the *Devi Mahatmayam*, whose three central episodes revolve around the allegorical slaying of ignorance by the Devi. Rapacious demons, symbolizing afflictions of the mind and ego, wreak havoc on heaven and earth, which are symbolic of one's inner environment, shattering the rhythm of life. In the first episode, which is a creation-myth, two demons attack Brahma as he prepares to launch a new cycle of creation. He calls out to Vishnu, who is asleep, for help. Brahma then petitions the Goddess in the form of Yoganidra, who withdraws from Vishnu, causing him to awaken and slay the demons. So while the actual slaying is done by Vishnu, it is through the enabling agency of the Goddess. She allows the world to come into being, literally, and the cosmic order (*rta*) to continue.

In the second episode of the *Devi Mahatmayam*, Devi makes her debut as the warrior goddess, Durga. The male gods are unable to deal with a demon, Mahish, whose ability to shift shapes has rendered him unconquerable. They invoke Devi, who materializes from their collective energies in her combatant form—Durga—bestride a lion. She engages Mahishasura in a fierce battle where he changes form each time she is about to kill him, which suggests to my mind the slippery nature of the ego and the many manifestations of ignorance that constantly defy the practitioner's attempts to subdue it. Eventually, Durga vanquishes Mahishasura with her alertness. Comprehending the exact moment he is about to leave the body of a buffalo, she swiftly decapitates its head, thereby killing the demon. To better the wiles of the ego, one needs to be ever aware of its movements, keep an unflinching eye on it, and as it begins to draw one's observer-consciousness into a play of emotions and thought patterns, act quickly in wielding the sword of discrimination to end its hold upon oneself.

The third episode of the *Devi Mahatmayam* comprises a cluster of stories that introduce an aspect of the Goddess that is perhaps the most fearsome and the least understood. In Kali, the dark one who is mistress of time and transience, who keeps cosmic balance by ensuring an end to created life, the Devi expresses her fierceness and wildness, and the ability to harness and utilize these attributes for the benefit of all. The reason Kali is such a powerful icon is because she uses the negative impulses of anger, retaliation, vengeance and violence to create balance and harmony. She is never a slave to these emotions, as happens with most of us, but their mistress. She channels the basest of human instincts to generate positive power, and is never overcome by them. She reigns by reining in and converting negative into positive. This alchemy of energy, whereby negativity is not to be destroyed but is transformed into its exact opposite, is central to the practices of Shakta Tantra. One could see this as a sort of 'energy optimization'—one kind of energy is converted into another, which is then used to attain spiritual goals, like deepening meditative absorption or uniting individual consciousness with cosmic consciousness.

For the Shakta devotee, Kali is as much a mother as the benign forms of Devi are. Her bloodlust is reserved for subverters of cosmic law; to her children she is mother-as-guru, she challenges their limited understanding of life and death, self and other, illusion and truth. With her terrifying figure, her nearness to death and decay, her garland of human skulls, she opens her devotees' perception to the realities of passing, change, renewal. In her nakedness, she personifies transcendence of conventional reality; in her darkness, she points to the undifferentiation and attribute-lessness of supreme consciousness, Brahman.

One of Kali's greatest devotees, the nineteenth-century mystic Sri Ramakrishna Paramahansa, said of her, 'My Mother is the principle of consciousness. She is *Akhanda Satchidananda*, indivisible reality, awareness and bliss. The night sky between the stars is perfectly black. The waters of the ocean depths are the same; the infinite is always mysteriously dark. This inebriating darkness is my beloved Kali.'

The impact of this new Devi-centric theology on the cultural psyche of the subcontinent was huge. The Goddess as Great Mother, along with her many manifestations, became an enduring and beloved fixture in its divine pantheon jostling with deities and heroes. Shaktism evolved an entirely new wisdom tradition, a new sadhana path that was based on worship, contemplation and ritual adoration of the Divine Feminine. The heart of reality, the core jewel of insight represented by a direct comprehension of Brahman, hitherto ungendered, came to acquire a feminine accent for the Shaktas. To know Her was to know all.

Shakta Tantra aimed to directly experience the Goddess in oneself, and not just as an external deity. One of the ways to do this was through the awakening of the kundalini. Literally, kundalini means 'she who is coiled', and refers to the energy that is believed to lie coiled like a serpent at the base of our spine. It forms the centre of the body's subtle energy system that consists of *nadis*, channels, and chakras, 'wheels' of energy, through which the life force, *prana*, irrigates our physical, emotional, psychic selves, performs life functions and keeps us alive. In most of us, this energic system remains semi-functional at best, and in disrepair at worst, leading to knots that obstruct free flow of prana and manifest at the physical level as disease.

One of the discoveries made by the yogis and practitioners of Tantra, in the laboratory of their own selves, as they practised what I imagine were disciplines to loosen ties that bind self to ego, and observed ever deepening levels of consciousness, was the possibility of arousing this somnolent network of subtle energy. Through certain techniques, the channels and chakras could be vitalized, creating an optimal flow of prana that would, in turn, dissolve any mental or physical disease or disturbance, and cause the adept to function with a greater fullness of perception, intelligence and self-effort. But what was a superior achievement, an awakening of unlimited potentiality, and therefore a greater challenge, was attempting to rouse the kundalini herself.

I would like to clarify that Tantric practices such as kundalini awakening are not easy to describe as they are part of an esoteric tradition and are best experienced for oneself, usually under the tutelage of an accomplished guru. Since I do not have a direct understanding of these nor can I claim any scholarly expertise in the study of Tantric scriptures or practices, the insights I share here are informed by accounts provided by practitioners and their understanding of the arcane literature of Tantra.

The conventional explanation seems to be that due to our fundamental ignorance, our bodies and minds exist in a state of defilement, caused by toxic assimilations and negative thought patterns, during which the goddess energy of the kundalini remains asleep, indifferent to our fate as it were. Kundalini energy has been described as feminine a spark of the Great Goddess in the human body. If atman is Brahman's reflection in the individual, it could be said that the kundalini is the Devi's. Both display the characteristics of their macrocosms—the atman is the essence, the core consciousness, to the kundalini's creative dynamism, in an echo of Brahman (or Shiva) and Devi (or Shakti) respectively.

To awaken the goddess within requires of us a dedicated effort to convert this inferior vessel of the afflicted body–mind into a receptacle fit to receive the grace of the Divine Feminine. Though she exists within all of us, male *and* female, we don't own her, we cannot claim her benevolence automatically. Her manifestation also depends on us—if we prove ourselves worthy, she might enliven us with her gifts of acuity, intellect and insight.

For this to happen, the yogi must prepare body and mind through rituals of purification and cleansing and those that enhance balance and concentration. The energic pathways are cleaned and strengthened to facilitate an unimpeded rise of the kundalini, and the mind is scoured as much as possible of afflictive emotions and bondage to the ego. A Tantric text, *Goraksha Samhita*, describes the process thus: 'Awakened through *buddhi-yoga* (mental discipline) together with [the combined action of] mind and breath, she rises upward through the *sushumna* (central energy channel) like a thread through a needle. Sleeping in the form of a serpent, resembling a resplendent cord, she, when awakened by the yoga of fire (mental concentration and breath control), rises upward through the sushumna. Just as one may forcibly open a door with a key, so the yogin should break open the door to liberation by means of the kundalini.'

If the body-mind is not thoroughly prepared or if there are impurities that haven't been dealt with, the immense energy of the rising kundalini will burn these away, causing great physical and mental agony. In fact, without proper groundwork, the ascension of the kundalini is considered dangerous and incomplete, a curse rather than a boon, leading the practitioner towards suffering rather than liberation from it.

If she has been properly aroused, the kundalini awakens and uncoils. Passing through each of the chakras located along the spine—the root chakra (*muladhara*), the sacral chakra (*swadhisthana*), the solar plexus chakra (*manipura*), the heart chakra (*anahata*), the throat chakra (*vishuddha*), the 'third eye' chakra (*ajna*)—she stimulates them, balances them and draws upon their concentrated energy to power her ascent. She thunders to the end of the energy channel and pierces the *sahasrara* chakra at the crown of the head, blossoming out like a hundred-petalled lotus, and unites individual consciousness with cosmic consciousness.

The impact of this event seems to get as close to a physical divinization of humanity as is possible. The goddess energy of the kundalini is said to radically transmute the body-mind of the practitioner, leading to a maximization of his or her inherent potential and a diminishment of negativity and the tendencies that foster its growth. Initially, however, the ascent is coupled with descent, and the kundalini will want to return to her position of rest at the base of the spine. To maintain a constantly elevated state, which is actually a permanent union of the self with the cosmic energy that characterizes self-liberation or enlightenment, requires tremendous effort on the part of the practitioner. To use Zen imagery, a one-time ascension of the kundalini is like entering the shallow end of the pool of realization; it must be deepened with practice and concentrated effort.

—

A question that suggests itself to me at this point is, how did this powerful feminine theology of Tantra and the kundalini affect the lives of real women? Did it make living in patriarchy any easier? Did it help them connect with their inner devi? Did it inspire some women to shake off the chains of conformity to gender stereotypes and follow this new archetype instead? Were there ever any living embodiments of the Devi, any real women in whom the Great Goddess came alive?

The Devi could not overturn patriarchy within which women continue to live restricted, circumscribed lives. In a tragic gap between belief and practice, a failure to connect divinity with reality, men who revere the Devi are usually unable to see any reflection of her in the women around them. They find no contradiction in extolling the Devi in worship while simultaneously subjecting women to discrimination and disrespect, devaluation and a lack of choices and, in some instances, verbal, physical and mental abuse. Women too suffer from this gap in perception because they often internalize the patriarchal power system and participate actively in its perpetuation, and are unable to connect with the Devi as a sacred presence that lives and breathes within and through them and other women.

Little girls are worshipped in much of north India as emanations of the Devi, their feet are touched and the aarti flame waved around them, on the eighth day of Navaratri, the festival of the nine nights sacred to the Devi, even as pregnancies are screened for the foetus's gender and the ones with the 'wrong' (read 'female') gender aborted, causing the female sex ratio of the country to plummet with each passing year. This disconnect between a robust and revolutionary tradition of worshipping God as Goddess and the way living, breathing women are treated is to my mind a testimony to the kind of hypocrisy ritualized religion can breed if it is not sufficiently rooted in actual, heartfelt practice.

—

Any day now
I expect
the great mother goddess
to rise in revolt
in this ancient land
that she has nurtured
with her breath and milk and love
whose rivers carry her blood-benediction
whose very earth is her body
in her we all exist...

Any day now
I expect
the great mother goddess
to shrug off her benevolence
and turn against her children
a terrible beauty
astride a rampaging lion
or perhaps
an old crone
who dances death
any time now...

For, hasn't she taken offence
at far less provocation
than presented by
scarred wombs
from which
have been ripped out
her own emanations
stopped from being born
because they are
what she is—female?

Any time now
I expect
the great mother goddess
of this ancient land
to fill the breasts
of us ordinary women
with her divine rage
her unstoppable courage
and then we, her daughters,
will rise
ululating and angry
adorned in red
millions of mother goddesses

carrying our own emanations
in ironclad wombs…

Then perhaps
this massacre of innocents
will stop?

—

The Goddess may not have been able to stem the tide of patriarchy, but she did rise in the bosoms of many ordinary women over the centuries, astride the lion she subjugated of fear–ignorance–male dominance, enabling them to connect with their inner devi, offering them an empowered archetype as an alternative to patriarchy's obedient wives and mothers. It would seem the Goddess *has* incarnated in flesh-and-blood women, women who are not pretty idols smothered in jewels and silk, venerated by successive generations of male priests.

These are real women who ignite their inner shakti to find the strength to overthrow the oppressive, stifling veil that patriarchy enforces upon them, who may wash the henna from their hands and wipe away any possibility of vermilion from their forehead and head out into the wilderness of spiritual seeking, and when they do stay in marriages, assume roles that are certainly not subjugated. And when they find the balance of unshakeable equanimity, when the fire of knowing burns steadily within them, when the river of their seeking flows into the ocean of wisdom, they become recognized and venerated as incarnations of the Great Goddess. As Karen Pechilis observes in *The Graceful Guru*, 'Female gurus are understood by Hindu tradition and by their followers alike to be manifestations of the Goddess; that is, as perfect embodiments of shakti…'

The idea of a woman guru in Hindu wisdom traditions thus often occurs in tandem with identification with the Devi, who is also the Great Mother, so it is with a sense of an all-encompassing motherhood as well. Women gurus are mother *and* goddess, compassionate caregivers *and* uncompromising teachers of truth, nurturers of the life of the spirit *and* destroyers of what is unwholesome and unneeded in the disciple's life. This triadic characterization, as guru, goddess, mother, accords great power to the woman as preceptor, which she wields to accelerate the growth and evolution of her disciple's spiritual life. It also makes for a phenomenon that doesn't quite occur in the male sphere of spirituality, for though realized masters do become like mothers in the quality of their care and nurture, as in the case of Nani Ma's and Sadhvi Bhagwati's gurus, they are not accorded the added patina of Goddess. The tapestry thus formed by the triple role women gurus play in their disciples' lives is unique to feminine spirituality and must be explored and studied accordingly.

In this part of the book, I will look at two contemporary women gurus through the triadic prism of guru, goddess and mother, and attempt to unearth how the impact of their work is determined by their intelligent assimilation of these three aspects in their selves. They also present a possibility of the rise of the Devi in our bosoms, igniting her fiery path through our consciousness, of the awakening of the Divine Feminine, and the fact that it is not as distant or incredible for us ordinary women as it may seem at first glance.

The choice of women gurus in this section—Mata Nirmala Devi and Mata Amritanandamayi—is not based on intrinsic merit alone, it is also a direct result of access and constraints of time and location. I was able to travel to Mata Nirmala Devi's home in Pune and meet Mata Amritanandamayi in Delhi and Jaipur. There are many other women gurus whom I would have liked to include in this section, such as the current head of the Siddha Yoga lineage, Gurumayi Chidvilasananda, Germany-based Mother Meera, Shree Maa of Kamakhya who lives in the US, among others. That I could not is either because they were not available for interviews, or because they live in places I was unable to travel to. Therefore, the women that are included in this chapter, indeed in this book, must be seen as representative of different aspects of feminine spirituality, and not an absolute list or a judgement on the value or merit of those that were included and those that were not.

—

The first time Mata Nirmala Devi made an impression on me was on a poster announcing a Sahaja Yoga camp she was going to lead, plastered on a wall somewhere. I distinctly remember the large red bindi aflame upon her *ajna* chakra (located between the eyes) like a blood-red sun rising in the horizon, and an authoritativeness that was palpable even in a grainy photograph.

Over the years, I have become familiar with her ministry, which has in large measure consisted of teaching Sahaja Yoga, a path of sadhana formulated by her that includes raising the kundalini in mass gatherings. This has earned her the ire of traditionalists who maintain kundalini awakening to be 'secret' knowledge that can be practised only by advanced yogis. For Shri Mataji, as Nirmala Devi is known among her devotees, it is a way to enable emotional, mental and physical healing, and she has steadfastly maintained in the face of opposition that this must be freely available to all those who need it, irrespective of their yogic credentials.

Providing what is needed without judging the receiver's capabilities is a quality 'universal mothers' characteristically display. For instance, it is said that while Sri Ramakrishna Paramahansa and his disciples were very strict about whom they initiated and gave the teachings to, his wife Sri Sarada Devi taught whoever came to her and asked for them. Once, Sarada was watching a play about Ramanuja, who is given a secret mantra to achieve enlightenment and is warned against revealing it to anybody, and who then begins shouting it aloud in the town square to benefit as many people as possible. She was so moved that she went into a trance. This quality of free-giving is to me the quality of Devi as Mother.

In December 2005, I travelled to Pune to meet Mata Nirmala Devi. I was unaware at the time that Shri Mataji was seriously unwell and would not be able to speak with me. In fact, the official Sahaja Yoga website had announced, in a message dated 16 May 2004, that Shri Mataji had 'completed her work', though she continued to travel and meet devotees and preside over pujas. Recent photographs posted on the website show her in a wheelchair, the lustrous black hair that framed her round face now thinned considerably. Yet she seems alert and happy in the company of her devotees and her husband, C.P. Srivastava.

I arrived in Pune with a heart full of hope, kindled by the possibility of being in the same room as a living 'guru–mother–goddess', one who was among the first few women gurus to come out of seclusion, publicly proclaim her message and travel around the world to teach. When I came to know that I couldn't meet Shri Mataji but that her husband would see me instead, I found in this a rare opportunity to look at the career curve of a hugely popular woman guru through the eyes of one who had been her constant companion. Married in 1947, at the cusp of India's independence from British colonial rule, they had negotiated their lives together. Nobody could have the kind of vantage point from which to observe the evolution of a guru than her husband, who lived with her and must have felt the inner workings of her consciousness, as he watched her evolve from the mother of his children to the 'Mother of the World'.

On a cold, sunless afternoon, I arrive at the barricaded entrance to Shri Mataji's palatial bungalow set amidst the wilderness of the Sahyadri hills, a few kilometres outside the bustling city of Pune. I am fortunate to be in the company of Dr Nikam, the genie whose presence causes the barricades to fall away and a path to open up to the main house. We are ushered in through a labyrinth of passages into a large room crowded with ornate fittings and gilded decorations, luxurious carpets and plush sofas. I look around in amazement at what appears to be a veritable Aladdin's cave of splendid things and exotic objets d'art from all over the world.

Upon closer inspection I find that many of the artefacts bespeak a connection with the Goddess. A particularly beautiful sculpture of Kwan Yin, the female bodhisattva of compassion, catches my eye, and I realize that the room is full of gifts that Nirmala Devi's devotees have brought her from all corners of the globe. They found in their culture something that resonated with the idea of mother and goddess, and offered it to their guru who, for them, is an embodiment of both. I am surrounded by gestures of adoration, offerings of love and gratitude, in this, the Mother's own boudoir.

Mr Srivastava's arrival is quiet and dignified, much like the man himself. A distinguished bureaucrat, he has held senior positions in the Indian Government and at the International Maritime Organization, United Nations, in London where he was secretary-general for three consecutive terms. He has written a seminal biography of Lal Bahadur Shastri, former prime minister of India, with whom he was associated as personal secretary from 1964–66.

Though the 'goddess' herself is hidden from me, she is present everywhere—in photographs where moments from her eventful life are stilled forever, in the living body of memories her husband will share with me, in the devotion of her followers evident in every object in this room, in the cloud of incense that wafts out from somewhere in the house, perhaps from her inner sanctum?

I begin at the beginning, with their marriage.

Mr Srivastava's gentle eyes turn to me in surprise. I suppose when one is married to a much revered guru, direct questions related to their marriage are not asked very often. Should I ask something else, I wonder. But he appears to have accepted my question and is contemplating a response.

In the manner people often have of recounting memories from long ago, Mr Srivastava seems to search within, as if peering into an interior place that houses the past. In his narration, he gives precedence to his wife's story, partly because that is what I have come to interview him about, though I suspect it might also have to do with a temperamental reluctance to receive personal attention or glory.

Nirmala, the 'pure one' (coincidentally also the given name of Anandamayi Ma), was born in 1923 to Prasad and Cornelia Salve, who were dedicated followers of Mahatma Gandhi. As a young woman, Nirmala too joined India's movement for freedom and was an active participant in the Quit India Movement called by Mahatma Gandhi in 1942. Somewhere along the way, the two met and fell in love, though they waited until the year India was freed from colonial rule to begin their married life.

'She was highly idealistic,' Mr Srivastava reminisces, 'and I was dedicated to my country as a government servant. Our commitment to serve our country was a common point. From then on, it has been a story worth telling. Initially, she was my wife and the mother of my children. Whatever she has done, it has been with a full heart. Once our daughters grew up, she decided it was time for her to do something else. So she resolved to dedicate herself to spiritual activities. She evolved her own philosophy, which she propounded with great success.'

With the kind of understatement characteristic of diplomats, Mr Srivastava makes his wife's emergence as a world guru sound almost as if she took up a hobby once her children were grown up and she had some spare time on her hands. It was anything but. What actually happened to enable the butterfly to emerge from the cocoon of her worldly, wifely self remains a mystery, perhaps fully known only to herself. But we can attempt a glimpse into that fascinating moulting that is a direct result of spiritual endeavour and lies at the heart of the mystical transformation of human to divine, or of a woman into a guru–goddess.

Nirmala Devi has spoken about a dramatic awakening she experienced on 5 May 1970, on the seashore of Nargol near Mumbai. In her words, 'The experience was like this. I saw my kundalini rising very fast, like a telescope opening out, and it was a beautiful colour that you see when the iron is heated up, a red rose colour, but extremely cooling and soothing.' This event has been hailed not just as the awakening of Nirmala's kundalini, but as the momentous arising of 'Adi Kundalini', primordial energy. Her disciple Gregoire de Kalbermatten calls it 'a milestone in the history of evolution' in his book, *The Third Advent*.

Nirmala spent the next few years refining a technique with which the kundalini energy could be raised and maintained in an awakened state by anybody, with her help. This method evolved into Sahaja Yoga, which also includes guidelines to integrate the psychic energy of the kundalini in all aspects of everyday life.

I ask Mr Srivastava about this period, when his wife traversed the many degrees that separated her homely existence from the world stage, determined to teach as many people as she could to use the purifying fire of kundalini to enrich their lives.

'To be honest, the first time she said this, I did not think she would become a world leader. Initially I would wonder, because I was a down-to-earth civil servant and she said she was going to take on the task of spiritual awakening of people. I said, "Are you sure? How are you going to do it?"' he tells me, revealing some of the bewilderment that might arise in a spouse when the other is transformed so radically, so completely. 'Gradually, I began to see for myself how she was going about it. It happened to one, then to a few more, and so on. When I saw that, I began to believe.'

Rather than hold her back or bind her to familial, feminine roles, Mr Srivastava became a willing participant in Nirmala's spiritual journey. Support that is unconditionally provided even when the spouse is unable to fully understand the demands of the spiritual life—especially a guru's work—is uncommon, and its absence prevents many practitioners and adepts from living *en famille* as their sadhana grows in intensity and scope. Conflict with the expectations attached to gender roles must have prevented several women adepts from growing into full-fledged gurus through the centuries. The few that did, had to fight their way through, like Lalla, Rabia and Andal, or simply practise where they were, like Meerabai. Only a fortunate few did not need to face this conflict, like Nirmala Devi, and perhaps the progressive ideals of India's freedom struggle under the guidance of Mahatma Gandhi, which included equality for women, during which this couple came of age, had something to do with this.

Mr Srivastava was able to grasp the full import of his wife's work only when he saw its transformative potential for himself. 'Once the kundalini is awakened, the person is transformed,' he says. 'I have seen people transformed miraculously. We went to London and the first man who came was a drug addict. He sat with her for a half hour and emerged totally free of the addiction. There were no withdrawal symptoms, no sickness; it just disappeared. Since I have witnessed this myself, I can tell you this honestly. That is the marvel. From the early days, I did whatever little I could to support that. In fact, now I feel this is the only way humanity can survive.'

Coming from a diplomat who has seen the world change so much, this is a crucial statement. That humanity must turn to spirituality to *survive*, and not just to get rid of its stresses or find an illusory nirvana. The spiritual life is no longer a luxury or an alternative. It has become an imperative.

'See what's happening in the world,' he continues. 'There is no peace. Iran is a problem, America is a problem, Afghanistan is a problem. This explosion of violence is because people don't know the reality. They get involved in this mundane world, but this is part of a larger journey. You are here only for a short while and then you are gone. Who knows who lived in this world 200 years ago? But people at that time must have thought, I am the one. I own the earth. Today many people feel the same way. A hundred years later, who would know, except for her? People remember Jesus Christ, Rama, Krishna and so on. But the rest are gone.'

What he seems to suggest is that Mata Nirmala Devi's role in our times is comparable to that of the prophets of old, who steered humanity towards spiritual evolution in their times. Is she, according to him, the prophetess of a new dawn, the seer of a new possibility of mass enlightenment that could fundamentally change the way we are, the way we can be?

'Basically, as I understand her, she says we have been created by the Almighty Power in His image. And in each one of us there is a congealed power called kundalini, which resides at the base of the backbone, which is dormant but if an individual finds someone who can help awaken it, it rises through the spinal column to the top of the head and connects you with the all-pervading power of God. God is everywhere and is everything—omniscient and omnipresent. That Power is there. So your power and that Power come together, you are connected with the Ultimate Power. Then you become the instrument of that Power, of good, and you think in ethical terms. You lead a pure life. You cannot think of anything else. All distinctions on the basis of caste, creed, community and language cease, for all are children of one all-pervading Power. So for her, all humanity is one family.'

Indeed, her following cuts across barriers of nationality, race and gender, and I have found people from Europe or the US to be as devoted to her, as eager to be her spiritual 'children' as those in the towns and cities of Maharashtra and other parts of India. Perhaps this quality of motherhood, of uniting people through a common spiritual bond, is the need of the century, as Mr Srivastava has pointed out. Seers of our troubled and divided age must have this quality of inclusiveness, of reminding people of their core humanity which remains unaffected by outer markers of identity and connects us with one another in ways we may not be able to comprehend without a deep spiritual experience, like the one Nirmala Devi is said to facilitate in her followers.

What is characteristic of most guru-mothers is their ability to bring people together, in her case from around the world, as children of one mother. Spiritual siblinghood under a Great Mother's tutelage can be a powerful instrument in breaking down barriers and encouraging warmth, camaraderie and cooperation between people who might otherwise be strangers. In the community around the Mother, they are all equal; one is as much her child as the other. Psychologically, this could be a union that is more genuine, and more effective, in fostering external cohesion and peace through their inner experience than synthetic slogans and political posturing that call for 'world peace' but have little impact on ground realities, which in turn are constructed by how people really feel about one another.

Mr Srivastava recalls an epiphany he had during such a gathering, as he observed people from diverse backgrounds collect around Nirmala, their shared mother. 'In London, the other day, about twenty people [were] sitting. That gathering had a former Catholic, a former Protestant, a Jew, a Muslim, a Sikh, a Hindu—they were all Mataji's children. Nothing else. They forgot what they were. They were Mataji and her children. They are a genuine family. So her family is not me and her two daughters, it is the whole world. And she believes in it. The love that she has given! People understand that. She said the other day, "In Sahaja, everyone is equal. There is no one superior, no one inferior. They are all my children." So the equality is important.'

If the sannyasi expands his or her circle of compassion by giving up ego-driven pursuits, the woman as guru seems to do so by dissolving her individual self into universal motherhood. To enfold everybody that comes to her, she has to be empty of the narrowness of the ego-self, her heart enlarged immeasurably to include countless 'children', their problems, the paths to their wellness. For this to happen, perhaps she does need to outgrow her limited gender identity as an individual woman and embrace her femininity to its full potential, raised to the power of infinity, where she is as complete, fulfilled and glorious a woman as she can possibly be. Who is to say that enlightenment can only mean a transcendence of gender; perhaps it might also occur in a form where it is the complete fulfilment of all the potential hardwired into one's gender? Is woman, honed to the extremity of her womanliness, goddess? Is this the alchemy that transforms Nirmala Srivastava into Mata Nirmala Devi, an ordinary woman into a mother-goddess?

Her followers, though, would not agree that Nirmala was ever an 'ordinary' woman. Having experienced her guru-goddesshood, it is perhaps difficult for them to comprehend that she could have been anything but this before, that this could be the result of an evolution, a process of growth. Somehow, to the devotee, to assume common humanity for their guru smacks of disrespect and is difficult to accept despite the centrality of seeking in Indian spiritual traditions. That Nirmala never acknowledged studying with a guru may have contributed to the view of her as an avatar, an incarnation of superior energy, as opposed to a woman whose self-realization occurred because she made a consistent effort towards it. As somebody who has known Nirmala long before she became widely regarded as an embodiment of Adi Shakti (the root energy of the Great Goddess), Mr Srivastava is the perfect person to ask about her spiritual sadhana.

'No, no penance,' he says categorically. 'I think she was born with it. Inborn. She always had it. I don't think anyone gave it to her. She had it but she became more and more aware of it as time passed. Initially, that energy was devoted to the country. At the age of nineteen, she was in the Quit India Movement. Then she got married and wholeheartedly devoted her energy to me and her children. They grew up, and she said, "Now I have done this part, now let me get into the other." And she did that with the same enthusiasm. She never tired.'

There *was* a progression of awareness, of becoming conscious of the hidden reservoirs of the mind and heart, of energy and its ability to raise consciousness, of the pure gold that lies under the dross of the worldly self. The spiritual process has been described as one that proceeds towards awakening to our true nature. In Nirmala's case, the process of awakening to her core self revealed Shakti, the goddess that creates the world on her loom, instilling each sentient being with a spark of her own energy. Who could uncork that latent energy in us but the goddess herself, arisen to a living presence, in the person of a charismatic woman guru?

Before Mata Nirmala Devi popularized its ascension as a spiritual path, the kundalini was a mysterious force that wasn't properly understood outside advanced yogic circles. If one casts even a cursory eye on the vast body of sacred literature on Kundalini Yoga, including testimonies from Tantric masters past and present, one realizes the extent of preparation and effort required of the adept to even approach the dormant goddess energy. Like all Tantric practices, this too requires apprenticeship with a living guru who would typically train the aspirant in the yogas of mind and body for several years (if not lifetimes!) before allowing him or her to enter the sacred sphere of the serpentine goddess energy.

Nirmala Devi has proclaimed the availability of the path of the awakened kundalini to all, provided they want it and follow her instructions in good faith. There seems to be none of the complex Tantric rituals of cleansing and orientating, though there is an emphasis on purity of mind and character. Her method of awakening the kundalini seems relatively easy and painless, a 'lite' version of heavy-duty Tantric stuff, without the angst and agony it is said to entail. There is no complex *bandha* (yogic ties by which energy is locked in certain parts of the body) or specific pranayam (breathing exercises), and the serpent is certainly not caught by the tail (a forceful approach characteristic of Hatha Yoga)!

Rather than being the climactic moment of the spiritual search, the rise of the kundalini is the first step in Sahaja Yoga. 'Sahaja Yoga is different from other yogas because it begins with self-realization,' Nirmala Devi has said. In fact, followers of Sahaja Yoga are referred to as 'twice born' in direct reference to their second birth into the spiritual life after the awakening of their kundalini, an event Nirmala equates with self-realization.

The first time a spontaneous awakening of the kundalini was recorded in modern times was by Gopi Krishna in *Kundalini: Evolutionary Energy in Man* (1971). His is a terrifying account of the pain and dread of impending death, as the kundalini forces her way through his unprepared body and mind. 'There were dreadful disturbances in all the organs, each so alarming and painful that I wonder how I managed to retain my self-possession under the onslaught. The whole delicate organism was burning, withering away completely under the fiery blast racing through its interior. I knew I was dying and that my heart could not stand the tremendous strain for long. My throat was scorched and every part of my body flaming and burning, but I could do nothing to alleviate the dreadful suffering... The effort exhausted me and I felt myself sinking, dully conscious of the scalding sea of pain in which I was drowning.'

In contrast, Nirmala Devi and all those who say they have been awakened by her describe the experience of the arisen kundalini as a 'cool breeze' that flows through the body and out from the centre of the head and the palms. The official website proclaims Sahaja Yoga as a unique technique of raising the kundalini devised by Nirmala Devi for the collective evolution of human consciousness 'spontaneously' and 'without any effort'. 'A little light is then lit within us (a new dimension becomes available to our awareness) and through Sahaja Yoga meditation we can then grow much faster, without having to go through any penances, while living normal lives amidst our own families and societies', the website states.

Mr Srivastava concurs with this during our meeting, and characterizes Sahaja Yoga as a simple way of leading a spiritually oriented life. 'She talks about a pure spiritual existence but she doesn't say you run away from the world, go to the mountains,' he says. 'Be here, do your job, but do it honestly, do it purely. Have a family, have children, but adhere to ethics and spirituality. It is a very simple philosophy. And many are following it. It is not easy to follow because there are temptations in life. But you have to get over them, and after some time they cease to be temptations.'

Apparently, Nirmala Devi's technique of raising the kundalini is so *sahaja*—simple and spontaneous—that it can be learnt off the internet as well! A video version is available where she takes one through the paces herself. One quiet afternoon, I switch off my mobile phone and take my place before the computer. I spend a substantial slice of my day here, but this time it's different.

There is going to be none of the usual stuff—writing, emailing, net surfing.

I log on to the Sahaja Yoga website, click on the button that promises self-realization, and Nirmala Devi comes alive on my computer screen. Her face looks tauter, fuller, years younger than the photographs I have seen. She is clad in an ivory silk sari, her coal-black tresses cascading down her back. She seems to be looking directly at me, her large, heavily kohled eyes piercing through the computer screen. She is the living devi of this online sanctum, seated on the throne of wisdom, surrounded by flowers and lights. The camera shifts into a wide-angled frame to reveal some of her students, mostly white foreigners, sitting some distance away on chairs facing her.

When she speaks, it is with a confident eloquence that pierces the skin of secrecy cast upon the kundalini by generations of male Tantrics. For those who comprehend her as an avatar of Adi Shakti, it must be as if the Devi is calling forth her own element in us.

Nirmala Devi begins with two preconditions, which she will repeat throughout the process—one must forgive oneself by letting go of any 'guilt', as well as forgive everybody else for anything they may have done to us. One mustn't judge oneself, she says, but allow the kundalini to judge, for she is the mother and 'she knows how to give you your second birth'. She then tells everybody to point their left hands towards her, and place the right one on one's heart 'where resides the spirit... the reflection of God Almighty'.

'Kundalini is the power of the Holy Ghost, the desire of realization of God... which is the all-pervading power which does all living work'. Perhaps because she is addressing an audience where most members were brought up in a Christian ethos, she often references vocabulary from that religion to better explain ideas that might appear difficult or esoteric otherwise, a skilful means the guru employs to connect with her students.

Next, the congregation is asked to place their right hand successively on various chakras on the left side of the body—the heart, the lower chakras, back to the heart, and then the upper chakras. Some of these actions are to be accompanied with affirmative statements addressed to the kundalini energy, such as 'Mother, I am my own master'. When one reaches the crown chakra, one must push at the fontanel bone hard with the palm and rotate it clockwise seven times, petitioning the kundalini with, 'Mother, please give me my self-realization.' While I do this, accompanied by the congregation onscreen, she blows into the microphone a few times, and the sound is like that of waves rising and crashing into the sea, of mountain winds threading the limbs of giant trees.

At this point, Nirmala asks the gathering to place one palm towards her and the other above the fontanel area and check for a 'cool breeze'. Sometimes there might be hot air, she warns. One must wait for it to stop and the cool breeze to begin. Then she tells everybody to put their arms up, push their heads back and ask any of these questions three times—'Mother, is this the cool breeze of the Holy Ghost?'; 'Is this the all-pervading power of God's love?'; 'Mother, is this the *Parama Chaitanya*, the *Brahma Chaitanya* (supreme consciousness)?' The response, I suppose, is meant to well up spontaneously within, assisted by the awakened force of the kundalini.

When Nirmala asks those who felt the cool breeze to put up their hands, mine doesn't wave in ecstasy like all the others onscreen. She consoles me, saying, 'If you are unable to feel it, you have probably not forgiven everyone. Say again from your heart, "Mother, I forgive everyone", a few times and check again if you feel the cool breeze above your head.' No luck for me again.

Perhaps my forgiveness is faulty, perhaps I wasn't able to abandon my researcher's mind, perhaps I only thought I wanted an awakened kundalini but didn't want it bad enough. I don't know which of these reasons it is but, at the end of it all, my kundalini remains stubbornly asleep at the bottom of my spine. If one doesn't feel the cool breeze in Shri Mataji's presence, it has to be an act of self-sabotage, Mr Srivastava had told me.

'She has helped many people with her blessings. She says this was given to her that she can through vibrations awaken a kundalini. You sit with her, she does that. Her vibrations flow to you and that awakens your kundalini. But you should want it. You can't come to test her, just to see whether it will happen or not. It won't happen. You should want it and desire it, only then will it happen.'

So the reason the kundalini is said to awaken almost spontaneously in her presence is because she *makes* it happen. She *gives* all those who come to her unconditionally the vibrational boost that sets their subtle energy systems whirring, and the kundalini stirs awake. She, the guru-goddess-mother, takes care of all energic requirements and possible side effects of the surging goddess energy, and ensures her disciples experience only the benevolent, enabling effects of the phenomenon.

How is this possible?

Part of Indian wisdom traditions, most of which emphasize apprenticeship with a living guru, is a process called *shaktipat*, which means descent of energy. A self-realized master is said to have the ability to confer spiritual insight or realization and, in Nirmala Devi's case, the reported arousal of kundalini energy upon a disciple through a touch, look, mantra or even through thought. Gurus are said to work with their disciples at multiple levels to enable their progress on the path. For the disciple, all this activity—whether it is giving instructions on handling samsara, or discoursing on scriptures, or guiding the mind out of the maze of its incessant chatter through meditation, or encouraging them on the spiritual path best suited for their temperament—is the fruit of the guru's grace. At every step, the guru judges the disciple's needs and guides him or her accordingly, sometimes conferring some of her own energy to spur them towards a breakthrough. How this grace is conferred and what its exact nature is remains a mystery to those of us who have not learned from a living guru, one who takes on the task of nurturing one over lifetimes, till the very end of one's journey.

In his discourse on the *Jin Sutra*, Osho Rajneesh talks of two tributaries that feed the river of spiritual seeking—*samkalpa* and *samarpana*, 'determined resolve' and 'surrender' respectively. These word-concepts seem diametrically opposed to one another in their meaning and effect on the psyche, yet they are inextricably intertwined for the seeker. Osho makes the point that there are paths, like the austerities practised by Mahavira, which require great inner resolve, a harnessing of will against the natural tendency of body and mind to fall into the familiar ruts of entrenched habit patterns. And then, I think, there is the path of bhakti, where the seeker surrenders the self, the ego, afflictive emotions and all, to the Divine.

One cannot possibly initiate one's spiritual quest without some resolve, some effort, some way of impelling one's mind to turn within. And yet, as one matures through contemplation and gains some insight into the way the wheel of reality turns, one can't help letting go of notions of the self and what it *does*, even if that doing is the doing of spiritual practice. For, often, spiritual practice too becomes tied to the ego, and becomes another thing it manipulates for its own fulfilment. Maintaining some degree of samarpana can be useful in this sense, to act as a check for the deceptions of the ego.

Apprenticing with a guru, where he or she becomes wholly responsible for one's spiritual growth and well-being, requires a higher degree of surrender. If the guru is mother as well, perhaps surrender becomes easier, for we were in a situation in early childhood where we surrendered entirely to our mother or primary caretaker. She took on the responsibility for our nurture and security so completely that when we were in her arms, the world was whole and so were we. Suffering was separation from her, and happiness was her nearness, her attentiveness, her good mood. A guru-mother seems to evoke a similar psychological space and, as a result, the task of spiritual surrender doesn't seem so daunting. It harks back to a lost innocence where the world was mother, and her benevolence the only bulwark that was needed against its storms. We grew up and learned otherwise. When a guru-mother holds out that same promise, primal in its call to our subconscious, we cannot but accept her invitation to turn ourselves over and allow her to mould and shape our potential. For those who were scarred by unhappy childhoods or lack of maternal care, a guru-mother's presence could become a source of profound healing as well.

In *The Third Advent*, Gregoire de Kalbermatten describes how his own energy was worked upon and raised by her. It is an unusual account because it provides a glimpse into the energy mechanics of kundalini arousal through Mataji's agency and presence, and the relationship of enablement that exists between a guru-mother and her disciple.

It was 1975 and Nirmala lived in England with her husband. De Kalbermatten heard of her spiritual prowess, her ability to instigate extraordinary experiences in those around her, and arrived at her doorstep one misty morning. He stayed on for a week, talking to her, emptying out his 'mental baggage, piece by piece'. She responded with a sort of 'soul therapy', which included responding to his angst with conversation that carried 'a pervading benevolence and desire to comfort, counsel and heal'. During this time, through sessions of guided meditation and 'chakra workshops', de Kalbermatten says, 'she awakened my kundalini...'

In his words, 'First, I experienced some vibrations flowing in my hands, which first caused a sensation of heat, tingling and a slight sense of burning in the fingers. As Shri Mataji worked on the plexuses along my spine, the flow stabilized, became cooler and it could be described as a light breath. She seemed to work mostly with her attention but also with her hands, making at times some concentric gestures towards the location of the chakras in my body... Progress translated in the relaxation of the thought process, the waves of thoughts calmed down and a soothing silence settled in... I saw successive curtains of light moving and rising within my closed eyes but these movements of lights quietened down after some time. Finally a cool breeze emitted from the fontanel bone at the top of my head. "You've got it!" Shri Mataji said and she looked very happy indeed... I, without particular skills or merits, experienced on my central nervous system the rising of my kundalini, leading to self-realization.'

De Kalbermatten says he was fortunate to have received 'tender, loving care' from a guru-mother, because his previous lifestyle had damaged his subtle energy system and it required much attention to be restored, healed and awakened. 'It was such a relief to discover that a Master of this calibre was also a very caring Mother, full of compassion and understanding,' he says gratefully. After his initial experiences with Nirmala Devi, he was drawn into a deeper commitment to the spiritual life, of taking care of this knowledge that had been transmitted to him and which he didn't want to lose by taking it for granted.

As Nirmala has maintained, an awakened kundalini is merely a first step in a lifetime of spiritual growth. By using her own realization to aid her disciples', she has shared the fruits of spiritual knowledge with countless individuals. She has taught and inspired, healed and protected, loved and soothed.

In her person, the guru merges with the mother merges with the goddess. The triad becomes One.

There are some old tales of the Devi where she decapitates 'demons' who propose marriage to her, whose source I cannot recall because I probably heard them in my nani's lap as a little girl. As I look at the gentleman sitting before me in the Mother's own boudoir, I cannot help think that this is the kind of man the Devi might agree to en-spouse. Calm, gentle, focused, unthreatened by his wife's eminence, one who actually defers to it. Who, I realize, has not referred to her by name even once. Only as 'she' and 'her', sometimes even with a capitalized emphasis. She. Her.

Shri Mataji has not been well? I ask him. No, he says. 'It was the purpose of the Divine to come for a while, take the human form, to be one with the creation, influence the creation and, when the time came, to take the journey to some other place.

That's what she has done. But there is a human body and the human body is susceptible to torment and human infirmities. So there is nothing strange about it.'

Will there be a successor, somebody who will carry on her work? I ask this because organizations and sanghas that arise around charismatic gurus often decline with their passing, and the question of succession may at times lead to acrimony among followers.

'I am glad you asked that question,' Mr Srivastava says quietly. 'She has given her message and the message of Sahaja Yoga is now recorded. There will be no successor at all. She is the leader today, tomorrow and for ever. All others are her followers. So there'll be no pope here, no guru. She has given the message, which is a divine message. The message is clear, it is available to people. All others, including me, are merely devotees, followers whose task it is to spread that message.'

Politics invariably exists in all organizations, even loosely held spiritual ones. The guru herself may discourage it, but it might still seep in through the inclinations, expectations and projections of others. I am unaware of its shape and texture around Nirmala Devi, but cannot help wondering if Mr Srivastava is attempting to deflect any attempts to equate him with the guru once she is not there in a physical form. He has already said earlier in our conversation, 'What she is, I am not that. I am an ordinary person—an administrator and civil servant, but devoted to the same concept of one human family.'

Still, I say to him, 'You must have a special place among Shri Mataji's devotees.'

'Because I am the oldest devotee!' he responds, his eyes twinkling. He rises, palms joined together, and my time with him is over.

I bow in namaskar, and words form on my tongue to express a desire that has grown in my heart over the past hour.

'Would it be possible to have a darshan of Shri Mataji? Only if it will not inconvenience her, that is.'

Mr Srivastava thinks for a moment, and tells me to wait. In a few moments he is back. I follow him to a connecting chamber that opens into a large cavernous space. 'Only from afar,' he whispers. Then he raises his arm and points to the other end of the room, directing my eyes, my awareness.

Mata Nirmala Devi, raiser of kundalini, discoverer of inner shakti, possible goddess incarnate, guru of many, mother of all, is seated in a chair. Her eyes are closed as if in unbroken samadhi. The large sun-like bindi has risen on her forehead, illuminating her being. Women attendants hover around her, combing her hair, it seems, though I cannot be sure in the jewelled dimness of this, the Mother's inner sanctum.

I touch my conjoined palms to my forehead.

Silence fills the air like dense, aromatic incense smoke.

5

In Her Circle of Love

MATA AMRITANANDAMAYI

She doesn't know me.
She doesn't know
the jealousy, anger
that sometimes sprouts
in my being.
She doesn't know
the pettiness
that can enfilm
my truth-seeking eyes.
She doesn't know
the half-moons
of goodness in my heart
or the penumbrae
of darkness.
She doesn't know
the chronicle of loss
I carry
upon my shoulders...

And yet
She will hug me
as if all those things
I think I am
don't matter,
don't define
me...
In the circle of love
Her arms draw around me
I am... just me...
a human hunger
for warmth, love
purged, merged
in her love
She is...
Mother to me...

So deeply is Mata Amritanandamayi Devi identified with motherhood that her name and the 'Devi' appended to it can both be easily dispensed with. If you simply refer to her as 'Amma', enough people will immediately know who you are talking about, though it is a popular way of addressing one's mother in the numerous dialects of north, middle and south India, and there are millions of women who answer to this informal, intimate title. She has mothered so intensely, so completely, that nobody confuses Amma with anybody but this one individual, who could be God in the form of Mother, if you were to think in those terms.

It is a motherhood almost too huge to comprehend, to judge using human yardsticks and standards. Amma is the only woman I felt I needn't actually interview for this book—her work, her being, her love are apparent and transparent, risen like the sun in an open, cloudless sky. One just needs to look up and allow the warmth to penetrate one's pores, seep through one's skin.

As a commonsensical Hindi proverb says, it doesn't take a lamp to discern the sun. One interview cannot gauge the measure of a Mother. Only an open heart can.

When words seem insufficient purveyors of intended meanings, what can a writer do but turn to that part of her self that is the seeker of secrets, the seer of unspoken truths? And shift away from communication and expression to become a conduit for darshan of the different ways in which truth reveals herself. A gesture here, a serif there, that must be pieced together to form a picture from its parts. Step back and allow the blind men from the fable to recount their bit-truths, which might coalesce to form some semblance of their original source, the elephant.

Often, while attempting to write about spiritual masters, adepts, the great mothers, gurus, living goddesses, one feels able to provide only a glimpse, a tip of the proverbial iceberg that comprises the entire extent of their journeys, attainments, teachings, and remains hidden under the surface. I sometimes feel like the blind men struggling to describe an elephant, using intuitive knowing to fill in the gaps, able to touch some facets and quite unable to access many others. I just hope to provide enough such patches from the quilt of truth so that a coherent picture might emerge of these remarkable women and the work they have accomplished, within themselves and without, which has not only transformed them but, like moist earth around a deep-rooted tree, has soaked into the ground of being of all those who came in contact with them and who changed too, as a result.

Stepping into the soothing banyan-like shade of Amma's presence, I try to gather as many darshans as possible into her nature and quest, her work and her extraordinary motherhood. With an open heart, it becomes possible to *know* a Great Mother. Who knows where this journey might take us, what inspirations might flash like thunderbolts in a darkened monsoon sky, what elephantine truths may be revealed?

—

Like Anandamayi Ma and Nirmala Devi and scores of gurus past and present, it is believed that Mata Amritanandamayi was born either enlightened or divine, or both. This places her in the avatar category of earthly manifestations of divine energy who do not suffer the consequences of ignorance and affliction like the rest of humanity, one is told, but are born perfect. Their human lives are not supposed to be the familiar jumble of faltering and learning and suffering; rather, they unfurl as leela—a healing play that reveals truths and illuminates through illustration.

Upon examining Amma's early life, one finds little overt proof of perfection, though. If we are to believe hagiographical accounts that anoint her an avatar who is thought to point towards the 'good life' through personal example, a life lived according to the rhythms of dharma, then Amma's early difficulties could possibly be a teaching in transcendence. Avatars are said to be conscious births, their circumstances coordinated to maximize the effect of their appearance on earth and their instructional roles. From this perspective, the slew of circumstances that surrounded Amma at birth could be revealing of, and quite appropriate to, an avatar's function as a corrector of glitches in the natural order of things.

In a twentieth-century India struggling with ancient burdens and modern dilemmas, Amma was born marginalized many times over. In a social system that privileges certain castes over others and rich over poor, Amma's family was at the lower end of both strata. They were fisherfolk who lived in abject poverty in a coastal village in Kerala, barely scratching a living out of their daily catch from the sea. When another mouth was added to the family's roster on 25 September 1953, one can assume there were no lamps lit in celebration, no sweets distributed, perhaps no smiles either, except the one that illumined the infant's face. For Amma was born smiling, her mother has reported, gazing silently around her, as if preparing for the play of pain and pleasure that was about to unfold in her, around her.

A difficult and unhappy childhood awaited the smiling newborn. She endured constant criticism from her parents for her unworldliness, her strangeness, her un-childlike behaviour that, in hindsight, is said to have been a result of ongoing sadhana, a stream of remembrance and practice that bubbled within her naturally. Without anybody instructing her, she seems to have become immersed in her own style of spiritual practice by the time she was five. When most little girls want to play 'house' or imagine stories around their dolls, little Sudhamani, which was her given name, was found sitting all by herself, her lips incessantly moving in a silent spiral of prayer.

About this period in her life, Amma has said, 'From birth itself I had an intense love of the divine name. I would repeat the Lord's name incessantly with every breath, and a constant flow of divine thoughts was kept up in my mind irrespective of the place I was in or the work I was attending to.' This inward wheel of prayer was so compelling that it would wean Sudhamani away from everyday consciousness into inner absorption. Sometimes it would whisper to her in the middle of play, sometimes amidst a household chore. As it swelled within her, she dropped whatever she was doing and retreated within. To her parents, relatives and neighbours unfamiliar with states of mystical intoxication, the child seemed plain crazy.

For someone who grew up to become a 'universal mother', it is ironical that Amma received little love from her own mother as a child. Being a dark-skinned girl child intensified her misery. In a country where fair skin is highly valued despite a majority of its population genetically predisposed to darker pigmentation, Sudhamani's dark, earth-goddess-like luminosity irked her mother. It was perhaps seen as a quality that would reduce her marital prospects, thereby adding to the family's burden of bringing up a girl child.

Sudhamani's mother was tragically unable to sense the beauty inherent in her little girl's gentleness and her loving disposition, and pined for a daughter she could have loved for her external beauty. Later, when Sudhamani had transcended her womanhood, in a sense, and all possibilities of marriage with it, this dark complexion would evoke the thought of Krishna in the minds of those who gathered around her, the dark lord, also an avatar, whose skin is extolled in sacred literature as having been a luminous blue-black reminiscent of gathering monsoon clouds ('Ghanshyam').

Young Sudhamani's strange moods only added to her mother's emotional withdrawal from her, and the little girl became increasingly isolated within her own family. She had no friends or playmates, her schooling was stopped even before it had begun properly and she was often saddled with more household work than she could manage.

I wonder if Sudhamani's inwardness was brought on by her agonizing circumstances, rather than the other way round as has been implied in various accounts of her life. Could prayer have been a way of creating a reality that was a comforting alternative to the one where she was treated cruelly, where her mother's love had retreated from her? Children who are maltreated or abused tend to withdraw into imaginary worlds where they are safe, where they don't feel helpless or confused, where they are loved and respected. Perhaps Sudhamani shaped such a refuge out of prayer, constant remembrance of divinity, and attempts to connect with it in some way.

I do recognize that this goes against the grain of the 'avatar narrative', where the avatar retains all power over his or her life circumstances and consciously places difficulties in his or her own path, and where these difficulties are thought to actually be tools for illustrating correct (dharmic) responses to tough life situations. But if we are to learn something of value from Sudhamani's childhood, it might be more useful to relate to her as a human child, an extraordinary one undoubtedly, but human nevertheless, who found a way to be happy through her misery, the flame of whose compassion never extinguished, and who grew into an oceanic mother despite the lack of maternal love that threatened to blight her own childhood. For me, the miracle lies in this self-healing, the little girl growing up unscathed and unscarred by the wounds of life, and her consequent evolution into a phenomenon of love. No miraculous avatar narrative can compare with the kind of effort and grace and alchemic growth imbued in this story of a sad little girl who would one day become 'mother of the world'.

Her own suffering possibly opened Sudhamani's eyes to others', and she began to see and feel and respond to their suffering as she would her own. This wearing away of the membrane that separates self and other is crucial on the spiritual path. As Nani Ma had said, once the sense of separation softens, one cannot help but be connected with another's pain as if it were one's own. Perhaps her cruel circumstances snapped close identification with an ego-self that is in any case tenuous and unformed in childhood, so that Sudhamani embarked upon a freewheeling journey armed with a sense of her self and the world as being inter-bound, where nobody was a stranger and nobody's pain was too little or too much for her to try and deal with. Risking her parents' wrath, she would share her family's scarce rations with those who turned up at her doorstep hungry, and would take time out of a day already crammed with household chores to visit elderly and sick neighbours and minister to their needs. One could possibly discern in this selfless seva of childhood, seeds of the mega-motherhood that lay not too far off in Sudhamani's future.

Friendless and uncared for, Sudhamani perhaps found a new purpose through this psychological shift away from her own problems to that of others. She roamed her village, observing the human condition at different ages and stages, a little mother who poured as much love and care as she could muster to better the lives of those around her. By becoming a node in the interconnected web of life, one that throbbed with a vital healing energy, Sudhamani transformed her own narrative from one of victimhood and despair to one that was empowered with compassion and sought positive change.

This was the beginning of the process of transformation that would draw Sudhamani into its quickening vortex, and when she emerged, it would be with the inner skills that would help her help the world. She would enter this phase of intense sadhana with a Buddha-like determination to find the cause and cure for human suffering. She has said, 'As a child, I always wanted to know the cause of misery of mankind and thought that if sorrow is a truth, then there must be a cause and a way out.' Her resolve to do so brought to her an understanding of her own life's work. 'I realized my purpose is to console—to personally wipe away tears through selfless love, compassion and service.' Her compassionate childhood was a preparation for this role, and the coastal village a microcosm of the enormity of suffering she would encounter as her activities broadened to include the whole world.

Meanwhile, the quiet stream of Sudhamani's sadhana had inched towards the tipping point where her individual consciousness would lose itself in cosmic consciousness. Amma has recounted this experience of enlightenment in her own words, and it is interesting to note that the arising of the Goddess accompanies and facilitates it:

> Each and every pore of my body was wide open with yearning, each atom of my body was vibrating with the sacred mantra, my entire being was rushing towards the Divine Mother in a torrential stream...
>
> O Mother... here is your child about to die drowning in unfathomable distress... This heart is breaking... These limbs are faltering... I am convulsing like a fish thrown on shore... O Mother! You have no kindness towards me... I have nothing left to offer you except the last breath of my life...

Swami Amritaswarupananda Puri who has recorded this incident in his book, *Mata Amritanandamayi: A Biography*, says that at this point, 'her voice became choked. Her breathing completely stopped. Sudhamani fell unconscious. The Will of the Mother designates the moment. The Divine Enchantress of the Universe, the Omniscient, the Omnipresent, the Omnipotent Being, the Ancient, Primal Creatrix, the Divine Mother, appeared before Sudhamani in a living form, dazzling like a million suns.

Sudhamani's heart overflowed in a tidal wave of unspeakable Love and Bliss. The Divine Mother benignly smiled and, becoming Pure Effulgence, merged in Sudhamani...'

This cataclysmic event triggered the metamorphosis of a gawky, adolescent Sudhamani into Amma, a Great Mother, after what is described as a literal permeation with the energy of the Goddess. This transformation was hardly painless. As in the case of Meher Baba, her direct realization of nondual cosmic consciousness completely obliterated any sense of ordinary self and thereby the facility to function in everyday reality. To those around her, her 'craziness' seemed to have intensified. There were no longer occasional lapses into contemplative reverie. Rather, her whole being had crossed over to another level of consciousness, one so vast that she was unable to rouse herself from it initially. Unwilling to face a samsaric existence filled with insensitivity and barbed questions, she began to dig holes in the sand on the beach and hide herself in them.

Says Swami Amritaswarupananda, who was also her first disciple, 'She spent her days and nights enjoying the perennial Bliss of God-realization and avoided all human company. If anyone had considered her mad before, they were firmly convinced of her insanity now. Who among these fisher folk could conceive of the plane of consciousness in which the little one was established?... The only recent change, if they had noticed any at all, was that instead of rolling in the sand she was now digging big holes.'

Examining an experience of self-realization with unenlightened human eyes, one cannot help notice the extreme isolation it seems to fling upon the adept in its immediate aftermath. Paradoxically, the instant when he or she experiences the oneness, the infinite interconnectedness of everything, is also when all connections seem to snap, all support systems collapse, all that was familiar no longer is. So intense is the fire of realization that it seems to burn away everything that has to do with the conditioned responses and ways and being of the self that once was, but no longer is. To us it might seem that the individual is turned inside out, upside down. In fact, there is no *individual* in the conventional sense any more. The flame of personality has been extinguished and in order to return to some sort of samsaric existence, the adept must relearn the rules of the game in the light of his or her enlightenment, discard the ashes of the old self and fashion a new functional, connected, empathetic self.

Initially, Sudhamani remained engrossed in the unconditioned bliss of non-personality. The world around her no longer mattered, and the seva that she had constantly exerted at until now was lost in the wide horizons of cosmic consciousness. Until one day, when a thought welled in her mind spontaneously, somewhat like Sri Anandamayi's non-self-bound kheyal. It was as if the call of the Devi, who said, 'My child, I dwell in the heart of all beings and have no fixed abode. Your birth is not merely for enjoying the unalloyed Bliss of the Self but for comforting suffering humanity. Henceforth, worship Me in the hearts of all beings and relieve them of the sufferings of worldly existence.'

Sudhamani had crossed over, realized the mystical oneness that underlay reality, the truth of everything, lost her self in the process, died, been reborn, awoken her inner devi, and lived to tell the tale. It was now time to begin another journey, one that would launch her head first into the wild whirlpools of samsara, and challenge her with the task of aligning her inner insight with the work of the world. There had been enough navel-gazing and blissful samadhi. The Devi had pointed her on to a new turn, a new path that would take her right into the muck of affliction and suffering, ignorance and disease. It was time to tuck in the corner of her sari and set to work. It was time to get her hands dirty and take on the task of mothering millions. Slough off sweet, gentle, odd, strange, sadhika Sudhamani, and come into her multi-armed, goddess-like Amma-hood.

And she has said, 'From that day onwards I could see nothing as different from my own Formless Self wherein the entire universe exists as a tiny bubble...' She became 'Mother... just an offering to the world... available to everyone'.

—

It is estimated that till 2008, when this was written, Amma had hugged some 30 million people around the world. She began when she was seventeen, a newly arisen Mother who couldn't help connecting with everybody by physically embracing them. Her self had become obliterated and its place was taken by this Ganga-like motherhood—unfathomably deep, compassionate, flowing wherever there was the greatest need for nourishment and alleviation. When I think of this profound motherhood that begs to be referred to with a capital 'M', evidenced usually in spiritually awakened, Devi-esque women, I cannot help wonder about its equation (or the lack of it) with biology.

In the natural world, motherhood is biologically connected to reproduction, a process indispensable to life. Organisms reproduce likenesses of themselves, young that carry their uniqueness and particularities forward in time, into the linear future. A variety of reproductive processes exists, and in species where genders are well-differentiated such as those that comprise the vertebrates, reproduction is sexual and results in a combination of genetic material from both parents. Biologically, a 'mother' is the female participant in this process, who contributes the egg that will be fertilized by the sperm of the male.

Amongst vertebrates too, it is the mammals that carry their young for comparatively longer gestation periods, give birth to them live instead of as eggs that need external hatching, and raise them through close personal contact over a period of time that varies from a few days to a few years. Therefore it is mammals that are likely to display a motherhood that is more than a biological contribution of genetic material, where it begins to touch upon the bouquet of qualities we recognize as 'mothering'—nurture, care, warmth, affection, encouragement. These become even more pronounced among primates, the order that includes humans.

The connection between femininity and motherhood is understood as a sort of genetic predisposition, that is, women are thought to be biologically hardwired to the crucial task of bearing and rearing the species' young. Because the continuation of the species depends on this, it does make some sort of survivalist, Darwinian sense. Motherhood is part of this nest, this collective impulse towards self-preservation, but can it explain the Great Motherhood of an Amma, a Nirmala Devi or an Anandamayi Ma?

Surely here we have a motherhood that is independent of biology, which actually has more in common with cultural archetypes related to the exaggerated divine qualities of goddesses of earth and forest, blood and fertility, glen and glade, in which pregnancy and childbirth, the having of children of one's own womb and blood, is immaterial and inconsequential to the experience of motherhood. Here the 'mother' relates directly to the soul, and is not related in any tangible way to the body that cloaks it. Amma has never borne any children. And yet, where does one find a deeper expression of motherhood than in her presence? Who would deny the potency of her motherhood, its overarching impact, its ability to turn the soul?

The singlemost visible and compelling act of Amma's motherhood is her hug. She hugs all those who come to her without discrimination; whether they are Hindu, Muslim, Christian, atheist, man, woman, child, beggar, leper, people with HIV/AIDS, they are welcomed into her circle of love. She has been known to sit for twenty-four hours and longer at a stretch to meet and hug each individual in gatherings that sometimes run into several thousands. Her point is, 'All are my children, and I am their mother. They must be able to come and give all their sorrows to their mother.'

The impact of this simple act is phenomenal, for it conveys loving acceptance at a basic human level. You may be scorned or rejected by the entire world, but in Amma's presence you are worthy of love. A hug, given without any judgement, with a mother's warmth, is an opportunity for the receiver to release feelings of pain and inadequacy, frustration and misery and divest oneself of the crusty layers, the thorny masks one puts on as protective gear to negotiate the world. If one is awake to the moment of the hug, it may also offer a chance to let go of tightly held notions of self and other, so that the wall that guards our ego-personality and separates it from all else is obliterated momentarily, and there is no 'other' any longer. Amma's hug can thus trigger a darshan of the fundamental truth of non-duality, an encirclement that merges boundaries and binaries into one ocean of truth. It is said that the most profound understanding of truth includes oppositions, rights *and* wrongs, this *and* that. If we are alive to the possibility, Amma's hug can catalyse its realization.

Amma's motherhood is beyond biology and unbound by conventions that govern man–woman relationships and gender behaviour in India. Though there is no dearth of teenage mothers in this country where early marriage continues to be a widely-practised norm, Sudhamani's awakening to a spiritual, universal motherhood as a seventeen-year-old must have caused surprise and heartburn in her village. And this reaction may have been exacerbated by Amma's expression of motherly love, her embracing everybody, literally and figuratively, through hugs and warmth, care and companionship.

Physical contact between genders is largely unacceptable in Indian society outside the confines of home and immediate family. Was Amma's motherhood ever misunderstood, was it looked upon as unbecoming conduct on the part of a young woman? One hears of some initial hostility and threats to her life. And one did hear some murmurs of disapproval of the sniggering, lascivious variety, but not for some time now. Anybody that comes in contact with her cannot but notice how completely Amma *owns* the mother's space. There is simply no question of any charges of undesirable conduct sticking. Enough people have recognized her universal motherhood, and the quality of her realization, to request her to mother them in a different way—through teachings and spiritual guidance. By 1979, a sangha had gathered around Sudhamani that had named her 'Amritanandamayi'—she who is imbued with immortal bliss—and had also begun calling her 'Amma'.

In 1981, Amma's spiritual children constructed the first few thatched huts around her family's home, the one where she had been born and spent her turbulent childhood, and this became the foundation of the Mata Amritanandamayi Math. Within a few years, the Math had grown exponentially and it now resembles a small city. It has taken the erstwhile fishing village of Parayakadavu in its embrace so that its name and character have been entirely subsumed in the Amma-centric world of 'Amritapuri', the city of Amrita (a reference to her name 'Amritanandamayi', and also perhaps *amrita*, the nectar of immortality).

Amritapuri has developed into a spiritual megapolis in step with Amma's ascendance to the stature of 'world guru', one who is loved and respected the world over, a rare woman to have achieved this honour. Amritapuri's complexion and character have been completely transformed since the days of Amma's childhood. Multi-speciality hospitals, institutions of higher learning and accommodation for the lakhs that come visiting every year now dot its skyline in place of palm fronds and an endless horizon stretching from land to sea to sky.

In the ashram, which is the nerve centre of Amritapuri, there are temples and halls for meetings and meditation, cooking and dining, puja and ritual, all oriented towards the adoration of the presiding mother-goddess, Amma. Even where deities from the Hindu pantheon might be worshipped, it is done in accordance with Amma's instructions. Her presence is palpable in each event, each building, each grain of sand, each weary heart that finds its way to Amritapuri.

Amma's global mission to nourish humanity's body and soul is headquartered at Amritapuri. Her initiatives, aimed at providing whatever is needed, wherever, are dreamt of here and ways found to make them practicable. In this sense, Amritapuri is not just an opportunity for a quiet retreat with one's guru, a temple where devotees may worship their personal deity, a replica of a sadhu's solitary cave. To me, Amritapuri is a call to duty, a hub of meditation *and* action, inwardness *and* meaningful activity. In this, it asks her disciples to follow the personal example of

Amma, who 'returned' from her enlightenment, as it were, to mother the world.

As Judith Cornell says in *Amma: Healing the Heart of the World*, 'Amritapuri Ashram is a centre where Amma has a thousand arms of compassion stretching worldwide to help nurture human beings spiritually, mentally and physically.' The image invoked is of the Devi, multi-armed in her quest to nurture her children as completely as possible. She, as the Great Mother, is responsible for us all. Indeed, according to the *Devi Mahatmayam*, She contains us all. Anne Lowenkopf says in her essay 'The Mother Goddess', 'The Great Goddess contains within herself not only all other deities but existence itself. Her children and all things reside within her, are of her substance, and she indwells inside them. The shortest distance to the Mother is within yourself.'

Those who are astounded, like I am, by the level of organization and resources that have been harnessed not only in bringing Amritapuri to being, but also in implementing charitable schemes globally, might find the answer in one of Amma's oft-quoted instructions to her disciples. 'Everyone in the world should be able to sleep without fear, at least for one night. Everyone should be able to eat to his fill, at least for one day. There should be at least one day when hospitals see no one admitted due to violence. By doing selfless service for at least one day, everyone should help the poor and needy. It is Amma's prayer that at least this small dream be realized.' The outpouring of selfless service on the part of her spiritual children is a response to Amma's entreaty, their attempt to manifest her dream in the real world.

—

I had the good fortune to interview Amma, and be hugged by her, in 2003. She entered the room where I was waiting, smiling broadly, diamonds glinting upon her nose, arms outstretched. Soon I was enfolded in her warm embrace. Holding me tight, she whispered in my ear, 'Meri beti, meri beti,' in Hindi, a language Amma otherwise doesn't speak. There was something completely accepting and unconditional about that hug, and a warm glow suffused my being for a long time after that. Even today, when I think of that moment, I can feel Amma's warmth and her loving presence.

With that embrace, I got a taste of Amma's mega-motherhood that draws one into a space of co-being with everything and everyone else. Moments before, I had been irritated by the fact that I could not have much time with Amma, partitioned as her day was, and always is, into millions of moments in which to attend to the crowds that flock to her wherever she goes. Her embrace awoke me to the fact of her vast love in which there is place for everybody. Nobody would be turned away. Time would be created, as would materials and resources, out of her huge love. Why was I bound to my agenda, my own little roster of questions?

In that moment, Amma's hug as if liberated me from a too-tight drawing of myself into a journalistic role. She was with me as she was with everybody else, I realized, looking to fulfil my need, even if it meant revisiting the painful circumstances of her childhood and retelling a story she must have told so many times before, and did again now, without an iota of jadedness. 'Amma is a beginner, living always in the present... the past does not exist, neither does the future, so why worry?' she asked me with an affectionate intimacy that usually comes only with people you have known since they were babies. She also endearingly referred to herself in the third person, much like Anandamayi Ma and many other self-realized masters seem to, having grown out of the 'I-ness' of ego.

Amma created an atmosphere of ease between us, almost of two friends gossiping. Though I couldn't understand what she was saying without translation, her continually changing expressions, like shape-shifting clouds, told me her story. Her eyes danced with mirth as she recounted her mother's taunts, her mouth turned smilingly downwards in self-deprecation, and she often covered her lips with her fingers in a gesture of modesty when I asked of her efforts on behalf of others, of the compassion that welled naturally from within.

Speaking of the years she spent in her village, she said she had begun to question the suffering she saw all around her. 'I would ask myself, why do people suffer? If it is their fate, then it is my destiny to help them. That is why I hug people, it is a spontaneous response of love to their grief.'

Those early seeds of awareness drew Amma to her lifelong mission of service. Today, wherever suffering comes to her notice, Amma feels compelled to respond, and this has resulted in humanitarian work at a phenomenal scale. 'We can never close our eyes to the world in the name of spirituality,' she has said. 'Self-realization is the ability to see ourselves in all beings. This is the third eye through which you see, even while your two eyes are wide open. We should be able to love and serve others, seeing ourselves in them. This is the fulfilment of spiritual practice.' She advocates loving and taking care of others as the true path to self-healing. 'Real devotion to God is to be compassionate towards the poor and the suffering. Feed those who are hungry, help the destitute, console those who are sad, give relief to those in pain, be charitable towards everyone.'

The extent and scope of Amma's humanitarian work is exceptional not only in terms of its sheer scale, variety and spread, but also because of her constant emphasis on compassion and the need to engage in service as part of one's spiritual practice. Some of the activities she has thus inspired are free food and clothing programmes, charitable hospitals, hospices, disaster relief programmes, free homes for the poor, medical camps, orphanages, schools, educational institutions, widows' pension schemes, free legal advice and environmental preservation, among others.

Amma has stirred people all over the world to walk the path of selfless service and compassion through her own example. Amma is not a guru who preaches from a pedestal nor is she content with living in ivory-towered comfort while others toil on her behalf. No work is too small or too big for Amma's hands.

I have heard stories of how she will pick up a broom and sweep away dust that has caught her eye, how she will lend a helping hand to labourers toiling in the hot sun, all unselfconsciously, as if it were the most natural thing in the world. And for her it is. Because she is not immersed in fulfilling personal goals or ambitions or in the mental chatter that keeps one tied to plans and worries and anxieties, she is ever ready for the task at hand. For the uncluttered mind, the present moment is the only point of real contact with life, and it remains anchored in this truth, doing the work each moment brings to it. The river of Amma's attention and affection flows in the direction in which it is needed *now*, which is perhaps why the Mata Amritanandamayi Math is usually one of the first to volunteer in disaster relief work, as in the Asian Tsunami of 2004, Hurricane Katrina in the US in 2005 or the Kosi floods in Bihar in 2008.

Amma's alacrity and lack of squeamishness about engaging in menial manual work is also a teaching in the dignity of human labour. India's deeply entrenched caste system categorizes working with one's hands—whether it is tilling the land, crafting things of everyday use, weaving cloth, working with leather, or the maintenance of hygiene and cleanliness—as a 'lower-caste' function. The so-called high castes reserve for themselves the 'higher' jobs of studying, worshipping, warring, trading, governing, even spiritual adventuring, in short, work that doesn't really require them to engage in backbreaking manual labour. Centuries of this kind of hierarchic division of labour has devalued physical work and worse, tied some professions to notions of uncleanliness, impurity and untouchability.

To bring our collective attention to the fact that we must be able to clean after ourselves, and to inculcate this essential work with the dignity it deserves, Mahatma Gandhi asked his followers to clean their own toilets, homes and the premises of ashrams where they lived together. This teaching was nested within a larger work ethic that required voluntary contribution of labour, *shramdaan*, in jobs of building, gardening, cooking, spinning yarn, taking care of animals, tending to crops and so on—work that the caste system had classified as menial, meant to be performed only by lower castes whose birth-given destiny it was said to be. I think with his emphasis on the equality and dignity of all labour, Mahatma Gandhi was trying to lift a society out of centuries of work-based discrimination and a distaste for certain kinds of work, educate it to treat the work, and its doers, with respect and ensure that each individual learnt to use his or her hands appropriately for the work of life.

When Amma picks up a shovel or a broom, and her disciples cannot but follow her, I discern a Gandhian quality of teaching, both in terms of the insight imparted and the use of her own self as proof of its viability and workability. Just as Mahatma Gandhi would never ask people to do what he himself had not or could not do, Amma never merely directs or orders. She does. And those who observe her every moment, in the hope of guidance, follow her lead. Not only does the follower learn a valuable growth lesson, a golden chain of service is formed, beginning with Amma and moving link by human link towards any place where there is some need to be eased, some pain to be assuaged. Once, when Amma was asked about the qualities of her ideal disciple, she responded, 'One whose legs rush to offer help, whose lips utter comforting words of love and whose eyes shed tears of compassion on hearing the cry of the distressed—such a person I would call a true disciple.'

Amma's mentorship of her children's spiritual lives is based on an axis of love and seva. To know one's true self is to know the reservoir of love that is ever present within, the 'honey in the rock' of our worldly, ego-driven selves, which we taste when we realize our real nature. The purpose of human life, according to Amma, is to make the effort to discover the truth about our selves, and use it to spark the flame of compassionate love in our beings, which will then illumine the path towards unconditional seva. 'After all, love is our true nature,' she has said. 'When we do not express love in our words and actions, it is like honey hidden in a rock. It is of no use to anyone.'

Once there is self-realization, a kindling of true knowledge, it must be put to use for the greater common good. It almost seems that to Amma, using the light of self-realization to brighten only one's own life, and doing nothing with it that would directly better others', would be a colossal waste. Wisdom too is a valuable resource, she seems to say. Let's use it for something. Let's not sit in a cave any longer. Let's not enjoy the honey of transcendental bliss on our own. Let's go out and find a hungry soul to feed it to.

This attitude of Amma, a kind of non-wasting of spiritual self-knowledge, is reminiscent of the Indian mother, the homemaker who must optimize all resources, stick to a budget, and do the best for her children within her limitations. Indian mothers, and perhaps mothers in most poor countries, developed ways of maximizing the use they got out of material things, such as clothes and books that were reused by younger siblings, scarce water that was recycled to water plants after washing vegetables, sturdy old saris that were sewn into blanket covers or curtains, kitchen scraps that fed poultry to substantiate family incomes, and so on. Because of a cultural predilection towards frugality and need-based consumption (rather than its increasingly prevalent greed-based version), dictated by necessity, Indian women have been innovators. They have raised broods and sustained families on the barest of means, relying on their creative resourcefulness to tide over the choppy bits. This has been part of my own experience growing up, and I too have an Amma who has never wasted anything, neither water nor fabric, nor her instinctive maternal love.

Mata Amritanandamayi has extended this sprit of motherly innovativeness into the spiritual sphere. As their beings open to the possibility of unconditional love, she asks her disciples to use it to empower themselves to contribute unconditional seva. If they are householders, no problem, they should try and devote at least an hour a day to help somebody in need. Whatever they contribute, whether it is time or skill, money or material, is immediately routed for use in Amma's multiple initiatives around the world. Nothing is superfluous, nothing is wasted. A few dollars from one part of the world could provide life-saving drugs in another. A few hours of a surgeon's seva time could ease the pain of somebody who wouldn't be able to afford the surgery otherwise. A lawyer's expertise given free of charge could help a marginalized group get justice.

In this way, Amma's love grows from a seed to a forest, her hug radiating out from the individual to embrace the whole world. Each lamp lights another, until the stain of darkness disappears. Amma ignites the seed spark. The individual must then pass on the flame, spread the love.

—

With each passing year, Amma's spiritual family continues to grow, her embrace circling its way through almost the entire globe. Whoever she visits—a village in India, a family devastated by Hurricane Katrina or an auditorium full of adoring followers anywhere in the world—Amma insists on a loving, maternal informality, a familial closeness, her ability to connect with each human being unaffected by the fact that she speaks only in her mother tongue, Malayalam. Though Amma's words are constantly translated by followers, as she chucks a grown man or woman under the cheek like she would a child, or quietens another who has dissolved into cathartic tears in her arms, words become secondary. Her foremost expression is of unconditional love which is instinctively understood by the other.

When she is thanked for her generosity and help, her response is usually something like—'I am your mother, and if a mother doesn't do something for her child, who will?' Once, somebody asked Amma about her seemingly infinite patience with people who came to her, and why she was never bothered by the close proximity of the ill and the diseased. When the automatic human response is to draw away from that which is unpleasant, how does Amma not experience this reaction? She replied, 'When a bee hovers over a garden of varied flowers, what it beholds is not the difference between the flowers but the honey within them. Similarly, Amma sees the same Supreme Self in each and every one.' Amma sees with the eyes of love and awareness, which don't judge appearances but unsheathe the innate humanity, the essence that lies hidden in us all.

If she *is* an avatar—a Krishna-hued, love-imbued one—responsible for balancing that which is out of whack in our world, Amma's spiritual and social work would reflect some of the crises that characterize our times. Indeed, her seva initiatives in medical care, education, free housing, environmental protection and legal aid attempt to fill the gaps that exist in crucial infrastructural and developmental areas, and make these available to the poor, the destitute and the marginalized, out of whose pale of experience they would otherwise be. Amma's immediate response to natural disasters at times shows the lack of it on the part of the government and administration whose designated work it is.

By responding selflessly, and effectively, to any instance of suffering around her, Amma brings it into the open and provides the rest of society with an opportunity to respond to it as well. If we are aware and sensitive to them, Amma's actions can be the truth-telling mirror each society must have held up to it. One might wonder, why does Amma need to engage in these activities? It is not just because she is a goddess-like universal mother and seva is her spiritual path. It is perhaps just as much because the need exists, because the misery-inducing circumstances exist. Can we, as a society, take up Amma's challenge and examine our flaws, our corruption, our disinterest in making things better for all and, like her, perhaps follow it up with some action too?

Another avataric role that might suggest itself, because of the circumstances of her birth and her life choices, is Amma's significance to the movements for social justice in the country. At a time when social justice is a complex and much discussed issue, Amma brings a different perspective to a debate that has at times threatened to splinter the ideal of universal equality enshrined in the Indian constitution. Democracy has attempted to deliver some of the promised constitutional measures to the oppressed and marginalized castes of Indian society so that they can have a little more than equal opportunity to purge themselves of the toxic effects of centuries of oppression, and grow towards economic, social and educational success. Caste-based reservations in education and employment do have the potential for providing opportunities to the oppressed castes that were denied these earlier. I say 'potential' and don't make a more emphatic statement because employment or higher education cannot be seen in isolation—reservations in these sectors must follow reforms in primary and secondary education, which must improve in quality and become freely available to all.

The rise of caste-based politics, where castes band together and vote candidates or parties affiliated to their own castes to power, has emerged as an important feature of the social justice movement in India. As a result, several key Dalit and OBC (Other Backward Castes) politicians have arrived on the national stage and reduced the monopoly of higher castes in power and politics. Whether this development has instigated any grassroots change, or has become subsumed in the wider phenomenon of opportunistic politics, is open to debate. What it has achieved is the opening of the gilded gates that guarded preserves of power, and the fulfilment of the political aspirations of Dalits (literally, those 'trodden underfoot') by enabling an ascent to elected positions of authority.

In the matter of religion, an overpowering distaste for the system that kept them in cruel bondage for centuries has led new generations of Dalits to cast caste out, so to speak, by turning away from Brahminical Hinduism and converting to other religions like Christianity and Buddhism. Without getting into the conversion debate and the rightness or wrongness of it, I would like to explore another kind of affirmative action, one that is not bound to legislation or politics or religious conversion. While all these are worthwhile ways of attempting to change an unjust system, I think Amma is emblematic of a radical affirmative action that can liberate the mind of its chains and set one free in the true sense of the word.

Exchanging one belief system, one religion, for another may

work well as a political and social statement, but will have no impact on the individual's quality of life if change is not striven for at a deeper spiritual level. If I don't begin to recognize my afflictive emotions and attempt to replace them with wholesome ones, for instance, I am still in the same place internally as I was before. I may have changed the label that I stick upon my identity, but I have not walked even one step towards the most important journey I will ever undertake—towards knowing my true self.

Through her own life and the choices she made, Amma points to precisely this truth about empowerment—that it doesn't work if it only remains on the surface of our being. I may overthrow the yoke of caste, but my soul may still be burdened by a yoke of another kind, of ignorance of its own true nature. Amma chose to overthrow this inner yoke and, by realizing her indwelling truth, the light that brightens the deepest recesses of the cave of our being and burns as brightly in one individual as it does in another, regardless of circumstances of birth, wealth or karma, she set herself free. Truly, deeply, eternally free.

As a social statement, spiritual liberation is unequalled in its impact. For it empowers one so completely, and marks the adept with such fearless dignity, erases their oppressed identity so decisively, that the rest of the world cannot see them as anything but a realized master. India has had a history of social empowerment through spiritual liberation, where people from marginalized castes, and women, established a direct connection with truth and divinity that was not dependent on the dominant Brahminical religion, and inspired others to do the same through freewheeling, unconventional verse rendered in dialects of common use.

The Bhakti poets of medieval India are remarkable in this regard and the movement, that was not really a consolidated event but a successive and sometimes contiguous appearance of saint-poets, led to the emergence of a counter-culture that rejected mainstream religion, ridiculed it as being stuck up and out of touch, and accorded greatest primacy to direct spiritual experience. Seekers from marginalized communities like Kabir, who was a weaver, and Raidas, who was a leather worker, forged spiritual destinies that were at variance with their circumstances, showing everybody that truth can never be the preserve of any caste or group or religion, nor does reality and realization dawn only on the high-born. Life flows through all equally and reveals its deepest core to those who are able to intuit its true nature, without the scab of ego blinding their consciousness. They claimed their freedom for themselves through spiritual practice and realization; nobody had to give it to them.

Kabir, for instance, rejects the dreary dissertations of both the mullah and the pandit, and gives precedence to the two-and-a-half letters of love in our hearts over the combined knowledge of all scriptures. Nobody ever became a real *jnani*, a knower of truth, without learning how to love, he says—*dhai akhar prem ka, padhey jo pandit hoye*. The emphasis is on the direct experience of selflessness that the touch of true love can bring, a transformation that cannot be expected by mugging up dead words inscribed on a palm leaf.

I see Amma as a contemporary jewel in this garland, a presence that may or may not be avataric, but that has successfully turned the hierarchies of caste *and* gender on their heads by realizing the fullest extent of her own potential and then some more, by refusing the grasp of victimhood and by growing into a role that embraces the whole world, as the arch of the sky. Because of this, Amma will never be just a woman who belongs to a particular caste or a place on the edge of the sea, in a small village, of one blood with a family. She has shrugged away all the identities that could limit her.

She is now mother—of earth, sky, water, air, the living and the non-living, the beloved and the unloved. The roots of her love continue to penetrate deeper into our collective unconscious, reaching out for the undernourished parts of our beings, spreading out further to accomplish their work as conduits of compassion.

Part Three

When Women Go Forth

6

Revolutionaries of the Spirit

SRI SARADA MA AND PRAVRAJIKA VIVEKAPRANA

Who am I?
A sari woven
from
the prickly yarn of
roles and responsibilities
—mother, mother-in-law
wife, sister, daughter
aunt, grandmother...

Who is I
when not
shrouded
in this sari?

A wind unbound
A wave of sound
A rhythm freed
A voice at ease

A keening call
Or nothing at all...

When knots of I
shrivel and dissolve

Who remains...
What dies...

—

In the cacophony of Delhi, walking into the city branch of Sri Sarada Math is like entering a secret garden of sorts. The entrance is through a school run by the sadhvis of the Math, and the chatter of children forms a trail I follow into the inner sanctum, the ashram. Young women in white saris—the uniform of the novitiate, the brahmacharini on the first rung of sannyasa—cheerfully bustle in and out of classrooms. One makes the bill and counts out change in the small bookstore, another ushers me into the shrine, her oiled plait gleaming on her shoulder.

Noise fades away, as if left behind in a parallel plane of existence. And my mind forgets its chatter for a moment, drawn into the silence of this womb-like space. There is nobody around, the young woman having left me alone to commune with the guiding spirits of the Math, their presence evoked through stiffly posed, turn-of-the-last-century photographs. Even so, a sense of these three individuals, and their distinct yet deeply interconnected paths of inner and outer action, becomes apparent.

Clouds of incense smoke soften the sunlight streaming in through latticed windows, accentuating the feeling of having stepped into a different dimension, an other-world convulsed into being by a creative impulse of the sacred feminine. For the triad enshrined here engineered a modern socio-spiritual movement that radicalized the feminine path to inner awakening and expressed a uniquely Indian ideal of the emancipated woman.

One man, a mystic, his eyes turned within. Another man, a saffron-robed sannyasi, arms folded in quiet determination, poised between contemplation and action. And then a woman, palms upturned in *dhyana mudra* on her lap, head covered with the edge of her sari, long hair flowing over one bare shoulder in the manner of women in rural Bengal. Each figure is distinct yet bound to the others by waves of history and destiny, love and service, teaching and learning. Their togetherness in this shrine evinces shared hardship and happiness, not unlike seafarers on a voyage to a distant land. Perhaps because they walked the thorny path to inner illumination together, and were guru and disciple to one another. In the case of Sri Ramakrishna and Sarada, the young woman was groomed into the spiritual life by her mystic husband, who also made her responsible for the spiritual welfare of his students. For the fiery Swami Vivekananda, Sarada's teaching complemented Sri Ramakrishna's. One was veiled, the other apparent. Both were mothers of his quest, co-gurus, his awakeners and encouragers.

Looking at this triumvirate, my mind wanders to the power associated with the number three in human imagination. The Father, Son and Holy Ghost of Christianity, the Triple Gems—Buddha, Dharma, Sangha—of Buddhism, and the triad of Hindu thought—Brahma (who originates), Vishnu (who sustains), Shiva (who ends one cycle of creation so another might begin). Considering their impact on the subcontinent's dharma, one could possibly think of Sri Ramakrishna, Sri Sarada Devi and Swami Vivekananda as a new creative triad, representative of three approaches to a common ideal—attaining the heart of the mystery of life.

—

I am escorted to a bare room to meet Pravrajika Vivekaprana, a senior nun of the order who runs their retreat centre in Pangot in the Himalayas. She has agreed to help me explore feminine spirituality through the interconnected work of Sri Ramakrishna, Sarada Ma and Swami Vivekananda which led to, among other things, Hindu women receiving the right to ordain as sannyasins for the first time in the wisdom tradition's 5000-year-old history.

Any wisps of a parallel realm that might have clung to my consciousness from the shrine are quickly dispersed by the quick-witted, no-nonsense attitude of a mercurial mind that refuses to romanticize or idealize. Vivekaprana tells it like she sees it, and is impatient with my questions on gender because, as she immediately explains, it is immaterial to the spiritual quest.

'The real identity of a human being is not gender-based. It *cannot* be gender-based. It's up to women all over the earth to deepen their sense of identity beyond the gender. Beyond the mind and the body there has to be something, some reality, which in our psychology we call the atman, and if I am sure of that, nobody can debar me from anything.'

With words as spartan as the room she is in, Vivekaprana sounds a figurative gong on the gender debate which, like the gong in Zen meditation, centres the mind and refocuses it. At a time when gender is assumed to be a basic, definitive marker of identity, she directs one's attention right at the beginning to the core self that is beyond biology.

The 'no-gender' state of being that Vivekaprana articulates stems from the Vedantin belief that gender is no more than a footnote in the journey through lifetimes, a variable in karmic evolution, which does not touch or affect the core. Reality and truth, atman and Brahman, have no gender. God is not man. Or woman either. And nor are you either this or that. Why not realize it, instead of operating from gender-limited mindsets?

Interestingly, postmodern feminist discourse has reached a point where gender is considered not given by nature but a constructible propped up by language, which can be deconstructed using the same. If gender is not merely biological, if it is determined by culture and conditioning and is a 'system of meaning', then it can be changed and interpreted anew.

It is not being suggested that this brings postmodern feminism in alliance with Advaita Vedanta, far from it, but one can reflect on the possibilities inherent in the fluidity that both seem to suggest by discarding the concept of fixed identity; a chance is held out to re-imagine and remake. Both postmodern feminists and Vivekaprana are looking at gender as something that is not cast in concrete, the latter more so because she suggests doing away with it for good. Gender and its paraphernalia, its tyranny of culturally encoded expectations and definitions, are not any more real than the world populated by the hopes and revulsions we create around ourselves. Nor the ego-self we build out of culture, ethnicity, gender and layers of thoughts and emotions that we cling to and attempt to own. Where the postmodern feminist tries to empower through modifying this ego-self, Vedantin Vivekaprana asks of us a more radical transformation, by letting go of the ego-self entirely.

While the truest aspects of our selves might be gender-free, I tell Vivekaprana, we still need to navigate the world, and the inner path, as men and women. Before we can leave gender behind and live as unconditioned beings, much work is required of us. And it needs to be done in this body and its circumstances. Therefore it is valid to want to explore the nature of gender as it exists, the way it shapes our experience of life and spiritual practice, and whether it can be used as a tool to facilitate inner growth rather than a hindrance that needs to be eliminated or bypassed.

Perhaps we can begin with a basic question: Is gender a condition of the body, or is it a state of mind, or both? In other words, what does it mean to be a woman? Or a man?

Vivekaprana points me to Sri Ramakrishna, the mystic who transcended gender by embracing it completely, and who worshipped the divine feminine variously as an idol in the temple, as a living, breathing mother, *and* as an all-pervasive presence inherent in everything, like water in ice, thread in cloth, salt in the ocean.

Sri Ramakrishna's story is too well-known to bear more than a brief repetition to refresh it in our minds. What I am really interested in putting in the spotlight are his experiences and experiments with feminine energy that had the effect of effacing *and* expanding gender boundaries. His gender-bending experiences, I believe, are so singular and profound that no discussion on feminine spirituality can afford to disregard them. They brought a fresh perspective on gender, femininity and the spiritual, and provided the initial impetus for a movement that would in time lead to the establishment of Hindu women's first monastic order.

As a boy, Gadadhar, which was Ramakrishna's given name, appeared to brood for long periods, lost to the world. When in the mood, he would sing devotional songs with great feeling, which endeared him to the women of his village, Kamarpukur. His older brother Ramkumar, a priest, worried about Gadadhar's inability to make a Brahmanical living out of conducting pujas and rituals, summoned him to Kolkata to din some sense into the dreamy lad. When encouraged to turn his attention to his studies, the young Gadadhar reportedly said, 'Dada, what shall I do with a mere bread-winning education? I would rather acquire that wisdom which will illumine my heart and give me satisfaction forever.'

The opportunity to embark upon the path of illumination came soon enough, in the form of a temple built by a 'low-caste' woman, Rani Rasmani. She had made money through her acumen in business and commanded much respect in Kolkata for standing up to bullying by the British, but was unable to shake off the shadow of caste. Ramkumar was prevailed upon to take up the position of priest at the temple, and Gadadhar joined him as an assistant. After only a year, Ramkumar passed away and Gadadhar became head priest of the temple at Dakshineshwar that would soon become the stage for the unfurling of his spiritual quest.

A detailed account of Ramakrishna's spiritual adventures was recorded by his close disciple Mahendranath Gupta, and published as *The Gospel of Sri Ramakrishna*. It is because of this book that we have access to spiritual practices and experiences that are not usually discussed with anybody save one's guru.

The *Gospel* introduces us to the seeker Ramakrishna, who is completely devoted to his quest, eager to explore diverse disciplines in his single-minded search for truth, and does not shy away from the hard work that this requires of him. In his quest for the wisdom that would 'illumine his heart', no practice is too difficult or obscure, no path too insignificant to pursue with all his energy. Indeed, the *Gospel* is much more than the portrait of a master. It is a comprehensive catalogue of the stages of spiritual seeking, a portrait of the master as a seeker, an account of the moulting and shedding that transforms the latter into the former.

From the beginning, Ramakrishna's spiritual path was moulded by an almost instinctive attraction towards the feminine principle. His tenure as head priest at Dakshineshwar began with an intense devotion to the deity of the temple, the dark mother, Kali. It is said that the only way to connect with the fierce goddess is to relate with her as her child. Perhaps this quietens the devotee's own fears, and makes it easier for him or her to learn the truth of transience that Kali represents.

His deepening contemplation of Kali drew Ramakrishna away from the ritualized worship of her idol in the temple, and towards an instinctive, heartfelt sadhana. Kali does not conform to rules of purity that modulate the practice of the Vedic Brahmanical religion. In fact, she represents the antithesis of the dos and don'ts that cast barbed wires in the mind and might keep us away from a direct cognition of dharma in its sense of 'the way things actually are'. With her garland of skulls, her skirt of human limbs, her weapons and her wildness, Kali attempts to clear the mind of the cobwebs of conditioned perceptions that compartmentalize experiences and things as pure or impure, good or bad, beautiful or ugly, thereby awakening us to the undifferentiated oneness of reality.

As Ramakrishna began to look deeply into the truths symbolized by the dark mother, he felt compelled to let go of some of the perceptions of purity that were part of his Brahmanical belief system. Kali demands her worshipper be immune to the exclusionist effect of caste purity in his quest for the truth that is by definition advaita, 'not two'. Essentially, there is no 'other'. To cure himself of caste beliefs that were too stubborn to drop away on their own, Ramakrishna deliberately did whatever was the most contrary to the call of caste. He swept the homes of 'low-caste' families with his long hair, it is said, chose a deserted burial ground for his sadhana and, while engaged in it, took off the sacred thread that symbolized the Brahmin personality he was trying to erase.

He explained his conduct to his nephew, Hriday, saying, 'Don't you know that when one thinks of God one should be freed from all ties? From our very birth we have the eight fetters of hatred, shame, lineage, pride of good conduct, fear, secretiveness, caste, and grief. The sacred thread reminds me that I am a Brahmin and therefore superior to all. When calling on the Mother one has to set aside all such ideas.'

At this time, Ramakrishna yearned to meet his beloved Mother in person. He wanted to *see* her, be near her, and he called out to her as a child would its mother. Soon, this came to pass. In his words, as recorded in the *Gospel*, 'I was overpowered with a great restlessness and a fear that it might not be my lot to realize Her in this life... Suddenly my glance fell on the sword that was kept in the Mother's temple. I was determined to put an end to my life. When I jumped up like a madman and seized it, suddenly the blessed Mother revealed Herself. The buildings with their different parts, the temple and everything else vanished from my sight, leaving no trace whatsoever, and in their stead I saw a limitless, infinite, effulgent Ocean of Consciousness... I was caught in the rush and collapsed, unconscious. What was happening in the outside world I did not know; but within me there was a steady flow of undiluted bliss, altogether new, and I felt the presence of the Divine Mother.'

This experience cracked open Ramakrishna's consciousness, as it were, to the immanence of Devi. Life appeared as a dance infused with her presence—a tantalizingly complex creation she choreographed as well as performed. There was no need to meditate upon her form any longer. Her femininity, her divinity, her motherhood had leached out of a defined image and coloured everything Ramakrishna looked upon. His experience of reality had changed from a masculine space, or even a neutral one, to a space that was decidedly feminine.

Everything was awash with the dark mother and the experience of pure consciousness she had come to represent for Ramakrishna. 'The Divine Mother revealed to me in the Kali temple that it was She who had become everything. She showed me that everything was full of Consciousness. The image was Consciousness, the altar was Consciousness, the water vessels were Consciousness, the door-sill was Consciousness, the marble floor was Consciousness—all was Consciousness... I saw a wicked man in front of the Kali temple; but in him also I saw the power of the Divine Mother vibrating.' So keen was this sense of the Goddess's all-pervasive presence that one day, Ramakrishna fed prasad to a cat, later saying, 'I clearly perceived that all this was the Divine Mother—even the cat.'

Ramakrishna's mystical ecstasy and absorption were suspected to be symptomatic of mental instability by those around him who had no framework in which to place it. Though his employer, Rani Rasmani and, upon her passing, her son-in-law Mathur Mohan, recognized the quality of his realization and supported him, his family was concerned about the reports of his perceived insanity that reached their village from Dakshineshwar. It was decided that the priest, now twenty-three, needed to be grounded with the anchor of marriage and, as per the customs of the time, a little girl of five, Saradamani, was chosen to be his wife. Though the marriage was solemnized, it would be a while before the child bride attained puberty and came to live with her husband, and a new phase began in both their spiritual journeys.

This interim period signalled an intensifying and focusing of Ramakrishna's sadhana through the catalysing influence of two gurus—Bhairavi Brahmani, who guided him in Tantric and bhakti practices, and Totapuri, who turned him towards non-dual Advaita Vedanta. The former, a rare woman adept who wore the robes of a renunciate, arrived in Dakshineshwar at a time when Ramakrishna was assailed by allegations of madness. 'My son,' she said, 'everyone in this world is mad. Some are mad for money, some for creature comforts, some for name and fame; and you are mad for God.' She clarified his doubts regarding the physical symptoms of mystical absorption that he often experienced, like tremors, tears, perspiration and so on, by explaining them as signs of *mahabhava*, 'the great emotion', a term used in bhakti literature to describe the ecstasies of advanced devotees like Chaitanya Mahaprabhu.

In Bhairavi Brahmani, Ramakrishna found a kindred spirit who understood his intent for illumination and was prepared to be a guide. Her arrival probably came as a relief from the suspicions that had been flung at him recently, and he asked her to take him on as her disciple. In doing so, Ramakrishna found a bulwark to secure his practice. And by requesting a woman to be his guru, untainted by the hesitation of patriarchal gender norms, he opened up a new space for feminine tutelage of the spiritual quest.

Under Bhairavi Brahmani's guidance, Ramakrishna's intuitive, self-made sadhana widened to include scriptures and formalized practices. Intensive Tantric practice enabled an experience where 'the whole world, animate and inanimate, appeared to him as pervaded with Chit, Consciousness, and with Ananda, Bliss'.

Ramakrishna's apprenticeship with Bhairavi Brahmani deepened his comprehension of feminine ways of truth-seeking, particularly as his sadhana entered a bhakti phase. Bhakti is a path of transcendental love. The devotee assumes the stance of a lovelorn woman awaiting her divine lover, usually Krishna. Metaphors of love are used to describe the fire of separation the soul undergoes in the turmoil of the world, away from its true refuge (Krishna), and the suffering it must endure in order to unite with him once more. Divine love is cast in the garb of human love and the bhakta arouses in himself an intensity of emotion for the divine which, like a lover, calls out and supplicates, entices and cajoles, threatens and complains, walks away only to return.

Through all this, the bhakta maintains a single-pointed focus on the object of sadhana. Emotionality, which may be problematic for both women and men, is hence drawn out from its shell of negativity and converted into a powerful and credible path of spiritual seeking.

Psychologically, it is easier for us to love a person, even if imaginary, than an abstract ideal. Emotions for an impersonal Brahman are difficult to arouse; but they might flow of their own accord if that ideal is attired in the garb of an endearing, butter-stealing, flute-playing, charming rogue of a cowherd. Having a point of focus helps the mind channel its thoughts in one direction, out of its usual scatter. As it matures in contemplation and gets closer to the truth, the form that clothes the truth usually drops away. Most bhaktas, like Meera, ultimately come to a realization of the truth of oneness, that the lover and the beloved are not separate after all. That separation is a state of mind, as is union. Then their supplicating voices fade away, their restless feet halt. Union is no longer an imagined ideal. For the goal is already reached. The Beloved is within.

In this way, the path of bhakti might lead to a similar realization as the paths of jnana or karma, but it does so with a richness of emotion. The practice is not of dry detachment or sterile breath-watching, or of the determined slicing away of afflictive emotions. It is one of becoming drenched with love, of allowing the sweetness of the relationship to percolate one's being and transform it, of creating an intimate equation with the divine. It is a path that opens up the heart to the Beloved, and in the process to everything else too. For there comes a point when one begins to see *everything* as a manifestation of one's Beloved—dark-hued Shyam appears in the grey, rain-heavy monsoon clouds, in the soot of the lamp, in the kajal stains tears elicit upon the cheeks of a woman sick with love.

A male devotee's loss of gender by consciously adopting a feminine identity is central to the transformative effect of bhakti. In patriarchal cultures, maleness (like femaleness) comes with its own preconceived set of characteristics. Boys are encouraged towards macho ideals that glorify brute force and aggressive behaviour as the hallmark of 'real men'. If women's individualities are suppressed and reined in, the male ego is nurtured as being desirable and even indispensable in the delineation and assertion of 'manliness'. A male personality that is low on expressive emotionality, which is derided as being 'namby-pamby', effeminate and high on egoic self-perception, ends up becoming the desired norm. (In the interest of clarity, I am compelled to generalize.)

It has therefore been surmised that male seekers in patriarchal societies have a greater issue with laying aside the edifice of the ego personality, having invested much in building it up, nudged to do so by key influencers like parents and peers. By deliberately severing the connection between the ego-self and the maleness from which it draws much of its sustenance, the bhakta might find it easier to proceed towards the goal of self-lessness. Nothing can be demanded of the Beloved; the lover must efface his own self to diminish the separation between him and the Beloved. That is the only way he will get close to the goal that has drawn him on to the path. He is a moth to the flame; he must allow his self to burn away in the incandescence of his Beloved.

In human love relationships it is often observed that the male tendency is to crave emotional space and individuality, while the feminine leap of love tends towards union, merger, togetherness. Women like to conjoin and cohere, which may have to do with genetic hardwiring that goes with being the birth-givers and nurturers of the biological world. Perhaps this feminine quality that seeks union, with the Divine in the case of bhakti love, also makes the feminine the ideal gender with which to enter the waters of devotion and endure the inner turmoil until union is achieved.

Like every other practice he had attempted on the path, Ramakrishna became completely absorbed in this gender-subverting sadhana of loving the Beloved in the garb of a woman. Another way of viewing this mental 'sex change', to use a contemporary term, is to understand the gendering of God in devotional traditions. I will examine two examples here that might provide an insight into this.

Lalla, or Lal Ded, the fourteenth-century Kashmiri Sufi saint and yogini, adopted a sky-clad existence ever since she felt her body and mind had 'dropped off'. She says in one of her *vaakhs* (poems):

Coursing in emptiness,
I, Lalla,
Dropped off body and mind,
And stepped into the Secret Self.

(from *Women in Praise of the Sacred*)

Because she was no longer tied to her body or its conventions, Lalla felt as free as the mountain air, one with God and nature. Clothes, to her, seemed a metaphor for mindless conformism, the kind that keeps one in earthly bondage and away from one's true self, and were hence discarded. Not everybody saw it that way, though. In a society used to unclothed male sadhus, a woman's nakedness out of enlightened choice is an idea so fiercely audacious and rebelliously fearless, that it has the potential of overturning the gender status quo. Lalla lived in the blissful ecstasy of divine love. She didn't care about being viewed as a female body. It is said that whenever she was rebuked for being naked before men, her response would be, 'But who is a man here?' The allusion being, there is only one 'man'—God.

A similar instance occurs in the life of Meerabai, the fifteenth-century mystic poet whose verses are suffused with her transcendental love for Krishna. As a Rajput princess, the taboos that bound Meera's feet and kept them from dancing to her inner song were tighter, stricter. She danced anyway, the song of the dark lord echoing in her heart until it burst forth from her lips—a love so great and intense that it wouldn't be denied. Meera withstood venomous attacks, both verbal and actual in the form of snakes and poisoned chalices, and survived to laugh at the ways of the world and sing of her liberation with carefree abandon.

It is said that Meera once went to meet the Goswami of a Krishna temple. She was stopped at the entrance because the celibate Goswami refused to allow any woman in. 'He does not even look at the face of any woman,' she was told. Meera laughed and, in words reminiscent of Lalla, said something to the effect of, 'Oh, is the honourable Goswami male? But I thought we were all gopis of Krishna. Only He is purusha. All else is prakriti.'

Meera not only played upon the philosophical ideals of Supreme Consciousness (Purusha) that permeates the created world (prakriti), she also pointed out the femininity of the true bhakta, who loves the lord like a woman, with the unreserved dedication of Krishna's gopis. There is a pointed questioning of who is in control, which the male automatically assumes to be his prerogative in patriarchy. Lal Ded and Meera use 'man' as a metaphor for the One who has the real power, thereby divesting human men of their petty notions of dominance. We don't answer to you, they seem to say, we defer only to Him. In any case, human beings only harbour an illusion of being in control of their own lives, and it is actually a larger pattern, a web of 'universal' consciousness, which they identify as 'Krishna' or 'God', that holds our lives in balance, that represents the ultimate reality we must all seek and revere.

As Ramakrishna became immersed in feminine bhakti love, he seemed to shift away from a hard-edged maleness towards a soft-contoured femininity. His manner became feminine and motherly. It is recorded in the *Gospel*, '... he began to regard himself as a woman. His speech and gestures changed. He began to move freely with the ladies of Mathur's (his employer's) family, who now looked upon him as one of their own sex. During this time he worshipped the Divine Mother as Her companion or handmaid.'

Even though he would eventually move towards a nondualistic perception of reality, to me it seems that Ramakrishna was deeply affected by femininity as a form of divinity, an object of worship *and* a determinant of the nature of the spiritual path, during this phase of his sadhana with Bhairavi Brahmani. This is evident in the way he would mother his students' spiritual lives as well as the unique partnership he forged with his wife, Sarada. His was a 'gender-fullness', to use Sadhvi Bhagwati's term, that was an enrichment, a completion, a full moon of femaleness *and* maleness.

Sri Ramakrishna's experiences and experiments with femininity on the spiritual path opened up radical new spaces for women and handed innovative techniques to both women and men with which to explore the truth of self and identity. The real import of these insights would be felt in the years and centuries to come.

—

According to Vivekaprana, the feminine stimulus provided by Ramakrishna's sadhana set in motion a sequence of interrelated circumstances, endeavours and ideas. 'You must remember,' she says, 'that in India in the nineteenth century, with the birth of Sri Ramakrishna, his worship of his own wife and accepting a woman guru, and then Swami Vivekananda's explanations about what real identity is, this power is functioning. Some of us are very aware of it, some of us are not… the mother principle, goddess principle, feminine principle, you can call it by any name, it is a kind of swell in the ocean.'

At the outset, this upsurge of feminine 'power' found expression through Sri Ramakrishna's solo sadhana and his Tantric and bhakti experiences under Bhairavi Brahmani's tutelage. These proved to be stepping stones towards a refinement of understanding through the exacting discipline of Advaita Vedanta, which brooked no duality and cast the mind through a fine sieve to divest it of notions of separation of self and other, self and divinity, self and everything else.

Despite his experience of undiluted oneness, Truth didn't lose its femininity for Ramakrishna. In what could be one of the most radical, and feministic, interpretations of the Advaita perspective ever, he said, 'When I think of the Supreme Being as inactive—neither creating nor preserving nor destroying—I call Him Brahman or Purusha, the Impersonal God. When I think of Him as active—creating, preserving, and destroying—I call Him Sakti or Maya or Prakriti, the Personal God. But the distinction between them does not mean a difference. The Personal and the Impersonal are the same thing, like milk and its whiteness, the diamond and its lustre, the snake and its wriggling motion. It is impossible to conceive of the one without the other. The Divine Mother and Brahman are one.' Perhaps the path of the Personal God is also where one forms an intimate relationship with divinity, where one needn't cast away one's emotionality but can cultivate it as a means to a deeper connection with Supreme Consciousness, and with everything else.

The Advaita perspective was, in Ramakrishna's view, a challenge of cohesion and commingling. Oneness need not necessarily be a cutting away, a negation, a withdrawal. It could be a plurality, an innumerability, a co-being, within a continuum of consciousness that provided the essence, the basic thread, the one membrane that held everything together, that contained it. It was this root essentiality, according to Ramakrishna, that was male in its silent form and feminine in its dynamic one, that was Brahman in its universal form and atman in its individual one. The trick was to recognize the simultaneity of both, that Truth lay in the realization of this *and* that, atman *and* Brahman, male *and* female. To endeavour to know only one was to blindfold oneself willingly, and opt for a half-measure instead of the Whole Truth.

This twinned interplay of energies soon became an actual, living, organic principle for Ramakrishna when his wife, the young Sarada, turned up at his doorstep to begin their married life together. For a seeker so completely immersed in sadhana as he was, this could have seemed a calamity equivalent to being delivered to the entrance of hell (misogynistic spiritual teachings labelled women as *narakasya dwaram*, hell's door). What actually occurred was an unprecedented, mutually enabling spiritual partnership that provided yet another opportunity, a groundswell, really, for the feminine principle to play itself out as an enriching, empowering influence.

Also, the implication of this alliance, what it *showed* to the world, was a spiritually workable togetherness, an inclusiveness and harmony of genders which was in keeping with Ramakrishna's understanding of the truth of oneness. In this, a new model for spiritual seekers was hewn out of the rock of their relationship, one that underscored the possibility for men and women to live together and seek together. The predominant model, which necessitated withdrawal from the world and relationships, and cut women out of the path most of the time, needn't be the only option any longer. There was no real need to go anywhere, or qualify relationships negatively as the bondage of maya, or wait to find ideal conditions like silence and aloneness. The practice could be done in the here and now, in the midst of the flow of life, by lighting the lamp of unwavering practice in one's heart.

Like the marital alliance of Anandamayi Ma and Bholanath, who succeeded them chronologically, Ramakrishna and Sarada's marriage was unconventional and oriented towards facilitating one another's sadhana. It is said that when the seventeen-year-old Sarada arrived at Dakshineshwar, her husband greeted her with a playful question. 'Have you come to drag me down into maya?' he asked, perhaps a smile lurking beneath his grim exterior. It was a trick question, for he had already resolved his doubts about married life in a discussion with his Advaitin guru, Totapuri.

'What does it matter?' Totapuri had said. 'He alone is firmly established in the knowledge of Brahman who can adhere to his spirit of discrimination and renunciation even while living with his wife. He alone has attained the supreme illumination who can look on man and woman alike as Brahman. A man with the idea of sex may be a good aspirant, but he is still far from the goal.'

This advice would form the bedrock of their married life—single-pointed concentration on sadhana (their own and each other's), along with an intimacy that came from shared values and goals, and a companionable celibacy that did not preclude emotional vibrancy. Indeed, Ramakrishna must have recognized his spiritual collaborator the moment she responded to his introductory question with, 'Why should I do that? I have come only to help you on the path of dharma.'

Much before she came to live with him, Ramakrishna had begun grooming his child bride during visits back home. It is said that he taught her everything, from the best way to trim a lamp to how to take care of guests, to methods of stilling the mind and focusing it inwards. Much later, Sarada would say that he *recognized* her, almost in the sense of re-cognizing, that he had somehow sussed her inner self out of its ordinariness and helped her became aware of its true luminosity. She would narrate a parable in explanation. A diamond lay embedded in the steps leading to the river. People would wipe their feet on the diamond, thinking it was an ordinary stone. One day, a jeweller came to the river. He was about to wipe his feet on the diamond too, but he recognized its worth and prised it out of the steps. The diamond was Sarada; the jeweller, Ramakrishna.

It is said that we all have the enlightened nature, the pure atman indwelling in our being at all times—the point of spiritual practice is not to create it but to uncover it and bring it into conscious being. In the same way, each woman and man who comprehends in their self their innate dynamic creativity, deep compassion and the capacity to nurture wellbeing, will have accessed their alignment with the Divine Feminine, or Devi, or Brahman, or Buddhanature, or God, or whatever we may wish to call our deepest fundamental reality. The essence is present, but it has to be roused and set in motion. This is what I believe happened with Sarada, under the watchful guidance of Ramakrishna.

As I have pointed out in earlier chapters, there is a general tendency to view enlightened men and women as avatars, pre-perfected divine creatures, whose suffering and seeking are geared towards teaching and presenting examples to followers. From this perspective, Sarada was an avatar of the Divine Feminine, a vessel for Devi to conduct another round of her leela in the world. But what if we were to imagine that Sarada was born human but *made* divine? Whose divinity was uncovered through the efforts and choices made by her and her guru-husband? Who was not *given* goddesshood but rather discovered it in her self, through her sadhana? I will try and explore this through an incident that occurred a year into their life together, and which stands as a singular testimony to Ramakrishna's mystical connection with sacred femininity.

Sarada had quickly become engaged in household work, a lot of which involved taking care of the tide of visitors that swelled with each passing day, as Ramakrishna's reputation as an authentic mystic and teacher grew. Her spiritual education continued alongside. Though they shared a room for some time, Ramakrishna's disposition, his disengagement with physicality and his periodic mystical ecstasies ensured that their space together remained non-sexual. As an adolescent who suddenly had to face much change, it would have been understandable if she had been liable to a restless moodiness. Contrarily, Sarada revealed a dexterity at self-transformation and adaptability, and a creative compassion that allowed her to manage the rapid emotional, mental and spiritual growth demanded of her quite well. So that on that fateful night, she was not exactly a wide-eyed, unprepared girl, but one who had embarked on the adventure of spiritual seeking and was able to grasp the meaning of the life-changing experience when it took place.

It was the night of the ritual worship of one of the forms of Kali—Phalaharini, the one who destroys the fruits of actions and cancels out karmic debts. There would be a grand puja in the temple, but Ramakrishna prepared for another, secret puja in his room. Even those who helped him prepare the altar had no idea what this second puja was for. Ramakrishna asked Sarada to finish her work by nine at night and meet him in his room. Which the young woman did, and discovered to her amazement that he intended her to be the living goddess in his altar.

Ramakrishna seated her upon the seat of the deity in place of an idol or image, and worshipped her in the form of Shodashi, Devi as a sixteen-year-old, also known as Tripura Sundari, mother of three worlds, the beneficent enchantress who is the object of her spouse Shiva's meditation. If Kali denotes the dissolution of attributes in nirvana, Shodashi embodies a comprehensiveness of virtues and qualities, an abundant completion. In this sense, she is the iridescent full moon to Kali's unbroken dark night.

Nobody knows what exactly transpired during the puja, since neither Ramakrishna nor Sarada ever spoke in detail about this unusual event. But we can surmise that the puja proceeded as per the rites of Srikula, the 'family' of Devi emanations in Tantra that includes Tripura Sundari. Tantric rituals, in their purest form, work with energy which is considered the fundamental building block of the universe. Energy is aroused, concentrated and directed towards a specific goal, which can range from revving up individual sadhana to purifying comprehension, acquiring insight, or even wish fulfilment. What was Ramakrishna's objective in this extraordinary puja? Was it to venerate Sarada, intensify his own practice, or was there something more to it?

Pravrajika Vedantaprana, in her essay 'Sarada Shodashi', points us to a deeper meaning not apparent on the surface. 'During the Shodashi Puja, Sri Ramakrishna consecrated Sri Sarada Devi's body by placing mantras on various parts of it, making it *mantramayi*, encasing the Goddess in human form. Was it because he wanted to manifest the special characteristics of Tripura Sundari in the Mother of this age?' Vedantaprana implies both an inherent divinity, 'Goddess in human form', and an effort to awaken latent Goddess energy, to evoke it out of its dormancy so that it might become an active force in Sarada's being.

I think Sarada's Shodashi Puja was Ramakrishna's leap of faith, which was borne out by Sarada's own inner transformation. Once Ramakrishna had invoked the Goddess energy in her, she felt inspired to try and become a worthy recipient of it. She grew into her role through rigorous sadhana, and by consciously cultivating the qualities of the Devi within herself. Devotees might differ with me on this point and say that these qualities were either given to her during the puja, or that she had them already. I would like to contend that it is equally plausible that these qualities were nurtured through resolute self-effort and practice, even if they were present in seed form in her prior to the event, as they perhaps are in all of us.

One of the ways Tantra brings about deep-rooted psychological change is through an inner alchemy wrought by imagination. Energy flows where we direct it, and the most potent way of doing so is through thought. When the mind is focused along a particular path, energy will follow and fill out the vision that we have created for it, thus manifesting at one level what has already been dreamt of at another. Quite literally, we can imagine our world, and our self, into being. Tantra harnesses this through the practice of contemplative visualization, where one imagines a deity and builds his or her image step by step in one's mind. This visual is then animated with qualities of the deity, like compassion and wisdom and so on, using invocatory mantras that usually consist of a string of adjectives that describe these qualities over and over and arouse them in the mind. When the vision is firmly established, the practitioner imagines the deity entering and merging in her being. The worshipper and the worshipped become one, and the perfected qualities of the latter are hoped to have become infused in the former.

One can assume that when Ramakrishna worshipped Sarada as an emanation of Devi, he *imagined* her goddesshood into existence. Whatever her abilities had been until now, from then on Sarada worked to embody the qualities of the Goddess and thereby made real the vision that Ramakrishna had instilled in her. Vedantaprana explains the embodiment triggered in Sarada after the Shodashi Puja by comparing her manifest qualities with adjectival descriptions of the Devi that were possibly chanted upon her that night. For instance, a mantra says that Devi is 'the Mother who gives birth to all beings, from Brahma to a worm'. Sarada, when asked directly, 'Are you the mother of all?', would respond with a simple 'yes'. 'Even of these birds and animals?' To which she said, 'Yes, of them too.' There are, of course, many other instances where her profound motherhood was in evidence, and this, if any, could be considered her greatest goddess quality.

Further, Vedantaprana says, 'Lalita (another form of Tripura Sundari) is *vairagini adbhuta charitra*, an extraordinary person full of the spirit of renunciation. All these qualities are found in full measure in Sarada Devi.' Indeed, it has been said that Sarada developed a quality of renunciation that was deep-rooted and creative. She showed a Devi-like facility in ably handling every form of maya, such as material wealth. Ramakrishna had to test the completeness of his renunciation by actually throwing coins into the river, and he would experience discomfort in the proximity of money and would want it removed from his presence. Whereas Sarada could handle money as and when there was a need for her to do so without her equanimity being affected at all by the transaction.

The Shodashi Puja culminated with Ramakrishna absorbed in mystical ecstasy, as was the living deity at his altar, Sarada. They were united; only, it wasn't the union of sexual intercourse or erotic emotionality. Their individualities had dissolved in co-samadhi, and their separate psyches now throbbed as part of the same field of consciousness. Two pots had crumbled, dropped their baked-mud-beings in the river. Where did one end and the other begin?

Sarada Devi's life, both the time she spent with the master and the period after his passing, is an exceptional example of what I have been exploring in this book as 'women's way', the uniqueness of women's approach to and practice of spirituality. Sarada's sadhana was an underground stream that bubbled below the surface of the business of a woman's day, finding the odd crack to gush forth momentarily and then retreating until the next moment of silence, the next respite from routine. The fabric of her day was woven with the thread of continuous awareness and remembrance, which looped around all the other activities and work that required her attention.

In this context, Pravrajika Ajayprana, in her essay 'Luminous Tracks in Space', quotes Sarada as saying to a disciple, Swami Madhavananda, 'My boy, we are women. We can't get away from household duties. When I make rice, I first pour enough water in the pot to cover the rice and keep watch over it. Now and then when I get a little time I do some japa. Then I place a pot of water on the stove to cook dal. Till the water gets hot enough for cooking I am free, and so do a little more japa. Once the dal is cooked I again sit down quietly and repeat the mantra. In this way, somehow, I manage my daily japa. What else can I do, my child?'

Like so many women before and after her, compelled to practise within the enclosed parameters of home and family, Sarada invented a rhythm for her sadhana that was attuned to the pulse of her everyday life. It is said that in a traditional home, a woman's work is never finished. She is the pivot that keeps the wheel of family life turning. When there isn't cooking there is washing, and when the home is clean the children aren't, and when the adults have been fed, the animals are next. During sowing and harvest in agrarian communities, women's hands join the men's. They are the first to rise and the last to put their weary heads down. Where is the time for sadhana, for the cultivation of single-pointed concentration on anything? And yet women like Sarada have taken the raw material of a woman's day and with the warp and weft of patience and dedication, spun a sadhana so fine that it fits in the interstices between successive motions of the hand, between two breaths, in the tiniest of punctuations between one act and the next.

In this, I am reminded of another great teacher who embodied this feminine characteristic of bringing spiritual practice within life's embrace, as opposed to going out of one's life to practise.

Dipa Ma is now considered a remarkable twentieth-century teacher of the Burmese *vipassana* (insight meditation) tradition. As a middle-aged woman, Dipa Ma hauled herself up by the bootstraps with a dedicated practice of vipassana from the torpor she had sunk into after the death of her husband and her own descent into ill-health. Realizing she couldn't leave her young daughter and her home and take off for long retreats as prescribed by the tradition, she carefully rationed free moments in her day to strengthen her practice of unbroken mindfulness. Sometimes her sister would come and live with her, and with six children in the house, the two women would somehow manage to patch together a schedule of meditation with whatever bits and pieces of silence that became available through the day.

When she began teaching, Dipa Ma would readily personalize the practice for women with demanding work and family lives. Because of her own experience, she understood the topography of a woman's life and the possibilities and impossibilities it held, and only demanded that her students be committed and consistent. Meditation was possible any time, she taught, by focusing the mind and becoming completely aware of whatever it was one was doing. 'Human beings will never solve all their problems,' she would say. 'The only way is to bring mindfulness to whatever you are suffering.'

In an article about Dipa Ma's life, Amy Schmidt and Sara Jenkins exemplify Dipa Ma's teachings through her students' stories. Sudipti was struggling to manage a business while caring for a mentally ill son and an invalid mother. During their first meeting, Dipa Ma asked Sudipti if she could meditate for five minutes right then. 'So I sat with her for five minutes,' Sudipti is quoted. 'Then she gave me instructions in meditation anyway, even though I said I had no time. Somehow I found five minutes a day, and I followed her instructions... I was able to find longer and longer times to meditate, and soon I was meditating many hours a day, into the night, sometimes all night, after my work was done. I found energy and time I didn't know I had.' Another student, a new mother, was asked to nurture awareness by bringing her attention to the sensation of her infant suckling at her breast.

Because of the everydayness of her teachings, Dipa Ma became the 'patron saint of householders', one who was more concerned with 'being the practice rather than doing the practice'. The aforementioned article quotes another insight meditation teacher, Michele McDonald-Smith, as saying why she, as a woman who needed to manage home and family, found Dipa Ma so moving. 'At the time I met her,' she says, 'there were mostly male role models—male teachers, male Buddhas. To meet a woman householder who lived with her daughter and grandson—and who was that enlightened—it was more profound than I can put into words. She embodied what I deeply wanted to be like. For me as a woman householder, I immediately felt, "If she can do this, I can do this too."'

This issue of practicability, of doability, of widening one's own sense of ability, is crucial to a woman going forth on the spiritual path. For, as McDonald-Smith points out, all or most of the role models of spiritual adventuring and accomplishment are male. Scriptures and their commentaries in most wisdom traditions have been written by successive generations of men. Lineages of spiritual wisdom have passed on from one man to another. If women don't see or come to know of other women who have 'done it', they might just begin to believe that it isn't for them, that it is something only men do. And teachers like Sarada Ma and Dipa Ma are exceptional role models for women because they lived in their worlds and practised amidst the chaos and untidiness that tend to surround women in patriarchal gender roles. They didn't need the solitude of a cave to make it work. Women need to know both these aspects—that it can be done, and done in the skin of their worldly selves.

A role model not only inspires, she also helps us re-imagine ourselves in the light of her achievements; what she made possible, perhaps we can too. A dream so audacious that we never dared dream it suddenly comes within grasping, happening distance in the presence of a role model. She did, therefore I can too.

I suggest this idea to Pravrajika Vivekaprana. Surely, Sarada Ma is an ideal role model for this age? A woman who multitasked, who practised and taught without taking off anyplace? 'Well, I don't know whether they'll accept her any longer,' Vivekaprana says, somewhat acerbically. I assume 'they' refers to us, the women of today. 'They can't accept Sita, Savitri, Damayanti—you think they are going to accept her! What she has come to show is that this feminine energy is alive. It is functioning. I don't have to imitate her, I have to understand that she is a representative of something very deep in this universe which has come up as a feminine face. This feminine face of energy is supposed to give me the courage to accept the challenges.

'It isn't as if I am going to imitate her and become the Holy Mother. That's not so. That's also very wrong, which perhaps Indian girls need to understand. I can take her as my base, as the representative of feminine energy which is so sure of herself. But she has taken on a role that is absolutely traditional. Who cares for that any longer? Nobody cares. One cannot imitate without understanding. So this new challenge that has come to women in this age is not a challenge to go back to the old ruts and become a *pativrata* or a sati, an obedient wife and a suffering wife. It's not as if there won't be suffering. There will perhaps be more suffering in accepting these challenges. But one has to think of new ways, original ways of functioning.'

Vivekaprana has enumerated several problems that could potentially grow around the figure of Sarada Devi today. One, there is the pitfall inherent in the very idea of adopting a role model. The temptation to imitate, to do exactly what the role model has done. This, of course, does not work because one must live in one's own reality and find the truth for oneself. The role model can only be an inspiration, a guide, a motivational force. One cannot substitute the hard work one must do, the insights one must come upon on one's own, by assuming the persona of the role model. The essence of each search must be fresh if it is to be real, current to the seeker's own time, place and context.

Second, Vivekaprana questions contemporary women's ability to understand the power behind the veil, so to speak. This is a complex issue that wraps within it the tension between modernity and tradition, the changing sensibility of women and the impact feminism has had on the way women in traditional roles are regarded in the twenty-first century.

India today is caught in a whirlwind of change. As old edifices of society, philosophy, ways of life come crashing down, ensuing clouds of dust sometimes obscure the fact that modernity is not brought about by mere demolition of all that is old, and mindless devotion to all that is new. Many of us in India today might be giving away too much of our cultural autonomy in pursuit of what are essentially Western notions of modernity and which may come coupled with a lifestyle that prioritizes consumerism and materialism and, in the case of the ascendancy of mainstream American culture, a cultural sameness that wishes to foster, and foist, a monoculture of the mind.

The challenge is not only to be modern in a way that includes a reinterpretation of ancient wisdom for our times, it also asks us to dig deep enough and be *truly* modern. Too often, modernity is equated with superficial and cosmetic changes—our clothes or the accent in which we speak might change, but deep down, we continue to cling to notions, 'ruts', as Vivekaprana calls them, that may be regressive and unenlightened and remnants of the social order of the middle ages. I think the challenge today is not just to find an Indian or Asian way of being modern but, for women especially, to access a modernity that is an amalgam of the freedom and fearlessness that are the fruits of empowering philosophies and humanistic movements for justice and equality of the last couple of hundred years, and the ability to be compassionate and kind that might be cultivated using the tools available in ancient wisdom traditions.

'To be modern means to understand what is happening right now,' says Vivekaprana. 'How much do I know? You can say Sri Ramakrishna is modern. He is ever modern because he is in touch with the base of reality. *He* is modern. We are not.

We are dreaming. We replace one dream with another dream. One space–time image with another. We are not modern. Being modern means being in control and in touch with what reality is.'

We can extend the same logic to Sarada Devi, that she was modern in the truest sense by being ever mindful of the present moment, by being 'in touch', and by aligning her self not with the drama of egoic emotionality but with the deepest core of reality. Yet, from the prism of Western feminism, which has to a large extent monopolized the discourse on gender and modernity, Sarada Devi would appear to be the antithesis of a modern woman. She would either be regarded as a prisoner of 'tradition, unenlightened and untutored in the ways of the modern', in the words of post-colonial writer Gayatri Spivak, or as possessing a sort of untouched, 'pristine purity', in the mould of the 'Bon Savage' (the noble savage, a patronizing idealization of non-Western cultures as 'pure' and 'innocent' of the influence of modernity). Both these representations miss the actual substance of the woman. They don't even begin to understand the complex gender narrative that a close analysis of Sarada Devi's life could yield, one that is enriched by silent subversion of gender norms and roles and their ultimate transcendence.

Because she spent almost her entire life behind the veil, cloistered in a traditional woman's role, Sarada Ma's role as a revolutionary innovator of the spiritual quest often goes unacknowledged outside her sangha of devotees. Indeed, the veil makes for an apt metaphor for her spiritual life. At all times, her sadhana and attainments on the path occurred behind the veil of ordinariness. Of all those who gathered around Sri Ramakrishna and learnt from him, his wife was the least visible. She was the imperceptible presence behind the bamboo curtain during Ramakrishna's spiritual assemblies, her dance of ecstasy confined to the thrumming of her heart, the vein of bliss beating in her being. As an aspirant, Sarada was the *anhada nada* in Ramakrishna's spiritual song, the unstruck note. It is this subtlety of presence, this hiddenness of endeavour and ability, that prompted Ramakrishna to liken her to an 'ash covered cat' that hides its actual appearance by rolling about in ash.

Another aspect of the veil in Sarada's life is said to have been her motherhood, which cloaked the true extent of her spiritual realization as well as her guruhood. One might be overawed by a guru's persona and hesitate in going up to him or her. As mother, anybody could approach Sarada Ma and share their problems with her, and she would find ways of alleviating their suffering, adding homeopathic doses of spiritual advice to homely wisdom so that it could be easily assimilated and practised by the seeker. She would never discriminate between people who came to her and asked for teachings. Her reasoning was, she was everybody's mother. And when they came to her as her children, whatever their flaws might be otherwise, they had the right to her love and care.

Swami Saradeshananda, a disciple of Sarada Ma who had the opportunity to observe her over a long period of time, says in his biography of her, 'In the endless process of the members of the human species in this planet of ours, the Holy Mother stands out as a unique example... whose love never made any distinction between the deserving and the undeserving, in whose eyes the saint and the sinner were alike her precious children, whose wide heart held all humanity in its maternal embrace and who considered it a privilege to labour and to suffer for even the least of them.'

At one level, Sarada Ma's profound and all-encompassing motherhood was the most obvious and visible part of her, and thereby veiled her role as an enlightened guru and guide. At another level, we can perceive her motherhood as being a skilful means, a tool that helped her reach out to as many people as she could, and teach and nurture their spiritual lives with greater facility.

Though the veil that covered her face never parted, and Sarada lived and taught and mothered from behind it throughout her life, Sri Ramakrishna's passing ended her solitude in many ways. During his last illness, he sent for Sarada urgently one day, while she was cooking for him. When she came, he said, 'I will not be here very long on earth. You will have to carry my burden. You will have to encourage people to lead spiritual lives. You must bless them and guide them.' Sarada was surprised, for though she was already mother to his disciples, she had never really stepped into their world. And now her beloved 'Thakur' was asking her to teach them, inspire them, carry on *his* work. 'What! Am I to do this?' she exclaimed. 'Am I to guide people? Am I to continue your work?' To which he firmly responded, 'Yes, that is what you have to do.'*

Ramakrishna's belief in her once again encouraged her to expand her horizon of capability and despite the numerous literal and metaphorical veils that surrounded her, she confidently embraced the role he had imagined for her and made it her own. For thirty-four years, she tirelessly worked as a mother-guru, a guide whose luminous love kept the fledgling sangha together and prevented it from disintegrating in the aftermath of Ramakrishna's passing.

The arcs of possibility that he had drawn, she attempted to bring full circle. She would give individual advice to his disciples and her own, and keep their spiritual lives on track. She would sort out discord, and encourage adherence to Ramakrishna's ideals. Gradually, the movement gravitated towards her and she was placed at its centre, a living conduit of the wisdom embodied by Ramakrishna. Indeed, in moments of spiritual ecstasy, she seemed to *become* him, and would often say, 'Are Thakur and I separate?'

She would give advice on matters related to administering the sangha when it was asked for, and encouraged Ramakrishna's

---

* Exchange quoted by Pravrajika Atmaprana of the Sri Ramakrishna Sarada Mission, New Delhi, in a souvenir to commemorate Sri Sarada Devi's 150th birth anniversary in 2004.

foremost disciple, Swami Vivekananda, in his global journey and his vision of 'spirituality in service' for the newly established brotherhood of monks, the Sri Ramakrishna Mission, which she had consecrated. Incidentally, this might be the only time in the history of Hindu wisdom traditions that a woman, and a non-renunciate at that, laid the foundation of a congregation of monks. In all this, she remained as the still point at the centre of the wheel, her presence crucial to its motion, her equipoise hardly affected by it all.

Sarada Devi defies the stereotypes both of a traditional woman and of a modern woman, thereby encouraging us to think these terms and definitions afresh. She transcended many boundaries and limitations—of social norms, of gender and, most importantly, the ones created by the mind, the voice that whispers 'you cannot do this' and keeps us from realizing the full extent of our potential. Whenever she came to a barrier, in her mind or around her, she found a way to overcome it, or flow around it. In this sense, Sarada is a feminist icon in her own right and of her own making. She, says academic Mitu Hirshman in her essay 'Negotiating the "Modern": Sri Sarada Devi and Feminism', 'displaces many of the dualities feminist thinking rests on: tradition/modernity, East/West, public/private and so on, and more importantly, the debate surrounding the notion of motherhood as a state of 'being' and mothering as a role defined by the sex/gender system of liberal feminism.'

As the mother of an Advaitin sangha, I suppose it is fitting that Sarada Ma adroitly reconciled seeming opposites and illustrated the truth of nonduality in the way she lived and taught. Another barrier she broke out of was that of race relations, where she could have been the 'native woman', the 'white woman's burden'. This term is with reference to the so-called civilizing mission, condescendingly termed 'the white man's burden', that colonial powers used to justify their exploitative occupation of parts of Asia and Africa. The 'white women' who responded to Swami Vivekananda's call and arrived in India to lead a life of service and contemplation considered Sarada Ma their mother and guru. Margaret Elizabeth Noble, better known by her Indian name, Nivedita, forged a deep bond with Sarada Ma and called her 'Matadevi', Mother Goddess. Within two months of their first meeting, Nivedita described her as 'one of the strongest and greatest of women'.

In her initial work in India with women and education, as Nivedita struggled to find a toehold in the face of orthodoxy and resistance to change, she drew sustenance from Sarada Ma's presence. She lived with Sarada Ma for some time in Kolkata, but realizing the inconvenience her presence caused other members of what was an orthodox Brahmin household, she shifted to a lodging not too far away. Sarada herself was ever welcoming of her 'Khooki', the name with which she affectionately addressed Nivedita and which means 'little girl' in Bengali, and in the manner of Ramakrishna, never allowed caste, religion or social taboos to restrict her in any way.

In many ways, some of the most poignant descriptions of Sarada Ma come from Nivedita's pen. Through her eyes, we see Sarada as a gentle presence that holds within her immeasurable love, wisdom matured in practice, incisive mental acuity and a graceful dignity that deals with all matters evenly, gently, whose 'stateliness of courtesy and her great open mind are almost as wonderful as her sainthood'. Nivedita refers to her as 'Sri Ramakrishna's final word as to the ideal of Indian womanhood'. Yet she wonders, 'Is she the last of an old order, or the beginning of a new?'

This insightful question relates to continuation and impact, seeds sown by Sarada Ma in the hearts of those whose spiritual lives she mothered, and successive generations that heard of her and read of her and saw her in pictures. According to Vivekaprana, Sarada was an ideal, the human face of divine energy, perhaps too unique to be replicated, and who should not, in fact, be replicated.

I think Sarada Ma encourages us to turn within, to find the notes of our own individual song, to be free and one with life. She cannot be the last, and she is not the first. She, as I see her, is a flower in the precious garland of spiritual seeking, a crucial link in the chain that connects women of all ages and areas and religio-socio-cultural propensities who found their inner song, new ways of knowing, and were never the same again.

—

Until the twentieth century and the birth of Sri Sarada Math, there had never been a formal order of women renunciates within the ambit of Hindu wisdom traditions. The Buddhist and Jain women's sanghas were founded almost at the same time as the men's, though not without friction and reluctance. And individual women who were so inspired had been walking out of their homes for centuries, learning with a guru or walking to their own tune, living a life of renunciation and contemplation. The earliest examples of such free spirits are the *brahmavadinis* mentioned in the Rig Veda—women seers who helped construct this ancient compendium of sacred hymns with mantras that bespeak their spiritual insights.

Though women continued to infiltrate the ranks of sannyasis at every point in the history of the subcontinent's spirituality, a social consensus was built up over the ages that, generally, sannyasa was not for women. The reasons were many—an overall inclination towards misogyny in society and religion, an intensification of patriarchy's repressive gender norms and roles, the idea of 'ownership' of women by their male relatives and their becoming emblematic of familial 'honour', the issue of physical safety, and so on. As we know, some women managed to duck the confines these measures imposed upon them and took to the path. And we can also assume that a far greater number that might have done so in a more encouraging environment, didn't.

This was about to change with the advent of the spiritual 'son' of Ramakrishna and Sarada—Swami Vivekananda. Vivekananda reinvigorated the dharma with an infusion of fresh ideas and perspectives. He pioneered for the Hindu dharma a way of looking at itself and the world that was rooted in ancient wisdom and was at the same time free from the jaundice of superstition and meaningless adherence to norms for their own sake. He presented to the dharma the challenge of modernity, and guided this negotiation towards freedom from mindless observance of tradition, a resurgence of the highest values of the Indic civilization such as nonduality, renunciation and compassion, and a new emphasis on a seva-based spirituality. This last bit of innovation resulted in the formation of the Sri Ramakrishna Mission in 1897, with the motto 'individual liberation and service to mankind'.

Vivekananda was deeply affected by Sarada Ma, recognized the kind of radical, empowering transformation that spiritual training could bring about, and the sad fact that it was inaccessible to most women. This became one of the ways he imagined 're-forming' the dharma, by making available to women the same opportunities and knowledge available to men, giving the former the same chance to discover their true selves that the latter had tried to retain solo control over for centuries.

'Without Shakti there is no regeneration for the world...' he said. 'Mother has been born to revive that wonderful Shakti in India; and making her the nucleus, once more will Gargis and Maitreyis be born into the world.' Gargi and Maitreyi were ancient brahmavadinis, seers who are mentioned in the Upanishads. Vivekananda intended for the women's monastic order to come into existence even before the monks', but due to repressive social circumstances and a lack of confidence among women themselves, his dream remained unfulfilled during his lifetime.

By extending the Advaitin oneness to hitherto marginalized sections of Indian society—women, untouchables, lower castes, and others—Vivekananda not only opened up new avenues for them to walk the spiritual path, he also revitalized the reservoirs of ancient wisdom that had begun to stagnate in the absence of rigorous application. 'It was Swami Vivekananda who had a very deep insight into the human problem, not only women's problem, but the human problem in today's age,' says Vivekaprana. 'Which is basically to do with the purpose of life, what is happening to society, and what is the way to connect daily life with some kind of meaningful activity and a purpose that would give the human individual, both man and woman, some kind of path to evolve from mere gender-based identity to some deeper identity.'

Vivekananda's vision for the women's sangha was unequivocal in its call for complete equality and much ahead of his time at the end of the nineteenth century, when the First Wave of feminism was just about beginning in the West and women were yet to get the right to vote. Vivekananda was emphatic that whenever it was founded, the women's Math would be governed by the sadhvis themselves, that it would not be appended to the Sri Ramakrishna Mission, that women would learn to manage everything on their own. This is exactly what happened. Sri Sarada Math was born free, though in its infancy it received help to stand on its feet from senior monks of the Sri Ramakrishna Mission. This independence was vital to instil in women a sense of their own worth, encourage them to gauge their own capability and challenge what they thought were their limits. The colossal endeavour towards realization of self as Brahman must begin with this first step, this fundamental realization that one's innate potential is much vaster than one believes it to be.

Says Vivekaprana, 'Swamiji has given a tremendous shock to society and especially to women by asking them to take up the challenge and find their identity and stand on that identity and then function in society. So it is up to the women, I believe. It isn't as if the government has to do anything or anyone else has to do anything! It is the individual woman who has to ask herself whether she is going to accept the challenge of the times, or whether she wants to get back to the same old ruts which I call the "bullock-cart age".'

To me, it seems that the women who have entered the Math since its inception have taken on an enormous challenge, not only of managing on their own and contributing valuable service to society, but also of deep study and contemplation of Truth, of unearthing the jewel of their true self. The simultaneity of spirituality and seva, the engagement of one with the other, makes for an inspiring ideal, but how does it really translate into a lived experience? Doesn't the noise of the world at times threaten to overwhelm the inner song?

'There are tremendous obstacles, and everywhere, every centre has to face tremendous resistance from the men they have to deal with,' agrees Vivekaprana. 'Suppose I want to build a house and I need a contractor, the contractor is male. The labour is basically male. And I have to be able to work efficiently with them so that they don't feel that they are working for a woman specifically. I have been dealing with all these problems. It does at times feel like something you need to break your head against before you can get things done. But even that I would say is not something insurmountable. The main thing is, am I sure of my identity as something beyond gender? Then the person I am dealing with cannot but accept it.' What she refers to is one of the problems of living in patriarchy, when women attempt what is basically a male enterprise, of 'getting things done' in a masculine workplace. To do so, they have to negotiate a space that is rife with preconceived notions about gender and gender roles—what a woman can do, what she should do, what her 'place' is and so on.

Opting out of the gendered space altogether, according to Vivekaprana, is an efficient way of sidestepping all the baggage that comes with it. Which is almost like saying, just know you are atman, not woman, and all will be well! It is handy advice for the women of Sri Sarada Math who are 'thrown into the public arena as soon as you become a sannyasini', as Vivekaprana points out. 'So you have to learn how to deal with the world.'

One must deal with the world, but one must also ensure that it does not intrude into one's sadhana and disrupt it, that outer noise does not instigate an inner cacophony. To pre-empt this, the ideal of 'being in the world but not of it' could be useful, for it seamlessly combines engagement with life, with society and its issues, with a measure of detachment and repose. It is a mantra that instantly creates an inner refuge by reminding one of the kernel of truth that lies at the heart of life. So whatever one's circumstances might be at that moment, one can draw back a few steps and access the larger picture, and become connected with the abiding core rather than remaining entangled with the surface. To not be *of the world*, to extricate oneself from the thorns of one's self-created samsara of likes and hurts and disappointments and the pursuit of pleasure, is imperative in the inward journey. This simple adage reorients the seeker's mind towards this fact.

Vivekaprana disagrees. 'These are old concepts,' she says. 'Is there anyone who is not in the world?'

You are *in* the world but not *of* the world, I try to explain.

'Who said that? Don't I take food from the world? Don't I breathe the same air? Don't I live in the same space?' One feels the Zen master's stick attempting to get one to focus.

I think it's a question of detachment, I say, somewhat subdued now.

'It's *not* a question of detachment. See, these are ancient words which are creating so much misery. People say, "Oh, you are telling me to be detached. How can I be? I have children, I have my duties." What is the point in talking about those old things? Give something new. Detachment today means standing first of all on my own feet, neither leaning this way nor that way on my husband, on my wife, on my brother, on my father. If you learn to stand on your own feet, you are automatically detached.'

I agree that women cannot embark upon the spiritual quest without a measure of self-confidence and a sense of their identity outside of patriarchal gender roles. How can you know your self, reality and truth deeply if you have no inner compass in place to guide you, no power of intellectual discrimination, no strength of character? Get real, Vivekaprana wants to tell us contemporary women. Begin with your identity in the world, and only then can you hope to begin the journey towards dissolving it.

Vivekaprana is impatient with ideas that are not immediately practicable in the human enterprise of negotiating the world, that even hint at divesting the spiritual from its roots in samsara, and therefore her umbrage with the term 'detachment'. It is a word that carries connotations of upping and leaving, which doesn't make sense to women with families that depend on them for nurture and support. Many women may actually be intimidated by the spiritual search and perhaps give up on it altogether, if they felt they were being asked to choose between it and their families. Though it is largely a misreading of detachment, it happens often enough. I see Vivekaprana's point about 'ancient words' that might actually be unhelpful because of the layers of meanings they have accrued that have obscured their original meaning.

I tell her that it is true, whenever they have a choice, women will almost always prioritize their relationships. 'It is not a question of priorities,' she says emphatically. 'It is a question of whether women are capable of looking at themselves from a very original point of view. Which is very hard. Because there are no examples. Suppose you take me as an example. They will immediately say, you never married, you never had children. You never had responsibilities. So the thing is, how do they look upon themselves? I cannot be a model for them. I cannot be an example for them. The example has to be set by people like you and her (indicates a long-time student of hers) who have fought and who are fighting, and who make it clear that it is not a question of becoming a mother or a sister or a daughter and then not being able to understand whether I can live my spiritual path or not. It's a question of understanding my real identity.'

Which is why I feel the examples of Sarada Ma and Sri Ramakrishna are as relevant today as in their own lifetimes, perhaps even more so. They represent a rich and dynamic inclusiveness, of relationship and sadhana, emotionality and prayer, tradition and innovation, feminine and masculine, laughter and solitude, playfulness and contemplation. Theirs is an integrative spirituality that offers to point the seeker towards a naturalness of effort and practice, an awakening of non-selfish love, a graceful femininity in sacred form and practice and the sweetness that comes with letting go of oneself in the ocean of the Divine.

Dusk stands at the door of my enquiry into the spiritual feminism of Ramakrishna, Sarada and Vivekananda. Lamps being lit in their collective shrine bring closure to this day. The tiny points of brilliance hold my eyes unblinking, reddening. So much done, so much yet to do. Each generation must find its own truth, each individual her own reality, I think, as I bow before the trio luminescent in lamplight. Those who have gone before ignite our minds with the fire of their insights. It is we who must set out to taste that truth in our own beings.

7

A Woman, A Buddha?

JETSUNMA TENZIN PALMO

I too will walk
the path
O Buddha,
I too will go forth…

My body
is a woman's
O Buddha
my mind
is sharp and pure…

Then,
why am I less
than your *bhikkhus*
O Buddha
why for me
nothing more?

The seed

of nirvana
is mine
O Buddha
as much
as it is yours…

I too will walk
the path
O Buddha,
I too will go forth…

—

It took the dawn of the twentieth century, a passage of some 5,000 years and the genesis of a complex spiritual feminism for the first order of Hindu women renunciates to come into its own. In contrast, the sangha of Buddhist nuns was created almost at the same time as that of the monks, some 2,500 years ago, during the Buddha Sakyamuni's lifetime. But like most changes that challenge patriarchy, this revolutionary statement of gender equality neither came easy nor was it uncontested.

One day the Buddha's aunt, Mahaprajapati, who was also his stepmother and had brought him up after his mother died in his infancy, arrived at his doorstep with a retinue of women and a request. They had all left their homes, shaved their heads and walked a few hundred kilometres to petition him that they too be included in his sangha. They wanted to 'go forth', they said, a term used by the Buddha to indicate initiation into a life of homelessness and dedication to the dharma. Until that point, there was no provision for women to follow the Buddha as renunciates, only as lay practitioners.

Mahaprajapati and her companions, dusty and dishevelled, presented a conundrum to the Buddha. According to some accounts, he had already refused his aunt-mother's plea for initiation thrice. Asserting something three times is thought to pretty much seal one's response. But Mahaprajapati would not be refused. She had sensed the truth the Buddha pointed to, and longed to study and practise his way. Her palace and jewels, her family and their concerns, her household and its needs did not appeal to her any longer. Restless and despondent, she had decided to seek the Buddha out once more, making a journey that was perhaps in the same spirit as his own all those years ago, when he had checked out of his prince's life and gone forth into the dark night to seek fulfilment for his soul-thirst.

Surely *he* would understand that her request was not merely a queen's whim? Surely he would not deny quenching a thirst he had known only too well? He must recognize the imperative that had driven this bunch of disparate and, might one add, desperate, women to him? As news of Mahaprajapati's intention spread, many women had seen mirrored in it their own spiritual longing and had stepped out of their homes to accompany her. Now, the soles of their feet cracked by the long journey, they stood before the Buddha and awaited his response in silence.

It is said that the Buddha didn't say anything for a long time. Neither did Mahaprajapati. Their previous communication on the subject perhaps weighed on both their minds. Until Ananda, the Buddha's attendant-disciple, pleaded with him to consider the women's case. When the Sakyamuni remained unmoved to all other pleas, Ananda used one he knew the Buddha couldn't ignore:

'Don't men and women have equal potential to attain nirvana?'

It was this intercession that reportedly won the day for the women. The Buddha could not deny the truth of this statement, for he shunned discriminatory distinctions like the caste system and sought to make the path available to as many feet as were willing to walk upon it. Yet it was a partial victory for the women, and one that left a bitter, misogynistic aftertaste that lingers till this day. At the threshold of the sangha, as the women readied to leap across the pit of prejudice, they were thwarted by what appears to be male mistrust and the heavy-handedness of patriarchy. With one foot in the door, the women were told they could enter, but they had to accept the overlordship of the monks. Eight additional rules were created which required them to submit to the monks in all matters and would, in effect, ensure the perpetuation of patriarchy in even this, the path to inner liberation.

Women in patriarchy often 'pay' for their freedoms by compromising with dominant power structures. Like women who are asked to settle for lesser wages for the same amount of work as their male counterparts and those who must expect no respite from housework if they choose to work outside the home, Mahaprajapati and the women who accompanied her were asked to pay for their spiritual quests by surrendering their right to equality and fairness. Because it came into being within a patriarchal society, the Buddha's sangha displayed the same characteristics and values, somewhat disappointingly so. The women led by Mahaprajapati had no option but to accept this conditional entry. The choice was between that and the courtyards and kitchens they had left far behind.

It is said that Mahaprajapati gracefully accepted the additional rules, even calling them a 'garland of lotus flowers' that she would forever honour and cherish. In doing so, she became the first nun to commit herself to the dharma as enunciated by the Buddha Sakyamuni, joined by the 500 women who had come with her. Shortly after the Buddha had initiated them, he is said to have lamented to Ananda that had women chosen not to go forth, the dharma would have lasted a thousand years, but since they had, it would survive for only half that time.

More than 2,500 years have passed since the sun set on that day, and the Buddha's dharma shows no sign of disappearing. On the contrary, the last century has seen something of a renaissance, where the dharma has found its way to continents it had never been to, astride new tongues, its eternal truths engaged in animated conversation with contemporary issues and knowledge systems, like science. In all of this, though, the shadow of that initial misogyny has relentlessly pursued women—lay and ordained, those born in Buddhism and those who came to it—and darkened their spiritual journeys.

Because of these continuing consequences, one can say that Mahaprajapati's compliance was not just on her own behalf or that of her immediate companions, but on behalf of all women who would ever elect to go forth on the Buddha's path. As the dharma blossomed out from the Indian subcontinent, that early acquiescence to gender inequality became amplified with each passing century and in the embrace of each Asian patriarchal society the Buddha's dharma encountered. The original prejudice gathered around it layers of local interpretation until it had grown into an edifice of gender discrimination, fed by those cultures' own biases, that had a debilitating effect on the status of women in general and of ordained women in particular. Today, when we are well into the twenty-first century and there aren't many preserves of male dominance where women have not left their imprints, women in the Buddha's dharma are still trying to break through that 2,500-year-old glass ceiling that invariably affects and directs the course of their spiritual journeys.

Before one lays the entire blame for what at times has amounted to second-class citizenship of the sangha upon Mahaprajapati and the Buddha, one must attempt to discern their perspectives from within their contexts. For instance, one can wonder whether Mahaprajapati's acquiescence was the subservience of a repressed woman conditioned to submit to patriarchal norms, or the courageous response of a seeker who was determined that her feet were not halted by any challenges the path might bring. I think she saw her chance and grabbed it with both hands and, like most women dealing with repressive conditions, resolved to make the best of her situation. Which she did and, with diligent practice, attained 'arahatship', the state of being an *arahat*—one who has realized the truths inherent in the dharma, and though not a Buddha yet, is well on her way. In this, Mahaprajapati not only redeemed herself to the women who followed in her footsteps and bore the fruits of her compliance, she also proved a point about women's intrinsic spiritual merit, their capability for intense sadhana and the fact that there is nothing inbuilt in the female body that prevents access to exalted spiritual states.

The Buddha's perceived misogyny is more difficult to understand. If one presumes he was a man of his time and was merely operating from within his cultural context, then one can argue, isn't one of the basic deliverables of nirvana the dropping away of the conditioned mind? Other reasons usually cited on his behalf are the practical difficulties of organizing two contiguous sanghas, the lack of appropriate housing for women (viharas or monasteries were built much later) and the threat that the close proximity of men and women might pose to a celibate order. Both Jetsunma Tenzin Palmo and Ven. Khandro Rinpoche discuss the issue in this chapter and the next, providing a sense of the evolution of the debate over the centuries and its continuing relevance for those who consider themselves *sakyadhita*, (spiritual) daughters of the Buddha.

There exists another possibility, that the Buddha didn't actually say those misogynistic words about the survival of the sangha, or perhaps not quite that way. Most of what is attributed to the Buddha comes from what others remembered about him, a corpus of memories and recollections gathered during the first monsoon retreat after his death in 483 BCE, and compiled into the Pali Canon, thus termed because of the language of early Buddhism.

In the Buddha's own lifetime, nothing was formally documented, including sutras, discourses and incidents. We depend on the memory of those who heard him, for his teachings, his life story, everything about him. Hence, with everything attributed to the Buddha, including this controversial remark about the ordination of women, one can never be completely certain whether that was exactly what the Buddha had said, or whether it was what the informer of that event remembered or chose to remember. The play of memory is often affected by our own imputations and expectations, and it is possible that the misogyny wasn't in the Buddha's mind but in that of the reporter(s) of the incident.

Karma Lekshe Tsomo, in her essay 'Mahaprajapati's Legacy', supports this view as a distinct likelihood. She adds to the unreliability of memory the possibility of women being seen as competitors by monks for 'material resources and spiritual achievement', for 'spiritual prowess attracts donations from the laity'. Thus, 'If nuns were perceived as competition and a threat to the material welfare of the monks and it was the monks who transcribed the scriptures, this could explain certain misogynist statements that appear in the texts, including certain discriminatory statements attributed to the Buddha,' she says.

We do know that the Buddha ministered equally to the spiritual needs of monks and nuns, and the nuns received as much instruction and opportunity for practice as the monks during his lifetime. Once, when the validity of Mahaprajapati's ordination was questioned, the Buddha spoke up on her behalf and said that since she had been ordained directly by him, there could be no doubt about her rightful place in the sangha of renunciates. Other women who expressed their wish to ordain after Mahaprajapati, and who came from varied caste affiliations and backgrounds and included courtesans and prostitutes, were welcomed and instructed in dharma practice. Many among them experienced profound transformations which they rendered into poetry, and which came to be compiled as the *Therigatha*, 'stories of women elders'.

The seventy-three poems of the *Therigatha* delineate as if an inner courtyard, a private world of women, where they shrug off veils of personality and the ego-self, bare their innermost experiences and swap stories about their struggles and insights. As women in patriarchy bound by rules of conduct, this personal, feminine space frees their voices to speak of what is important to them in an idiom they are comfortable with. One can almost picture a huddle of women with shaved heads, some young some old, sitting companionably during a *vessa* (monsoon) retreat, amidst the fragrance of wet earth ploughed by rain, talking their hearts, revealing their selves.

They lament the darkness that hung heavy upon them, woven of loss and sorrow, dissatisfaction and frustration until the light of dharma pierced that coal-coloured cloak and set them free. The famous parable of the mustard seed, where a mother learns to accept the truth of death, is one such. The mother, Kisa Gotami, begs the Buddha for a miracle that would revive her dead son. The Buddha says he would indeed do so, provided she bring him a mustard seed from a home that had never been visited by death. Kisa Gotami hunts for such a mustard seed and by the time she returns, she has understood the play of change and impermanence that is the nature of life. She says:

It's not just a truth for one village or town,
Nor is it a truth for a single family.
But for every world settled by gods (and men)
This indeed is what is true—impermanence.

(from *Thig* A X.1, translated by Andrew Olendzki)

The soul-songs of the *Therigatha* provide an intimate look at the concerns and issues particular to women on the path in a non-preachy, non-judgmental way. These have little by way of pulpy, lethargic sentimentality and aren't dry and clinical either. One could describe them best as examples of 'telling it like it is', with a clarity of mind and memory that might be expected of an arahat (which most of the *theris* reportedly were). The concerns mentioned therein feel immediate and true, even across the chasm of centuries that separates those women from us.

Whether it is Patacara, mourning the loss of her family, or Gutta, who yearns for a child, or Vimala, the courtesan who exults in her own beauty, or Anopama, the wealthy heiress who is restless with her materialistic lifestyle, the theris articulate a uniquely feminine perspective on life, and life on the path. Their contexts might be dated, but when they speak of emotional issues, deep attachments, the rigours of relationships, obsessing about the body and its appearance, women of any era cannot but find their own challenges reflected in the theris'.

Patacara's is a remarkable story of redemption which she composes into song. As a young woman, she fell in love with a servant of her family and eloped with him. They were deliciously happy, as only lovers can be, and had two children. Then a terrible change swept in and destroyed their idyll. Patacara lost her husband and children and, in the ensuing emotional storm, her mind as well. When the Buddha met her, she was dishevelled and destitute, a madwoman. In her song, she quotes the compassionate words of the Buddha that lifted the veil of insanity off her mind:

> Unasked,
> he came from there.
> Without permission,
> he went from here—
> coming from where
> having stayed a few days.
> And coming one way from here,
> he goes yet another
> from there.
> Dying in the human form,
> he will go wandering on.
> As he came, so he has gone—
> so what is there
> to lament?
>
> (from *Thig* 6.1, translated by Thanissaro Bhikkhu)

These words, says Patacara, brought home to her the nature of 'coming and going' and pulled out 'the arrow so hard to see, / embedded in my heart'. She is 'unbound' now, she says, and has gone 'for refuge / to the Sage'. As a nun, Patacara not only attained arahatship, she also helped many other women ford the turbulence of emotionality with the raft of dharma.

Bhikkuni Sujata recounts how she was 'awakened' from the languorous stupor of her pleasure-filled life that was fun, but little else besides. There was no depth or meaning to her days, which she spent decked out in veils, garlands and sandalwood perfume, surrounded by servants and 'eatables of many kinds'. Indeed, it is an existence similar to the wasteful, consumption-driven lifestyle of the wealthy today, termed 'affluenza', the disease of affluence. Sujata begins to experience a restlessness, an unease, a lack of fulfilment with her single-minded pursuit of pleasure. And then she awakens with a pinprick of realization, as the Buddha explains the true meaning of life, a teaching received fortuitously as she returns from a picnic one evening. The balloon of her insular, self-preoccupied existence is punctured, and she takes a nun's vows to know more. In her own words:

Having enjoyed and sported there,
We turned our feet to home
But on the way I saw and entered
Near Saketa, a monastery.
Seeing the Light of the World
I drew near, bowed down to Him;
Out of compassion the Seeing One
Then taught me Dhamma there.

Hearing the words of the Great Sage,
I penetrated Truth:
The Dhamma passionless,
I touched the Dhamma of Deathlessness.
When the True Dhamma had been known,
I went forth to the homeless life;
The three True Knowledges are attained,
Not empty the Buddha's Teaching!

(from *Thig* 6.4, translated by Hellmuth Hecker, Ayya Khema)

The very language of the *Therigatha* is redolent with imagery and metaphors related to women's work, words that evoke the warp and weft of their world. In this verse by an anonymous nun, for instance, the quietening of the mind is compared with a 'pot of pickled greens / boiled dry'.

Sleep, little theri, sleep comfortably,
wrapped in the robe that you've made,
for your passion is stilled—
like a pot of pickled greens
boiled dry.

(from *Thig* 1.1, translated by Thanissaro Bhikkhu)

For the women of *Therigatha*, liberation clearly has more than one connotation. The primary one, of course, is liberation from suffering, from afflictive emotions, the extinguishment of the ego-personality in nirvana. At another level, it also means liberation from the stranglehold of feminine roles and the expectations of a tradition-bound, socially conventional life. For in that society, if you were a bit of a wild spirit, and a woman, and wished for something over and beyond the marriage-motherhood grind, available options, respectable ones, were next to none. This may be another reason for their having been denied the option of a wandering ascetic's life till then, and the hesitation in letting them in when they demanded this option for themselves.

With the foundation of orders of women renunciates almost simultaneously by the Buddha and Mahavira, a new opportunity opened up for women. As nuns, though bound by the rules of the sangha, they were no longer the familial property of their male relatives, confined to a life where their intellect received little or no stimulus, where their functionality as mothers, cooks, cleaners, farm workers dominated their existence and left them with little opportunity to explore avenues of growth.

In contrast, nuns were homeless, parentless, possessionless, childless, spouseless. They survived by begging and spent a large chunk of their time meditating, contemplating, practising the dharma. The compass of their lives had shifted from the outer to the inner. There was no need for them to shape their selves according to others' notions of what they should be. They were learning just to be. A tremendously creative endeavour with the chance to transform, re-create, re-imagine the root of one's being. Where one was breaking out of moulds and masks and setting oneself free.

For the earliest *bhikkhunis*, their first taste of liberation came with the stripping away of gender roles. Between this liberation and the ultimate one, of nirvana, they traversed deep into the territory of the self, whittling away at those aspects of the mind that keep us in continuous bondage even if outwardly we appear to be free. For the theris, external freedom came twinned with a shot at inner liberation, as seen in this verse by Mutta who rejoices in the multiplicity of freedom she experiences, triggered and enabled by a nun's life.

So freed! So thoroughly freed am I!—
from three crooked things set free:
from mortar, pestle,
and crooked old husband.
Having uprooted the craving
that leads to becoming,
I'm set free from ageing and death.

(from *Thig* 1.11, translated by Thanissaro Bhikkhu)

In the *Therigatha*, there is even evidence of a co-seeking, a co-realization, where the husband–wife duo of Maha Kassapa, one of the Buddha's foremost disciples, and Bhadda Kapilani ordain together and attain a similar depth of spiritual experience. Bhadda says in her verse:

Seeing the world's deep misery, we both went forth
And are now both free of cankers, with well-tamed minds.

Cooled of passions, we have found deliverance;
Cooled of passions, we have found our freedom.

(from *Thig* 4.1, translated by Hellmuth Hecker and Ayya Khema)

I think Bhadda's verse is crucial for its self-confident use of 'we', denoting an equality of spiritual status. That both the man and the woman, when provided an equal opportunity for dharma study and practice, emerge with similarly 'well-tamed minds', should have been enough of a deterrent against the misogyny that steadily crept into the Buddha's dharma after his death. In fact, the 522 stanzas of the *Therigatha* alone could have become the swell that crashed through the dharmic glass ceiling. But it didn't, and couldn't, and the ceiling exists till today, in some form or another. What it has meant for women aspirants is restricted access to avenues for spiritual growth, implications of inferior intelligence, denigrating and de-motivating comments like those that characterize women as 'lustful' seductresses, and claims that enlightenment is not possible in a female body, that even if one reaches the penultimate stage, one would have to be reborn as a man to come into the fullness of nirvana.

—

The dharmic glass ceiling was still in place as the twentieth century dawned and the Buddha's path began to interest a wholly different kind of seeker—one who was not born Buddhist but was attracted to the promise of a non-theistic, reason-based spirituality that harnessed the mind in the process of transformation. This was also the century that witnessed women organizing themselves in movements for equal rights, now classified as 'waves' of feminism. Feminism fundamentally altered the way women related to themselves, their selfhood and identity, and impacted every sphere of life that functioned on the presumption of gender constructs.

From the relative margins of activism and academia, the gender debate entered mainstream social discourse and began to impact the hierarchies and structures that propped up society, culture, economy, politics, language, history and so on—initially in the 'first world', and then in the newly decolonized democracies of the 'third world', forming a crucial part of their postcolonial discourse. Fundamental changes were wrought in the way women were perceived and portrayed, and spaces were opened up for their rightful participation in processes they had previously been kept out of.

Organized religion was predictably the slowest to respond to this call of change, but there was a general acceptance, in Christianity, for instance, that certain overtly misogynistic theological ideas like the 'spare rib' origin of womankind would have to be downplayed to accommodate the sensibilities of a new generation of women. In some Christian denominations, like the Church of England, women won the right to ordain as priests. Judaism too found many members questioning its patriarchal tilt, which women from the Reformed stream of Judaism recently attempted to balance by collating a commentary on the Bible comprising women's voices and interpretations.

In this milieu, where religions were being forced to acknowledge and engage with women's issues and concerns, the new global version of Buddhism couldn't but be drawn into the conversation. It was a conversation that had as much to do with the Buddha dharma as the Asian cultures where it had thrived and mutated into richly varied forms and which were its emissaries to the new world. In the vessels of the traditionally patriarchal cultures of India, Sri Lanka, Burma, Tibet, Japan, China and south-east Asia, the dharma had intermingled with prevalent norms and customs and acquired their accents, tastes and nuances. The core remained the same, the garb changed considerably with each new migration and moulting. As a result, what the West encountered in the twentieth century was one philosophy that was being spoken in different tongues, clothed in different cultures, each form coupled with its own structure, rituals and hierarchies. All of which tended to be overwhelmingly patriarchal.

Buddhism's interaction and interface with a post-feminist modernity, both in the personae of Western followers and increasingly aware women adherents from traditionally Buddhist societies, exposed the misogynistic faultlines that had become deeply entrenched in the way it is taught and practised. Over the last few decades, a new discourse has slowly and painstakingly been constructed to bring the dharma in alignment not so much with modernity, as with its own avowed aims of spiritual egalitarianism.

This movement has been spearheaded in tandem by women of the dharma across boundaries of school, branch, tradition, *yana* (vehicle), teacher, nationality, geography, and so on. Beginning with dissatisfied whispers and murmurs of dissent, the movement has intensified into a roaring river of feminine voices that cannot be ignored. Its prime endeavour is to sift the gold of the original teachings and insights from the dross of interpolated cultural conditioning and values, and ensure gender neutrality in all matters of the dharma.

One could describe this urge for reform as a 'wave' of Buddhist Feminism. But is a 'Buddhist feminist' a contradiction in terms, for it seems to bind a doctrine characterized by 'no-self'—the essential emptiness of notions of a permanent, self-existing entity called the 'self'—with a philosophy that came into existence to strengthen the 'selfhood', the individuality, of women? Can a true Buddhist ever really be a feminist, or any other 'ist', for that matter, which pegs him or her to some sort of a solidity of self and identity, instead of the kinetic fluidity of the dharmic notion of an interconnected, impermanent, inherently empty non-self?

Women in Buddhism today are grappling with these issues that directly affect their practice, and are attempting to effect on-the-ground change. In this, Buddhist feminism treads that disputed ground between samsara and spirituality, seemingly divided by a thought-fence to keep out interlocutors that might mix the two.

A Buddhist feminist does exactly that: by crossing into a no-(wo)man's land, she tries to re-form the dharma into an equal vehicle for both men and women. If gender and body and physicality are samsaric issues that have no place in a dharmic discourse, then they should truly be so and have no effect, leave no stain, affect in no way, the journey of those who come to the path as women. And if they do, the dharma must submit to rigorous interrogation by those it marginalizes, and allow them to turn the flashlight upon itself.

Jetsunma Tenzin Palmo is one such re-former, re-imaginer, re-tooler of an appropriate dharma-yana for contemporary women. She is among the prime architects of the movement for which I have coined the term 'Buddhist Feminism'. Her personal grit, her journey as an uncompromising dharma practitioner and her compassionate understanding of multiple perspectives make her the ideal spokesperson for a gender-sensitive dharma. The clarity of mind she carried out of the cave where she spent twelve years in solitary retreat helps her speak an unclouded, unshrouded truth to power. Her own experience as a woman on the path, as well as her hands-on work with other women, particularly nuns for whom she attempts to make available a sturdy dharma education, have provided her with the insights and the means to become an agent of change, even as she attempts to stir a turgid establishment to follow suit.

And to think that her life very nearly didn't take the turn that led her to the Buddha's sangha. Right this moment, she could easily have been a grey-haired English matron having afternoon tea by the wisteria in her garden. Instead, a maroon-robed nun with a shaved head and a long-term meditator's rounded shoulders, pours chai for an inquisitive writer in a nunnery ringed by a panoramic view of snowy Himalayan peaks aglow in the late afternoon sun.

Her blue eyes turn to me with a flash of diamond-edged quickness.

'Shall we begin?'

To really begin, we must retrace Tenzin Palmo to *her* beginning, as Diane Perry, a fishmonger's daughter who grew up in Bethnal Green in London's East End. She was born in 1943, on a day the German Luftwaffe was bombing London, in Hertfordshire where her mother had been evacuated to. Growing up in post-war London while the physical and emotional scars of war were still palpable must have left an impression on the child. Her father's demise when she was two, and childhood battles with meningitis, high fevers, a spinal condition and a fire accident deepened her acquaintance with the Buddha's first noble truth, of the inevitability of suffering.

Tenzin Palmo, though, is more likely to attribute her spiritual journey to the enigmatic processes of reincarnation than a Buddha-like quest to find the truth about suffering. In the bestselling book about her life, *Cave in the Snow* written by Vicki Mackenzie, Tenzin Palmo casts her early life in the light of this belief and comes up with instances that could be read as imprints from a previous existence. Like germinated seeds, they perhaps required some more nourishment to ripen, a process she feels drew her into situations she had no reason to be in otherwise, and provided her with circumstances that acted as the wind in her sails, navigating her course towards the dharma.

For her, the very fact that she was born to a mother who was a 'spiritualist' who organized séances in her home and had a keen interest in the mystical, could be such a marker. Through her mother, the young Diane was introduced to the possibility of planes of reality that lay beyond the superficial and the obvious, at a time when her dominant cultural environment offered little such information. Later, when she would decide to leave home for India to pursue her interest in Buddhism, her mother would provide crucial, enabling support and an acceptance of her choices even when she didn't fully comprehend them.

There were other 'clues', occasional whiffs of another life that turned up in the most unexpected ways. For one, Diane always felt uncomfortable and out of place in England. 'I had this intense feeling that I was in the wrong place. Even now I never feel "right" in England,' she says in *Cave in the Snow*. Interestingly, for someone who would become a passionate proponent of women's rights in the dharma, she didn't feel 'right' about being in the female body either. She recounts how as a little girl she would hear people talk about physical changes during adolescence and be relieved because she assumed it meant she could 'go back to being a boy'.

Then, when she was eighteen and had already spent a few years on a spiritual quest, searching for a path to 'perfection' that had taken her through the main religions without quite resonating with any, she chanced upon a book on Buddhism. Published in 1961, *The Mind Unshaken* by John Walters seemed to encapsulate all that she had been looking for, guided by an instinctive inner compass. Halfway through the book, she turned to her mother and said, 'I'm a Buddhist.' Like Ramakrishna had recognized/re-cognized Sarada, Diane recognized a truth about herself. She had stepped into a pool of light, it seemed to her, that illuminated recesses in her being she couldn't quite grasp earlier. Now came the challenge of re-cognizing, or re-imagining her life to align it with that in herself which she had recognized.

The past-life influences hadn't run their course yet, and they seemed to be focusing her towards something specific. Possibilities that didn't fit in got eliminated, like her initial interest in Theravadin Buddhism. She found she couldn't identify with the arahats, the heroes of Theravada, nor did she find much of use in what to her seemed like a loveless, dry philosophy geared towards personal salvation. Instinctively, and without any theological study of Buddhism, the young Englishwoman had walked into one of the abiding fractures between the older and newer schools of the Buddha's dharma.

About a century after his death, the Buddha's sangha split along the issue of change, the Theravadins preferring to preserve the dharma in its remembered original form, and the Mahayana adherents calling for openness to evolution and change. Gradually, Mahayana absorbed cultural influences and other philosophical ideas and began to fork out in different directions while retaining its link with the core. Hybrids such as Tantrayana (a commingling of Tantra and Mahayana Buddhism) and Vajrayana (a fusion of Mahayana, Tantrayana and elements from Tibet's Bon Shamanism) were birthed from this process of assimilation and inclusion, and in time developed into sophisticated dharma lineages with their own scriptures, commentaries and interpretations of the Buddha's path.

Somewhere along this journey, Mahayana Buddhism, the central root of this complex system of philosophies and sub-philosophies, had expanded out of the notion of self-nirvana as the goal of the path. Salvation for oneself was too constricted, too selfish to be the rightful outcome of as momentous an event as enlightenment. It seemed almost churlish and self-seeking for a Buddha to salvage himself or herself out of samsara while countless other beings continued to suffer in it. This new idea could have had something to do with the growing primacy in Mahayana of the Buddha's teaching of *pratitya samutpada*, 'interdependent origination', according to which everything exists because of everything else, nothing exists by itself. Every event, every birth, every circumstance can be traced along a series of linkages, a set of interrelated causalities, to its source, which too does not independently exist.

So if our becoming is a result of a series of interlinked events, how can nirvana be an unrelated, standalone absolute? Logically, it too must be an expression of interdependence, where an individual practises the path to perfection with the intent of sharing it with *all sentient beings*. Where nirvana, when achieved, would be a combined co-event, for the compassionate Buddha-to-be cannot possibly evolve out of the swirl of samsara in a candyfloss haze, leaving everybody else struggling under the yokes of ignorance.

The Bodhisattva ideal, where one pledges to the rigours of the path not for oneself but for everybody else, arose out of this philosophical tilt towards an interdependent, interlaced nirvana that irrevocably binds the individual to the collective. It was a radical shift and one of the reasons why Mahayanists tended to look down upon Theravadins as passengers of a 'lesser vehicle' (Hinayana) who continued to cling to, what was in their view, a selfish nirvana.

When Diane felt an aversion to the 'lovelessness' of Theravada, was she unconsciously articulating her position as a past-life Mahayanist? Apparently so, as it soon became evident with further instances of re-cognition—once, when she came upon the bodhisattva ideal in a book by Nagarjuna, the second-century champion-philosopher of Mahayana, and then, when she was introduced to the Vajrayana, the 'thunderbolt' vehicle of Buddhism in Tibet. As she read about the schools of Tibetan Buddhism—Gelug, Sakya, Kagyu and Nyingma—a 'voice' from within told her she was Kagyu. It was the kind of deep knowing she couldn't ignore, and which had stood her in good stead as she attempted to navigate her way through the thorns and brambles that currently hid the path from view.

Diane sought out somebody who knew about Tibetan Buddhism, and was promptly handed a biography of the beloved yogi-poet of Tibet, Milarepa. Milarepa's story plays out a well-loved theme of spiritual lore—that of a sinner-turned-saint whose redemption is secured through a cataclysmic inner transformation. Wronged as a child, Milarepa turned to sorcery to avenge himself and his mother, wreaking immense damage and taking many lives. Caught in a vicious cycle of violence, he could not sustain the tremendous hatred it required of him, and the blindfold finally slipped off his eyes. Awareness of the destruction he had been responsible for filled him with remorse, and he sought a guru to help him out of the karmic pit he had dug for himself and in which he now felt trapped.

The wise guru, Marpa, recognized Milarepa's tremendous guilt as well as the unutilized potential that lay buried under it. To extract the toll of karma, Marpa set Milarepa the task of building a stone tower. When it was done, he asked Milarepa to dismantle it and place every stone exactly where he had taken it from. Like Sisyphus, who rolled the boulder constantly uphill and never reached the culmination of his task, Milarepa was asked to do the same thing again and again until he was exhausted, and the guilt, which could have been a psychological barrier to new learning, had been cleansed from his psyche. Marpa then instructed him in the dharma, and Milarepa withdrew to a mountain to practise.

In solitude, Milarepa immersed himself in the work of watching the mind and bringing it into an unbroken, non-reactive balance. The dharma truths his teacher had taught him illuminated the path ahead and acted as touchstones against which he verified his insights. Gradually, Milarepa cognized them in his great sadhana and they went from being heard truths to felt-in-the-bone, bred-in-the-heart truths. During this time, his only possessions were a cloak, a staff and a bowl, and he survived on soup made from nettles that tinted his skin a curious green. Several miraculous powers (*siddhis*) are said to have come to him almost as by-products of his intense practice, such as *tumo* (the art of raising bodily heat), flying over long distances, and so on. Fascinating as these might be, I do think his real miracle was the transformation he wrought within his mind and being, dislodging old negative habit patterns completely, stitching his fragmented consciousness into one vast, continuous sky.

Milarepa's life and dharma journey came to Diane studded in the most exquisite poetry, like jewels crafted into an intricately carved piece of gold. Though she read the English translation of his original *Hundred Thousand Songs*, which is said to be nearly not as striking and poetically rich as the Tibetan, she was deeply affected by the possibility that Milarepa held out to her. Here was a sinner, an evil sorcerer no less, who had turned his life around with the tools of dharma and achieved the acme of human perfection—enlightenment—in the course of a single lifetime. If he had done it in this manner, couldn't she try as well?

Her path was emerging out of the underbrush of confusion, illuminated by the fireflies of Milarepa's songs, embedded with stepping stones of intuitive insight that may or may not have had something to do with past lives. What happened next is best expressed with this verse from Milarepa:

I renounced all affairs of this life;
And, no longer lazy, devoted myself to Dharma.
Thus I have reached the State of Eternal Bliss.
Such is the story of my life.

(from *Sixty Songs of Milarepa*, translated by Garma C.C. Chang)

To devote herself to the dharma, Diane had to first find a wise guru who would agree to take her through the treacherous razor-edged path. Because of its Tantric character, which comprises a step-by-step ascension through practices that at each stage unlocks the next, a guru is thought to be indispensable to the practice of Vajrayana. A guru not only transmits knowledge, he or she also works closely with the student. As one who has already completed that stage of the path, the guru is able to advise course-correctors like a change in, or continuation of, a particular practice. At each stage, the guru *empowers* the student with practices and teachings specific to that stage, tailored to the needs of the student. The guru, in this sense, adapts the path as much as possible to quicken and support the student's progress. This is perhaps why the guru became the fourth jewel of the dharma in Tibet, and was worked into the trinity of traditional Buddhism—Buddha, dharma, sangha.

The timing of Diane's guru-hunt was opportune. It was the early 1960s and a large number of Tibetans, including several 'precious gurus', Rinpoches, had been forced out of their insulated existence on the roof of the world by Chinese invasion, and had arrived in the heat and dust of India in 1959. As she was wondering how to contact them, she got news of Freda Bedi, an Englishwoman who had been initiated as a Tibetan Buddhist nun and was at the time running a school for young *tulkus*, reincarnate lamas, in Dalhousie. In response to her request, Diane received a warm invitation from Freda to visit and so, after saving some money for her passage to India, she set sail for Bombay in 1963.

At the time, Dalhousie was the main Tibetan refugee settlement. Diane eagerly absorbed the atmosphere, fragrant with the dharma even amidst great hardship. The Tibetans were unused to the climate and the food, and most of them had nothing. They were being put to work as road construction workers, and many became seriously ill and died in the harsh living conditions. Diane was housed in a nunnery where the circumstances were pitiable, and was given the job of Freda Bedi's secretary as well as a teacher of basic English to the young tulkus.

The past-life stepping stones continued to appear at crucial points—points of re-cognition—to fine-tune her progress on the path. Soon, others began to 'recognize' her too. In one goosebump-raising incident, Diane, dressed in a Tibetan laywoman's *chuba*, had gone to meet the Dalai Lama. He greeted her with, 'You look like a lady from Lhasa.' To which she replied, without thinking, 'I'm a Khampa,' a resident of Kham in east Tibet, when she didn't know anything about Tibetan geography. Or at least not consciously.

What the Dalai Lama said next was even more significant. '*Oh, Ani-la, tukdam gong phel*?' (Oh, nun, is your practice progressing well?) His translator was confused because Diane was obviously not a nun, nor was she a practitioner in the formal sense, yet. It was clearly a recognition of some kind—but was it of a dharma-drenched past, or of a future he sensed her truth-seeking would sooner or later bring her to? It was a possibility that was about to emerge from its chrysalis. A week after the Dalai Lama's prophetic words, Diane would experience another crucial recognition, that of her guru, and embark upon an adventure of a lifetime, or many.

On Diane's twenty-first birthday, a visitor arrived at Freda Bedi's school—the eighth Khamtrul Rinpoche, who had recently fled the monastery that had been the seat of his reincarnations for some 450 years, in Kham, the Tibetan province Diane had inexplicably claimed affiliation to. In his presence, she felt an instinctive connection, an intuitive recognition, which she describes in *Cave in the Snow*. 'One was seeing somebody you knew extremely well whom you haven't seen for a very long time... And at the same time it was as though an innermost part of my being had taken form in front of me. As though he had always been there but now he was outside.'

The moment she *recognized* her guru, the young woman's spiritual apprenticeship began. She immediately requested the ceremony of refuge in the Buddha's dharma and, soon after, initiation into sannyasa. The Khamtrul Rinpoche agreed to both these requests. Confronted with decisions that would define her life forever, Diane reports feeling remarkably unconflicted and clear-headed. All other considerations that could have posed doubts melted away like the last snowflake in the spring sun, including the possibility of marriage to a young Japanese man she had met during her sea voyage to India, and thoughts of country, home and family. This was the moment that everything that had happened to her till then seemed to have been leading up to. The moment when a centuries-old saga picked up its thread and began to unspool once more.

Looking back at that moment, what she most clearly remembers is her motivation, her goal of attaining the moon of perfection she had glimpsed through the lens of Milarepa's poetry, rather than a compulsion dictated by a past life. 'The point was, I was searching for perfection. I knew that Tibetan Buddhism not only gave the most flawless description of that state but provided the clearest path to get there. That's why I became a nun. Because if one was going to follow that path one needed the least distractions possible.' This reminds me of Nani Ma pointing out that 'it is very easy not to stuff yourself with cream cakes if there are no cream cakes'; if you wish to learn tennis, it is helpful to join a tennis club. Sannyasa provides not just the blinkers that shut out distractions, it also means one gets into the club, the sangha of seekers, where guidance and essential tools are available and where there are others doing the same thing to compare notes with.

What Diane Perry, as the newly-minted Tenzin Palmo, would soon discover was that this particular club was an all-male one, and that to make good on her goal of perfection, she'd have to eventually leave the sangha with its glass ceiling for the empowering solitude of a cave.

Her life was about to take a Milarepa turn.

—

I sing the song
of formlessness
in the cave
of my heart...

My song
has no words
no notes
no melody
it soars upon
each in-breath
it thrums within
each out-breath...

My song
needs no body
no sound
no voice
it swells in silence
it hums in solitude...

My song
is a jewel
pregnant with light
The womb resolves
the form dissolves
an insight is born...

In the cave
of my heart
I sing the song
of knowing...

Though Tenzin Palmo never specifically sought information about the previous lives she had felt murmuring in her being like underground streams ever since she could remember, she was told she had been a close disciple of the Khamtrul Rinpoche across the span of several incarnations. In the life immediately preceding this one, at the beginning of the twentieth century, she was apparently a yogi instructed by the sixth Khamtrul Rinpoche.

If she had been a man, and Tibetan, in most of her past lives, what had instigated this current birth in the body of a woman who, notionally at least, belonged to a culture and country so many degrees removed from Tibet? I feel both her gender and her nationality are directly related to the challenges modern Buddhism is grappling with, and which have been impacted by Tenzin Palmo making the choices she made, holding her form and her practice in balance, and by growing into the kind of sincere dharma practitioner that she has come to represent, irrespective of race, gender or nationality.

After her ordination, Tenzin Palmo went to live near Khamtrul Rinpoche and worked as his secretary, the changed circumstances of exile enabling a woman to work in this position. This helped her spend time in her guru's proximity and learn from him through his presence, his way of being. Though a formidable teacher who was considered an incarnation of a fierce form of Padmasambhava, the establisher of Buddhism in Tibet, Tenzin Palmo found the Rinpoche to be gentle and nurturing. A bond developed between them where he was 'a father and a mother combined' to her.

At this time, she was invited to visit a friend in Thailand, John Blofeld, a scholar of Asian thought and religion. Suddenly, she was face-to-face with the biggest hurdle yet to her intention to ordain as a nun. Her Japanese suitor was waiting for her in Thailand and renewed his proposal for marriage, despite Tenzin Palmo's status as a novitiate nun. This time, she was sorely tempted. She was twenty-one, and she was renouncing forever all possibility of romantic love and the fulfilment that comes from nurturing a relationship, a home, a family. She was going forth into a life where she would take a vow of poverty, never own anything, never have a home, never know the warmth of nestling in loving relationships. She was choosing the silence of sannyasa over the cosy babble of samsara. Suddenly, it all seemed too much to give away without a thought. She wanted to try out samsaric happiness for once, experience it for a while.

Too many times, an emotional stimulus draws us into impulsive reaction, as opposed to a carefully thought out action. To act from a place of balance, from one's centre, where one is not being manipulated by the needs of the ego-self, one must sit with oneself and allow the impulse to react to quieten and fall away. Tenzin Palmo reflected on the fork in the road she stood at, and came to the conclusion that since there is no lasting fulfilment in anything but the realization of truth, it is far wiser to choose the opportunity to study with a guru. She returned for good.

In Khamtrul Rinpoche's establishment, Tenzin Palmo was the only nun among a hundred monks, the lone woman in an all-male club. For her, this worsened the sexism of Tibetan Buddhism. For along with the stain of misogyny already woven into the Buddha's dharma, Tibetan nuns have had to bear the misfortune of full ordination being unavailable to them. In the two stages of ordination, the novice and the full-fledged renunciate, Tibetan nuns can only enter the former. The reason usually given is that the lineage of full ordination for women in the Mulasarvastivadin School, the parent school of Tibetan Buddhism, never reached Tibet from India. And even if it did, it died out at some point.

To be fully ordained, a nun must be tested and accepted by both the nuns' and the monks' sanghas. If enough nuns are not present, a new nun cannot be inducted. Once the number of nuns had depleted, no new nuns could join the sangha, and a vicious cycle formed that stamped out the lineage of fully ordained nuns. In Sri Lanka, the order of nuns had died out and was reseeded with the help of nuns from other parts of Asia. The Tibetan religious establishment has as yet not accepted this solution and has resisted importing the nuns' lineage from a school of Buddhism other than its own on the ground that it will not be authentic.

Due to their perpetual novice status, and by virtue of being women in a patriarchal society, Tibetan nuns were relegated to the margins of the monastic universe. In a society where monasteries were repositories of spiritual, economic and political power, nuns remained 'second-class spiritual citizens', in Tenzin Palmo's words. They were not educated in philosophy and dialectics, they did not receive empowerments and initiations into higher stages of the path, they were kept out of discussions and debate. Basically, they were not in the line for enlightenment. They could not, still cannot, receive the degree of 'Geshe', equivalent to doctor of philosophy, given at the culmination of twenty-five years of intensive study, because the final examination includes a test on Vinaya, the monastic code of conduct, which one can study only after being fully ordained.

Thus deprived, nuns in Tibet were relegated to backroom jobs like preparing for pujas and rituals, chanting and praying for patrons and often, the 'women's work' of cooking and cleaning. Unlike Mutta in the *Therigatha*, their robes didn't free them of mortar and pestle, though the 'crooked old husband' was of course nothing to worry about! When Tenzin Palmo entered her guru's establishment, centuries of this kind of misogyny fell upon her like a heap of soot. She who had entered the sangha intent upon studying and practising her way to perfection, felt thwarted at every step, her past-life lore as Khamtrul Rinpoche's brilliant, and male, yogi-disciple, notwithstanding.

As a woman, Tenzin Palmo couldn't live in the monastery or participate in communal activities. She was isolated physically and emotionally, for all the monks except her guru regarded her, an attractive young woman, warily. What was the most devastating for her, however, was the denial of teachings, scriptural study and practices because of her gender. She was repeatedly told that there was no precedent of women being given the kind of access she demanded, which was essentially the same as men. When she requested to be taught the scriptures, she was delegated to a teacher who told her simple Buddhist stories. In *Cave in the Snow*, Tenzin Palmo likens the situation to a banquet laid out before her, and all she could get were some measly crumbs.

Faced with this kind of discrimination, she was not surprised to find that nuns pray to be born in a male body, and monks pray never to be born a woman. There is another reason for this prayer—belief in the myth among certain sections of the establishment, completely unfounded as far as the Buddha's teachings are concerned, that women can go right up to the penultimate stage of enlightenment, but to actually attain nirvana they would have to 'change into' a male body. When she first heard this myth from a high lama, Tenzin Palmo was so appalled she burst out with, 'What is it about a penis that is so essential for becoming enlightened?' She asked the same lama if there were at all any benefits to the female form. His answer was 'no'.

Tenzin Palmo was frustrated and dismayed. Here was this splendid tradition, with sure-shot, radical ways of transformation, reputed to deliver one to enlightenment in the flash of a thunderbolt, and it was as if its wheel was stuck in a bog, in a deep denial of femininity. As she hit against the glass ceiling again and again, Tenzin Palmo made a vow, one that would inspire countless women across the world and challenge Tibetan Buddhism to address its misogyny. It was a vow to attain enlightenment in *this* form, as a woman. She says, 'I was so exasperated by this terrible male chauvinism that was all around me. I thought, "Forget it! I don't want to be born in a male body under these circumstances." And so I made this strong prayer, even if I can't do that much in this lifetime, in the future may this stream of consciousness go forward and take on the transitory form of a female rather than a male.'

This vow rejuvenated Tenzin Palmo, acting as the flint that sparked her urge to study the dharma once more. Finally, after she had spent six years in this repressive environment, her guru accepted her request to go into retreat somewhere that would be more conducive to her practice. He suggested Lahoul, a remote area in the Buddhist belt of the Indian Himalayas, and fortified her with relevant teachings and valuable, practicable advice as to the future course of her practice.

It was here, in Lahoul, six years later, that Tenzin Palmo would do a Milarepa, entering an extended solitary retreat in a cave in the snow, at a height of 13,200 feet, for a period of twelve years. At that time, she was the only Western Buddhist woman to have attempted such a feat, which was as much an act of physical and psychological bravery as it was a test of spiritual growth and resilience. Which, in conjunction with her vow, created a credible spiritual heroine for our times, one whose story was real, and whose transformation authentic and believable. She found her golden mean, her balance of being and, like the women of the *Therigatha*, she was willing to speak of it in a language that was simple and clear.

In 2006, when I sit down with Tenzin Palmo in her Himalayan nunnery, watching the clear mountain lake of her mind reflected in her eyes, she has been out of the cave for eighteen years. Much of her dharma work in this period has been related to women—building the Dongyu Gatsal Ling nunnery to provide nuns with an opportunity to study and practise, campaigning in Buddhist ecclesiastical forums for equal rights for women, especially on the issue of full ordination for Tibetan nuns, building a consensus for change within the sangha and inspiring women across the world by sharing her own experiences on the path. Spiritual realization may have rendered gender irrelevant to her own present, but as far as other women are concerned, Tenzin Palmo is still intently smoothening the way.

I want to ask her about the cave. Tenzin Palmo declines. 'Really, it was another lifetime, I hardly remember anything any more,' she protests. Life after the cave, like marriage after falling in love, is the true test of the depth of the insights that occurred in the previous experience, I think, as I turn my flashlight towards other areas, wider questions.

To consider the Zen parable of taming the ox of the mind, which describes progressive stages of the path with the ox being a metaphor for the mind, Tenzin Palmo has sought the ox, found its tracks, glimpsed it, caught it, tamed it, ridden the ox home, let go of the ox, let go of her self, returned to the source that is the elemental truth of interdependence and impermanence. Now, I feel, she has 'entered the marketplace with helping hands', the tenth and final stage in the parable. Free, wise, compassionate. Ready to give of herself, unencumbered, a bodhisattva-in-being.

Or is she a lady Buddha?

—

Immersed in the pool of the present moment, I ask her about this nunnery, built for nuns of the Kagyu Nyingma tradition of her guru. It began in the way that much of her choices seem to—she was led in its direction by unseen undercurrents and propitious winds. After the (s)lumbering Indian bureaucracy rudely ended the last part of her retreat because of an unrenewed visa, she left for Assisi in Italy at a friend's invitation. There, she felt a natural affinity to the hometown of one of the most famous Christian contemplatives, Francis of Assisi, a saint she has been compared with because of the animals that would come to her cave and leave her undisturbed, a gentle co-being like St Francis and his birds.

'When I was in Italy, I tried to do longer retreats several times but it didn't work out,' she says. 'Again and again a big wall came down. I said, all right, I am not supposed to go in retreat, what then am I supposed to do? I have given my life to Buddha, Dharma, Sangha, what do you want? I can't spend all my life having a good time! What am I supposed to do if that's not it? Then I thought of coming back to India.'

At the time, the new incarnation of her guru, Khamtrul Rinpoche, was twelve years old, and Tenzin Palmo felt a need to renew her connection with him in his new lifetime. Soon after her return, the high lamas of the tradition asked her to start a nunnery. The time was just right. She had been thinking and speaking about the difficulties that women in Buddhism face at every opportunity she got. Now had arrived the moment every activist longs for, when he or she can extend their ideology out of the realm of thought and into the real world.

Though the template for establishing a nunnery existed in Tibetan Buddhism and in her own lineage, Tenzin Palmo was obviously not going to help create something that perpetuated the very circumstances that had almost blighted her own dharma journey. She saw this as an opportunity to re-envision, re-cognize, re-make the life of a nun, to think into being a system that would empower and liberate women by using the very tools and practices they had been denied for so long.

'Traditionally, nuns were not really educated and played a very minor role. Some of them, because they were not educated and were ignored, became great practitioners. In fact, meditation has been regarded as the thing nuns do. There were undoubtedly many great practitioners but because they were uneducated, they didn't really have an influence or much of a voice. And normally they would not become teachers because they lacked the confidence to do so.' I think of the spiritual heroines of Tibet—Yeshe Tsogyal who was Padmasambhava's consort and a realized master in her own right, Machig Lhapdron who founded the lineage of the powerful ego-severing ritual *Chöd*, Nangsa Obum who resurrected herself from an abused wife into a stellar dharma practitioner, among others. They broke out of stifling servitude and opted for the liberation offered by the dharma, but instead of the equally stifling life of a nun, preferred to strike out on their own as individual meditators and practitioners, like Tenzin Palmo had.

At Dongyu Gatsal Ling, rather than tell the nuns what to do, she decided they must be empowered to make their own decisions. They would have to dive deep into their selves and identify their individual aspirations and motivations. Did they want to study formal disciplines like scripture and philosophy and become teachers one day? Or perhaps act as nunnery administrators, who would figure out how to run a nunnery so it could become self-sufficient and function independently? Or would they want to do a Milarepa, or a Tenzin Palmo for that matter, bringing the mind's ox home in silence and solitude? Nuns were now going to have a say in the shape of their own spiritual lives, and they could choose their path depending on what suited them best.

Tenzin Palmo has consciously chosen to step away from the 'guru' space by taking on the role of a facilitator of another kind—one who makes avenues and opportunities available for other women to walk the path. Driven by the larger cause of women in dharma, she has chosen not to become a one-on-one teacher but a behind-the-scenes presence who works silently and steadily, raising funds for the nunnery, overseeing its administration and growth, inviting teachers to instruct the nuns, forming alliances with other women dharma activists to bring positive change. I am reminded of 'universal mothers' like Ammachi and Mata Nirmala Devi and think Tenzin Palmo too is a mother, just not the guru-goddess kind. She is mother of an entire sangha, enabler of their quests, remover of obstacles in their paths, inspirer of potential lady Buddhas too, perhaps?

As she tries to leap across the hurdles tradition has placed in the path of women, there is one old tradition Tenzin Palmo is keen to revive, that of yoginis, called *togdenma*. The *togdens* were yogis and the *togdenma* yoginis, who spent almost their entire lives meditating, their bodies gradually quietening to form an undisturbed cave for the wakeful mind. Inspired by Milarepa, they attempted to experience directly the essence of dharma teachings, rather than study to become scholars and debaters like intellectually ambitious monks. They would wear white cotton, like Milarepa, and not the ubiquitous maroon robes of Tibetan monasticism, this subtle difference placing them outside the ambit of usual monastic duties and activities. They were the ones who were marked for life, perhaps lifetimes, by their determined practice of the yoga of emptiness, the path to self-extinguishment, to nirvana.

This excerpt from a song by Milarepa could well have been sung by the togden-togdenma, a poetic description of the way of the yogi who practises the 'Path Profound':

The Great Lioness of the upper snow mountain
Poses proudly on the summit of the peak;
She is not afraid—
Proudly dwelling on the mountain
Is the snow lion's way.

The Queen Vulture on Red Rock
Stretches her wings in the wide sky,
She is not afraid of falling—
Flying through the sky is the vulture's way.

(...)
In the wood on Singa Mountain,
I, Milarepa, meditate on voidness,
Not because I fear to lose my understanding—
Constant meditation is the yogi's way.

Those great yogis who have mastered the Practice
Never desire anything in this world.
It is not because they want fame
That they remain in solitude;
It is the natural sign springing from their hearts—
The true feeling of non-attachment and renunciation.

Yogis who practise the teaching of the Path Profound,
Dwell always in caves and on mountains,
Not that they are cynical or pompous,
But to concentrate on meditation is their self-willing.

Unfortunately, in the maelstrom created by the tragedy of Tibet, this unique lineage of practice was all but lost. Only a handful of togdens, and no togdenmas, survived. The togdens were rehabilitated at the reconstituted Khampagar monastery, the seat of Tenzin Palmo's guru in Himachal Pradesh, not far from this sunlit room where we are, with its panoramic view of the Himalayas. In fact, not long after our conversation, I will find myself in a deceased togden's hut, perched high on a mountainside, facing a box festooned with lights in which his body has been preserved in herbs.

I will once more be reminded of a mountain cave in that space, isolated and womb-like, though it is only a tiny room with a view of the Himalayas. Here, Yogi Amtrin spent decades in 'self-willing' silence, meditating on 'voidness'. I will sit down on a mat and find the dreadlocked yogi watching me from a photograph. And I will know this is what you look like when you have spent all your life quieting the mind. Gentle, wise, still, a deep pool creased only with the ripple of a smile. I will smile back, close my eyes, focus on my breath, and try to empty my mind...

One can imagine Tenzin Palmo's excitement when, after all the misogyny, she chanced upon a tradition where women were equal practitioners of the 'Path Profound'. Because the togden tradition has been preserved, all one needs are enough women who will take up the challenge of a lifetime spent in retreat, snow lionesses unafraid of spending their lives at the summit of spiritual endeavour. 'We hope some of them will show the ability to be trained as togdenma,' she says. 'We are also hoping that nuns, with their practice and educational background, will be able to become teachers.'

Training women to become teachers and ascend to positions of spiritual and intellectual power is fundamental to the task of correcting the skew towards male authority figures in religions. A greater number of women teachers would serve as visible, positive role models for other women, and do far more for their self-image and esteem than assertions of equal potential of Buddha-hood that tend to sound hollow in the absence of any historically recorded, venerated, female Buddhas. In Tibetan Buddhism, particularly, great women practitioners have almost always been 'hidden' yoginis, never properly recorded or discussed or followed, so that when stories about them did become known, they almost always sounded like supernatural myths rather than credible accounts of a practitioner's journey. This garb of fantasy may have done a disservice to the cause of women by laying their spiritual quests open to charges of irrationality and disbelief, and one wonders about the solidity of inspiration or example they could have provided other women practitioners with.

Tenzin Palmo testifies to the power of example with an incident from her own time in the cave. A book was published in 1984 which, for the first time, attempted to document the lives of historical women practitioners of Tibet. It was written in English by Tsultrim Allione, an American woman whose early life mirrored Tenzin Palmo's, until she gave back her nun's vows to get married and have children and find her path in the babble of samsara, almost at the same time that Tenzin Palmo had retreated into a cave. *Women of Wisdom* became a revolutionary guidebook for postmodern, post-feminist women who came to the dharma and were bewildered by the lack of iconic women ancestresses, teachers and authority figures. In selecting actual women as her subjects, in whose narratives the powerful and plentiful feminine deities of Tibetan Buddhism played supportive rather than central roles, author Tsultrim Allione influenced a shift from the make-believe towards the real. While not failing to acknowledge the obvious value of the former, her book served to strengthen the credibility of the latter.

When I spoke with Tsultrim in 2007, some months after my conversation with Tenzin Palmo, she told me that *Women of Wisdom* actually grew out of her own search for the 'women's way', for a spirituality that integrated specific feminine experiences, like motherhood, into the practice of the path. When her own children were born, Tsultrim had immediately recognized the potential of motherhood as an effective means for challenging the ego-self. The problem was that no text or teacher spoke about it as such.

'If it was 99 per cent women writing Buddhist texts instead of 99 per cent men, then some of those women certainly would have written about and delineated motherhood as a path,' she said. Tsultrim took on the task of excavating feminine role models, the 'women of wisdom' in Tibetan Buddhism and, in telling their stories, found a way to create her own dharma path through the joys, confusions and conflicts of marriage and motherhood. 'The process of finding the stories and writing *Women of Wisdom*—for me personally that work, that challenge, was a tremendous development and it was very healing to me,' she said.

A friend sent a chapter from this groundbreaking book to Tenzin Palmo in her cave. It told the story of A-Yu Khadro, a yogini who was 113 years old in 1951, when she was interviewed by Namkhai Norbu Rinpoche. Namkhai Norbu was then a fourteen-year-old, sent by his teacher to A-Yu Khadro to learn from her. When Namkhai Norbu left Tibet, A-Yu Khadro's story travelled with him around the world and one day fell into the hands of Tsultrim, who was collecting stories of the wise women of Tibet, which is how it came to be preserved.

'A-Yu Khadro and her companions wandered all around Tibet,' recounts Tenzin Palmo, 'to various pilgrimage places and cremation grounds, doing Chöd. Chöd is a ritual-cum-psychological technique designed to cut away attachment to the body and the ego-self. 'They met with all the great lamas of the late nineteenth century and received teachings from them, often personal teachings, because obviously these lamas thought them to be extraordinary. A number of her companions, when they died, attained the "rainbow body".' This is a sign of a great practitioner—when the physical body is said to dissolve at the moment of death into light, a rainbow appears, and only the hair and nails are left behind.

It can safely be conjectured that A-Yu Khadro was neither the first nor the last nor the only woman practitioner in Tibet of such exceptional merit. Yet nobody would know of her if it weren't for a curious teenager who would subsequently be cast adrift into the world by an unexpected turn of events.

Tenzin Palmo concurs. 'A-Yu Khadro spent years and years in dark retreats, and was astonishing as a practitioner. But who has heard of her? And she must have been one amongst so many. We know of her because it happened that Namkhai Norbu asked her for her story. Normally, nobody would have done that, and there would have been no trace of her. So there are a number of these women who nobody ever wrote about because they didn't build big monasteries, they weren't high lineage holders, and so they weren't regarded as being worth writing about. Undoubtedly for women who feel they need inspiration, these are great examples.'

Was A-Yu Khadro an example for her too, in her cave in the snow? 'It reduced me to tears, partly because she was such an incredible woman, and partly out of despair because how could one ever hope to emulate someone like this!' she exclaims. I can almost picture Tenzin Palmo, alone, poring over the only printed matter she has seen in years, to find rising from it a co-journey, a mirror half, a doppelganger of a quest that ran through mountain and cave, ritual and practice, to infiltrate peaks cordoned off by the glass ceiling, to what could possibly be a fullness, a fulfilment?

A thought occurs to me: If a woman had already become a Buddha, or did in the future, would she simply be missed? Overlooked, ignored? When a tree falls in the forest, as the Zen koan asks, does it really make a noise if nobody hears it?

'These women were there... these women were there,' murmurs Tenzin Palmo, the handful we know of indicating the possibility of many more, the vast unknown iceberg that lingers below the tip, below the surface of our collective consciousness.

—

By choosing the way of the independent, unaffiliated free spirit, the snow lioness who roams in splendid isolation, the yoginis circumvented both bondage to patriarchal social gender roles and the yoke of second-class spiritual citizenship that kept ordained women from making much headway on the path. I would like to think they redefined the meaning of the term 'marginalized', that they thrived and came into their own *because* they were on the margins, and therefore free to sing their own song. In the secret life of spiritual endeavouring, this is often the case. What is of consequence happens outside the mainstream of religion and society, in unseen crevices and margins, in silence and solitude.

As an activist, Tenzin Palmo would like some of this free-spirited marginalization to seep into the mainstream, for the yogini's spiritual self-assuredness to permeate the life of the nun, the working woman, the homemaker, the mother. She puts the onus for this squarely on women themselves, for strong women will compel religion, and society, to change. The status quo will remain stolid and static until somebody changes it. And the impetus for this change must come from women rather than it being 'given' to them, if it has to have the kind of impact that would give greater meaning to their lives. Tenzin Palmo's now famous vow, to become enlightened in *this* body, was the beginning of the storm that would stir the turgid misogyny of Tibetan Buddhism, shake things up and begin the process of creating them anew. Her efforts with nuns are a widening of that vow, from one to many, to ignite in newer generations of women the dream of an empowered, enlightened femininity.

Things are already beginning to change. The delay in the biggest issue of all, that of full ordination for women, has not stopped the nuns from effecting small changes that are gradually changing the landscape of Tibetan Buddhism. 'It is a two-way thing,' says Tenzin Palmo as she explains how women are claiming their place in the dharma sun, inch by inch, footstep by footstep. 'As the nuns themselves are more educated and gain more confidence, the lamas begin to respect them more, and are more open and willing to give them teachings and instructions. If you are dealing as a lama with a group of nuns who have lots of devotion but don't really know what you are talking about, then you are not really inclined to teach them. Once the nuns have had basic dharma education and understanding, they are more likely to come forward to offer to teach them. This is what is happening. So the whole attitude of how you treat a nun is changing, even within the monasteries.'

Big changes usually come in the wake of a series of small, crack-in-the-edifice ones that do the crucial spadework of influencing attitudes. Sometimes it is just a matter of the way things have always been done, and continue to be done, because nobody has thought twice about them or questioned their legitimacy or rationale. Those of us who live in tradition-bound societies often witness this, and are complicit in an unthinking continuation of systems and values. When we become conscious of their import, their true meaning, and the effect they have on us and those around us, only then can we discern their actual significance and choose to follow them or not, in a form that we find acceptable.

For instance, in India, most of us who fall within the swathe of Hinduism are born into the caste matrix which has rules to govern every moment of our lives—how we eat, bathe, study, interact with others, work, worship, marry, die. Too many Hindus follow these strictures blindly, or as much as is suitable to them, without particularly questioning their need or relevance in a twenty-first century, postmodern world. Those who question will be a minority. It is they who are most likely to nurture the seeds of a positive, required change.

Tenzin Palmo is one such questioner who has sowed the seeds of change not just in the minds of nuns, but into the very heart of Tibetan Buddhism. She tells me the story of a seemingly small change that marks 'a big development in their (the establishment's) mind's perception'. It is the kind of change that can have a huge incremental impact, like tornados created by wind patterns set in motion by a delicate flutter of a butterfly's wings. 'Last year, at the end of one of the long pujas that the monks do, they were going to have a blessing by the head lamas,' says Tenzin Palmo, animated and excited. 'Normally the nuns wait outside with the lay people for the Rinpoches to come out. But then we got a call from Khamtrul Rinpoche saying that the nuns should be in the temple. So I herded them in.'

As the monks saw the nuns coming, they began to roll up the mats on which they had been sitting. Tenzin Palmo interceded.

'The nuns are here now,' she pointed out.

'But the mats can be sat on only by monks,' was the reply.

Tenzin Palmo was not about to give up.

'These are Khamtrul Rinpoche's nuns,' she said, 'and Rinpoche asked them to come. Are they supposed to sit on the bare ground?'

Tradition was trotted out once more, the ever present refuge of the unquestioning mind.

'Oh, but this is the Khampagar custom.'

'Well,' said Tenzin Palmo, 'Now we have a new custom. Monks *and* nuns can sit on the mats.'

Who blinked first in this tussle between tradition and change?

'The monks looked at each other, shrugged, and rolled out the mats!' laughs Tenzin Palmo. 'Now when we go in, the mats are already laid out ready for the nuns and the monks are even giving the nuns texts so that they can join in certain parts of the pujas. So, more and more nuns are being accepted as part of the sangha. I mean, they still sit at the back, but they are accepted as part of the assembly. Slowly, the monks are accepting the nuns as being, if not their equals, at least worthy of some kind of attention.'

Does the fact of Tenzin Palmo's 'otherness', her having come into Tibetan Buddhism from the outside, from a culture where women had already begun to find their equal space in the sun in the post-war years when she was growing up, place her in a unique position as an interrogator of tradition? The issue I speak of is two-fold. One, women who grow up in patriarchy are more liable to fall into stereotypical gender roles than women who come in from the outside, who would have perhaps a different vision, and for whom the genuflection to patriarchal norms would be distasteful and unthinkable. Two, the 'feminine intruder' will not only have a perspective with which to discern injustice, she will also have a language, an idiom to place it in and question it. The mats must have been folded up a million times when the nuns arrived, only, nobody questioned it. Tenzin Palmo did. And thus, patterns began to subtly change, each question, each challenge setting in motion whispering winds that could potentially grow into a tornado of positive change.

As a dharma practitioner ever mindful of the seduction of ego-fulfilment, Tenzin Palmo refuses to consider herself important to this process, brushing it aside with a casual, 'Who knows? I don't think about it.' I persist, curious about her understanding of the way social structures influence a woman's goals, of what she thinks is doable, believable. Can a woman whose spiritual journey has been circumscribed by patriarchy really think of enlightenment as the ultimate aim in the same way a man can?

'Can a man? I mean, honestly and truthfully, how many people get fully enlightened?' Tenzin Palmo's reaction is quick, razor sharp. And yet, she was the one who vowed enlightenment as a woman. 'Yes, the nuns can hope to definitely get genuine spiritual realizations and experiences. Definitely they can hope they can transform their minds and obtain a definite nondualistic perception of reality. Absolutely. There is no difference between male or female. Definitely they can hope that at the time of death, they will die in a very auspicious manner and go up. To become a fully enlightened Buddha, radiating thirty-metre lights all around you, who does?'

It is clear that she no longer holds on to that vow, made in the heat of her frustration with the barbed wire of misogyny that sought to lock her into a gendered space where her body was her prison. Many years filled with much solitude and patient practice have flown by, and with them, she too has flowed and surged, welled and withered, charged and changed. An ever present, conscious non-grasping, a letting go of pleasure and pain gradually dissolved the rock-hard ego-self into a fluid core being that no longer *sticks* to anything, not even to vows to attain enlightenment.

I feel her innate fluidity, her non-wanting, but surely what she says can be mistaken for a letting go because the goal was too difficult, simply out of reach? Even if we can't actually become Buddhas, surely that can be an aim to fuel the spiritual journey?

'Well, it's a curious thing because they all agree that the next Buddha is Maitreya,' she says, pointing to a myth beloved to most schools of Buddhism. 'And he is not coming for 2,500 years. In the meantime, to become realized is one thing and to become fully, totally enlightened is another. To be completely enlightened, I mean, even the Dalai Lama doesn't claim that, nobody does. Even the greatest lama, even the Karmapa, doesn't.'

How would she define the difference between *realization* and *enlightenment*?

In response, Tenzin Palmo uses the metaphor of a clear mirror for the enlightened mind, a quality we all have intrinsically, only, it is overlaid with ignorance and incorrect ways of knowing that cover the original luminescence like a thick layer of dust. 'When we look at the mind, all we see is thick dust. We don't see the bright, clear, mirror-like reflection. Now, you get a pin and you make a little hole through that dust, and you reach the mirror, and you see there's a mirror underneath the dust. That's an incredible breakthrough. You suddenly realize you are not dust. That bright clear shining mirror *is* there. But you still got all the dust over the mirror. And until we have wiped away absolutely every single speck of dust, we are not a Buddha. There are many levels of a bodhisattva, but to become an actual Buddha means not even a speck of dust is left. There are many levels of more and more dust being removed, of more mirror and less dust. But until there is no dust at all and no possibility of dust falling again, you are not completely there.'

While it may be rare to wipe away every mote of dust and become fully enlightened, different levels of clarity, the mirror shining through in bits and pieces, are goalposts on the path to nirvana that each spiritual practitioner, irrespective of gender, can aspire towards.

In the light of this moment ignited by the fire of the jewel of true knowing, where the mind is genderless and free, what does she make of that lama from long ago who told her there was no intrinsic benefit in being a woman? As a woman practitioner of the dharma, has she managed to uncover anything about her gender that might actually be considered an advantage on the path?

Tenzin Palmo smiles at the memory, and perhaps, at how much of her frustration she has allowed to ebb away, holding on to nothing, not even justified anger. 'I think all the lamas are saying—we all have Buddhanature. It is neither male nor female. If you have the opportunity here to study and practise, there is nothing you cannot achieve in a female body. Having a female body is no impediment at all provided you have the opportunity, which you do have. So go for it. They (the nuns) hear this again and again. On one level they take it in. One of the things for women is that they often have tremendously strong devotion. They really have a lot of faith. So by educating them, we are trying to make sure their faith is not blind and that they understand what they have faith in.'

Is faith, then, a negative on a path such as the Buddha's dharma that brings so much of the scientist's rational, practical, testable-in-a-laboratory sort of rigour to inner practice? For faith appears to be wrapped in the muslin of irrationality, with the aroma of the unknown, the indescribable, of spontaneous unreason if you will, clinging to its folds. In common language, faith is a matter of the heart, and it is assumed that it therefore must preclude logic. Nobody follows a step-by-step path to faith; it is born in your heart for reasons you usually cannot quite pinpoint, and it draws on the energy of emotion for sustenance. Perhaps it is this connection with emotionality that places faith in a dodgy position as far as women are concerned, for they are known to have a precarious relationship with emotionality and it is what their occasionally volcanic hearts and tumultuous moods are attributed to.

Tenzin Palmo places women's emotionality in a different context, one that comes from consciously cultivating its transformation from a potentially destructive force to a constructive, a spiritual asset no less. 'A number of teachers bring this subject up with me, I don't. They have mentioned this in different ways. Somebody said that women's minds are naturally more volatile, they go up and down much more. This could be a disadvantage. But if they could learn to control that and use that force, then they go much faster and higher than men.'

She recollects the great Burmese meditation master, Sayadaw U Pandita, telling her, 'Actually speaking, women are better at meditation than men. I have many women, even laywomen, who are far better at meditation than monks. And the reason is that women feel at ease within the intuitive. Most men have the kind of mind that likes to analyse and keep their feet on the ground.'

This is interesting—the prioritizing of the intuitive over the analytical in meditation. I think what is being pointed towards is an ability to make a leap, of faith or of the heart, into the unknown inner world that confronts us when we begin to meditate. Sometimes there is a jumble of emotions and at others, a roaring whirlpool of thoughts and ideas. To retain the sliver of awareness in all of this, perhaps one has to stop judging, expecting, wanting, guiding. 'The men don't want to jump, they want to go step by step,' explains Tenzin Palmo. 'Eventually they will get there, but will be much slower. Women are much happier to *just do it*. Therefore they get the realization much faster.'

Emotionality, apart from acting as a portal to the intuitive aspects of our beings, is also the Vajrayana practitioner's doorway to the constructive emotions that act as powerful antidotes to afflictive emotions, and which must therefore be actively cultivated. Isn't it possible that women, who have an easier access to their emotionality, could also be better equipped for the yoga of transforming it into a spiritual tool? For instance, one needn't tell a woman to love like a mother loves her only child—a metaphor used to describe the quality of a bodhisattva's intense compassion for suffering sentient beings.

'Yes, but without the attachment,' Tenzin Palmo interjects. 'That's the problem for women—attachment. To learn to love as a mother loves her only child, but without the clinging, that is what the Buddha said. Then you've got it. Women need to learn and understand how not to cling. Keep that love, have that love that you really wish for the well-being of the other, without wondering if the other is going to give happiness to us. Just want that happiness for the other.' She remembers her mother, who never tried to hold her back from her quest, who 'always understood I have to live this life, and she was just happy she had been able to bring me up so that I was prepared to do that'. There was never any hint of 'emotional blackmail', any attempt to draw her daughter back to herself to fulfil any need she might have had.

Monastics who leave their families behind have to contend with a certain measure of guilt, often because of the burden of unfulfilled expectations that is thrust upon them by disappointed family members. The kind of unconditional love which her mother embodied demonstrated to Tenzin Palmo the power of true love to set one free. 'Attachment keeps you in samsara. But love doesn't keep you in samsara. Love liberates. And we confuse the two, because we have such an impoverished language when it comes to love. I love my children, I love ice cream! And we get confused also. We think love means attachment, that the more we cling, the more we love. It's not love at all. That's just self-love, because this person makes us feel happy. Love really means I want you to be happy. Attachment means I want you to make me happy.'

It is this duality, this Janus-faced nature of emotionality that makes it a double-edged sword that cuts both ways, a fact that was harnessed by Tantra in the cause of quick spiritual progress, for combating a negative emotion by accessing and bringing into play its mirror opposite. While other spiritual traditions tried to weed negative emotions out individually by negating them, Tantra, especially Vajrayana, used its mirror emotion to accomplish the deed, like a thorn that is used to gouge out another thorn wedged in one's flesh. Or a poison used in a small dose to counteract another. So, mindfully cultivating compassion will counter clinging and self-cherishing; experiencing happiness in the happiness of others will dispel the thorn of jealousy, and so on.

Emotionality thus became a tool, an aid, but only when one knew how to effect the crucial transformation from negative to positive, as Tenzin Palmo cautions. 'Merely great emotionality in itself is not the path, it will not liberate us. It will only happen if we are genuinely capable of (she claps her hands) transforming it, seeing through to its essentially empty nature. That releases the spiritual energy, instead of the very heavy energy that pulls us down. It could go either way. But Tantra is certainly not a vehicle of licence, which is why in Tibet most of its practitioners were monks.'

What about women? Were they ever entrusted with Tantra? 'It seems this happened more in India. Often you read stories of Mahasiddhas where their teachers were women, but you don't hear who they were because the emphasis is always on this male Mahasiddha and not on the women around him. Who were these women? They were definitely there. In Tibet, there were these women practitioners at quite high levels. But again, you don't know what they were practising and who they were.' Again, the problem of recording herstory, of women's voices finding their own space, the lack of more *Therigatha*-like compendiums of women's perspectives.

What *was* written down, in the form of scriptures and commentaries, perpetuated a view of women that was coloured twice over by misogyny—one that came from being part of patriarchy, and another that was a result of enforced, as opposed to conscious, celibacy. My conjecture is that it is easier to keep away from something you have vilified, and for the celibate monks, women, whose company and presence was taboo for them, came to represent all that was negative and therefore to be shunned. Women were more prone to afflictive emotions, they said, almost as if women could infect them with anger, jealousy, and... 'And lust!' exclaims Tenzin Palmo. 'I love that. I mean, it is said women are so lustful and lascivious. All the millions of prostitutes in the world, who are they for, if women are so unable to control themselves? Human beings naturally have the five poisons and some have them in bigger doses than others. I think for some women, who are within a very narrow structure like a house and never go out much and nothing much is happening, it could be that their emotions become stronger because they don't have any release. Whereas men are going out and meeting people and have much more of an outlet. But if left to themselves, in their nature, I don't think women are especially prone to these emotions or defilements. Who writes the books? Who is writing all this? Who starts the wars? All these big businesses, who is running that?'

As somebody who lives in a community of women, Tenzin Palmo asserts from experience that women actually work very well together in harmony. 'I don't think if women were in charge on the whole, and were really relaxed within their female roles and not trying to compete with the men, that most of them would choose not to be in harmony. They tend to be, on the whole, more harmonious. Watching the nuns, they work together very nicely and enjoy it. There is no screaming or shouting or jealousy or uncontrolled emotions of any sort. They are on the whole happy little puppies!'

We smile at what I presume are concurrent mental images of the young nuns as playful puppies, just as some of them emerge in the sun in the large quadrangle in front of the nunnery. Okay, so some of the texts that were written during the long and eventful history of Buddhism became contaminated by misogyny for various reasons, but what about the core teachings? Are they untouched by the tar brush that painted women in monochromatic, denigrating terms?

'The teachings themselves, especially the meditation teachings, are not geared in any direction. They are gender neutral because they are basically, certainly in the Kagyu Nyingma tradition, dealing with the mind and the nature of the mind. And how to become more conscious of our thoughts and our inner world, and how to see beyond the thoughts to our unborn awareness. That's not male or female. There are certain texts that seem to have been put down for women but they are written by monks who were frightened of anything female. So naturally they project their fear onto the women. But you can see through that. You don't have to get caught up in that. These references occur mostly in the commentaries: the Buddha doesn't talk about it. On the whole, the teachings are relevant to everyone. They are analysing what is ignorance and how to get beyond that to realize your natural wisdom-mind. Even though in Tibetan Buddhism, the perfection of wisdom is female!'

Yes, I exclaim, Prajna-paramita, the mother of the Buddhas, the essence of understanding, the womb of wisdom in which insight is born. Wisdom itself is neither male nor female. What has been her personal experience in dharma practice? How deep do the roots of gender go into the soil of the mind? Where does form end and formlessness begin?

'When you are really sitting and meditating properly, there is no male or female,' she says. 'You are not even thinking about that. It does not even exist. And we all, male or female, have our innate ignorance, and from that our greed and aggression and jealousies. Some have more, others less, depending on the personality. But we all have the same problems to deal with. As thoughts come up, we recognize whether they are skilful or not skilful. Male or female, it makes no difference. In the end, we are all dealing with our very deluded frame of mind to transform it into something that embodies wisdom and compassion.'

Broadly speaking, the Madhyamika (middle way) branch of Buddhist philosophy explains the dichotomy most of us feel between teachings of spiritual truths and our own everyday experience of reality, by using a dual explanation of reality. Ultimate Reality is *the way things are*, the core truth that is omnipresent if occluded by our everyday sense of reality, which is termed Conventional Reality, *the way things appear to us to be*. Perhaps gender is an issue of conventional reality, the view that we are stuck with until we have polished the mirror sufficiently for it to reflect the actual truth.

At the level of Ultimate Reality, gender doesn't matter, it doesn't exist, the Buddha-mind is neither male nor female. But at the level of conventional reality, there is a need for women to find their own balance with the path and its practice. Tenzin Palmo agrees. In the matter of actual practice, 'sometimes women like to get together because it gives a kind of energy and they like to practise together. They can also talk about things that they can't in men's company because it upsets the men. This is nice, we should support each other all the way. In the end, as human beings, we have much the same problems to deal with. If it is not one thing it is another. The point is just to get on and deal with it.'

There remains the matter of the Buddha Sakyamuni's initial hesitation to let women in, which perhaps cast a more lasting shadow on women in Buddhism than any other text written afterwards. Every woman who walks this path, even now, must contend with that original stain, especially somebody like Tenzin Palmo who has been involved in issues of gender inequality within the sangha.

'It seems that the Buddha originally was not very excited at the thought of women becoming nuns,' she acknowledges. 'And we don't know why. But my feeling is that it is because it was his stepmother, Mahaprajapati, who at that time was of a fairly advanced age. She was a court lady brought up in luxury who, along with a large number of her court women, arrived wearing ragged robes, barefoot, in a terrible state. This was a time before monks lived in monasteries. What was he going to do with these poor women? As we know, they didn't have the protection of a nunnery in those early days, so it was dangerous to have women wandering around just like that. Why? Because of the men! In the *Vinaya*, there are accounts of nuns being raped because they are very vulnerable. And I can understand that the Buddha hesitated to let them go forth.

'Also, monks and nuns traditionally depend on alms rounds. If a person had only a limited amount of food and she had a choice, she would almost certainly give it to the monk because he is male and should be served first, and the idea is that it would be more meritorious to give it to him than to give to the nun. So, throughout history, nuns have had a tough time because people don't think it is sufficiently meritorious to give to them. Women are often not very supportive of other women. I think the Buddha foresaw that it would be difficult for the nuns to survive. Of course, now we have 60,000 fully ordained nuns around the world. So they did survive.'

Yes, they did, and even as we speak, they are right outside our window, throwing their hands up in the air and bringing them back down with a resounding thwack of the palms in the famous gesture of Tibetan debate, as they question one another on the intricacies of philosophy. Women have survived, nuns have survived, into this new century where they can take wing and fly. I am suddenly filled with an un-Buddhist irrational thought—I wish the Buddha could have seen these nuns, *his* nuns, right this moment—confident, self-assured, rosy-cheeked with excitement. His hesitation would surely melt away instantly, like snow around a tumo-practising yogini.

Our conversation about women in dharma has centred on nuns and their issues for obvious reasons, because Tenzin Palmo is an ordained woman and is concerned with changing their status quo.

If one were to step back and look at the resurgence of Buddhism in recent times and the rise of a sangha of its newest practitioners in the West, one might observe that the centre of gravity seems to be shifting away from a monastic-oriented discipline. Now, more than ever before in its history, people are coming to the Buddha's dharma for a lot more than just religion. They want answers to their existential dilemmas, mindful ways to live in an era shot through by materialistic frenzy, tools to quieten the mind that are longer-lasting than Prozac, for a non-theistic code of ethics, for depth and meaning. What they may not necessarily be looking for is commitment to a life of wandering homelessness and voluntary poverty.

Tenzin Palmo's own example points towards the importance of ordination for practitioners, and the significance of the solitary 'cave experience'. Yet, with the influx of serious practitioners who are householders, including women with careers and children, isn't the traditional life of contemplation challenged, and newer models required that will accommodate householders' needs more skilfully and holistically? Is the cave becoming obsolete, in a way?

'Ninety-nine per cent of people interested in spirituality these days are not monks and nuns, especially in the West. And if the dharma has any relevance at all, it must be relevant for everybody. One of the problems is that people sometimes think that spiritual life means meditation. But that is only one component, and there are so many other components. In Buddhadharma, there are six *paramita* or perfections—generosity (giving, openness of heart), ethical conduct, patience under provocation, energy needed to bring your life in harmony with the spiritual path and then meditation and the wisdom that arises from it.

'Anything we do is dharma practice, provided we bring our attention to it properly. Being a mother and a wife is very much a dharma practice if one uses one's intelligence. Where do you need more generosity, patience and so on than when bringing up a child? All these qualities are needed for the heart to open up. It is not just a matter of sitting on a cushion, meditating.

And learning how to be present, how to be here. Whatever we are doing can be a dharma practice. Either we are present or we are not. It doesn't matter whether we are in a monastery or workplace or home, it is the same. The mind is the same. The mind doesn't have a shaved head!'

For centuries, official dharma practice did have a shaved head, and to be a serious practitioner on the Buddha's path more often than not meant formal ordination. The emphasis on practising core teachings, as Tenzin Palmo has stressed, as opposed to taking the vows and robes of a renunciate, is another aspect of this new turning of the wheel of dharma. After a long period of ossifying into just another religion, Buddhism has an opportunity to rediscover its essence, its roots, go back to its basics—the nuts and bolts of spiritual practice—and weed out the junk of politics, misogyny, hierarchy and power play. This twist in the dharma's tale brings a fresh lease of life to the core teachings of the Buddha, and a chance to test them on the touchstone of today and discover their meaning anew, in our context(s). The Western sangha is largely responsible for this challenge, for providing the impetus for this de-ossification that has spread back to traditional Buddhist societies as well.

One of the challenges for non-cultural Buddhists is to separate the dharma from the culture it came wrapped up in. The culture, which is merely the vessel, is often mistaken for the truth. Tenzin Palmo recognizes the potential danger of mistaking the vessel for its contents. For her, Buddhism came boxed in what another contemporary master, Dzongsar Khyentse Rinpoche, has referred to as 'Tibetanism', the clinging to the outer symbols of a culture and mistaking it for the dharma.

'I think it is important to remember when I take up Tibetan Buddhism that I am not a Tibetan,' says Tenzin Palmo. 'A lot of Tibetan Buddhism is cultural and sociological, and you have to adopt it to a certain extent because you are living within that environment. But I don't want to be a Tibetan. I don't favour butter tea over cappuccino—both are nice in their contexts. By shaving your head and putting on your robes, you don't change.

You don't have to take up everything because that is what the Tibetans do. The culture is like a cup, a container for the elixir of dharma, but it is not the elixir. We don't want to end up worshipping the cup. That cup is necessary for holding the elixir, but it is only a cup. You could pour the elixir into anything—a glass, a tumbler, anything. It is important not to mix up the two.' This is a message Western Buddhism needs to hear, and Tenzin Palmo, who straddles both East and West in her being, is a perfect conveyor of it.

The nuns have retreated with the last warmth of the sun, and the quadrangle lies empty in the encroaching twilight. As Tenzin Palmo speaks of the distinction between the vessel and its contents, I think of how, for her, the formlessness of form has been a recurring refrain, a theme song that plays out in her life ever so often. She has realized the inherent emptiness of form, whether it is the form of the body or culture or scripture. She has incessantly searched for the core, rather than becoming stuck in the outer garb. In her body yet out of it, in the world yet not of it, in the thick of the gender debate yet beyond the form of her self.

As our conversation draws to a close, Tenzin Palmo goes over to the glass doors that let the Himalayas into the room. Peering at the construction work going on in the nunnery, she mentions how she would love to see all this completed. I think I detect a yearning for the cave, for a return to the life of contemplation. When I get up to leave, she puts her arm around me in an unexpected gesture of warmth. Her eyes are quiet and deep once more.

Right here beside me, she *is* in her cave—in quiet awareness of her innermost reality.

8

Rinpoche, Re-imaginer, Re-creator

KHANDRO RINPOCHE

Imagine, you are a man... You are interested in meditation and Buddhism. You approach a beautiful Tibetan-style temple. Taking off your shoes, you enter.

And there you see her on the wall across from the entrance: Buddha Tara on a beautiful Tibetan mural... Of course, you recall, the Buddha was female. All of the thousand teacher-Buddhas of our fortunate age are women or so the tradition would have it. On the thangka, she is surrounded by sixteen of her closest disciples, the sixteen Arhantis, liberated, free women...

You are lucky. Today a famous Buddhist woman teacher will give a lecture. You wait with hundreds of others for the arrival of the 14th Dalai Lama, winner of the Nobel Prize for Peace and beloved leader of the Tibetan people. You know that the Dalai Lamas are the incarnation of the Lotus Goddess, the manifestation of love and compassion on earth, always in a female body. The Dalai Lama is accompanied by high dignitaries, each of whom, like their honoured leader, has decided for centuries to reincarnate as a female for the well-being of all living beings.

Now the Buddhist nuns enter, strong, self-confident, beautiful women in shimmering red and yellow robes. They are led respectfully into the places reserved for them in the first rows. The monks scurry in behind them. A little shy and ashamed, they take their places in the back...

The Dalai Lama's lecture is enlightening and inspiring. You feel that you have been understood in the deepest sense. You feel good in this circle of people striving for insight and love. But something bothers you. Probably, it is your 'ego'...

Imagine now—remember, you are a male—you turn to a female Buddhist teacher the next chance you get... 'I value the teachings and the practices of Buddhism very highly but why are there almost only women who teach? Why are the teaching Buddhas always women? Why do the nuns sit in the first rows and the monks behind them?' The honourable nun... looks somewhat surprised but at the same time very compassionate and says: 'Young man, don't worry about this. Sex and gender play (almost) no role along the spiritual path. Practise, and then all problems will resolve themselves.'

'Yes, but why are there only female teachers?' you ask further. 'Well, in some scriptures it is written that a male reincarnation has less value than a female reincarnation. However, that does not mean that men are discriminated against. That is only a compassionate description of the social reality. It is simply more difficult for men; their lives are full of strain and work. I will pray that you are reincarnated as a woman in your next life. Then it will be easier for you. You can also pray for a female reincarnation.'

You... meditate tenaciously and with dedication. At times, you experience moments in which sex and gender really play no role—in your meditation and on your pillow. But almost every time you attend a lecture, open a book or hear a story, a woman is the central figure, surrounded by a squad of young women or men, who serve her with dedication.

Then a famous woman lama, a tantric yogini, comes to your city… Once again, you… ask: 'I honour and treasure Buddhism, but how do I fit as a man in this women's religion…' The tantric lama beams at you charmingly and opines…: 'Don't worry young man. You are a wonderful and valuable person. You are a wonderful Daka (masculine for 'Dakini'). You can help us women to awaken our kundalini-power and thus to become enlightened to the welfare of all beings.'

With that, our fantasy-trip ends.

(from *Heart of the Lotus: Women and Buddhism* by Sylvia Wetzel, translated from the German by Jane Anhold)

This poignant visualization was created by the German teacher and campaigner for women's rights in Buddhism, Sylvia Wetzel, and presented to the Dalai Lama and other participants during the first Western Buddhism conference in Dharamsala in 1993. By grafting what is commonly a woman's experience in Buddhism onto a man, she attempted to help male leaders connect with women's plight in what has become, for all practical purposes, a 'masculine religion'. Which, despite its fundamental egalitarianism and belief in nirvana for all, has become a hotbed of 'spiritual sexism', the most obvious symptoms being a lack of female teachers and role models and a dearth of equal opportunities for women practitioners.

The current debate on gender in Buddhism has largely been initiated by the dharma's adherents in the West, who continue to provide much of the fuel to enable a process of change towards a new order that is more supportive of women's spiritual aspirations. This is not to say that women 'from the East', traditional or 'cultural' Buddhists, have not joined in and raised their voices alongside their sisters in other parts of the world. Indeed, they form crucial contingents in intercultural, intra-Buddhist dialogues where they are able to provide a bridge between tradition and culture and the processes of questioning and change.

It has been my experience that when women speak from within their contexts, when they interrogate the parent culture that has shaped their consciousness of themselves and of the world around them, the process is far more complex and filled with a grey, curved ambiguity, rather than sharp distinctions between this and that, right and wrong. Closeness distorts vision and makes it harder to focus. It also ensures that one remains aware of one's interconnection with the object of one's scrutiny, and is able to bring what one knows of its nuances and undercurrents into the course of questioning and, if possible, extend it to a re-imagining, a re-creating.

After listening to Jetsunma Tenzin Palmo's passionate insights, and the groundbreaking efforts of dharma activists like Sylvia Wetzel to sensitize the dharma to its at-times overwhelming masculinity, I am curious for an 'insider's view', of somebody who was born into the dharma, so to speak. Would it be worse for such a woman because she didn't really have the means and the language to put the dharma in the dock? Or would it be easier because she knew the system, which might also mean she had the facility to subvert it? Would she feel the same degree of frustration that led a thwarted Tenzin Palmo to vow to attain enlightenment as a woman? Or would she be accepting, like Mahaprajapati, and try and make the best of what she got?

So I set off with my trusted, well-worn bag of questions, a few more miles stretch before my dusty feet. I once again head to the Himalayas, to their foothills rather, to Dehradun, recent capital of a new state, a development that has thrown the once charming hill town into a tizzy of construction and unfortunate tree-felling.

My destination is thankfully well beyond the official limits of the city and its congestion, noise and pollution, near a suburb encircled by thick forest and an army cantonment. This minor township with a quaint colonial name, Clement Town, is the seat-in-exile of the Mindrolling Trichen, head of a dharma lineage in Tibet's Nyingma school of Buddhism. It is also home, and refuge, to a Tibetan community whose vibrant chaos accentuates the suddenness of order that greets one upon entering the gates of the monastic complex. The lawns are neat, the hedges trimmed, the lanes devoid of any maroon-robed presence in what I imagine is mid-afternoon siesta time. A singular structure, 185 feet tall as I later discover, looms ahead in pristine white glory. From the crown of its façade, the Buddhas of this age and the next regard me with wakeful watchfulness. Beyond, a pine forest strains at the barbwired boundary walls, unruly branches stretching muddy fingers towards the perfection of this dharma oasis.

Like so many Tibetan institutions set up in India in exile, the Mindrolling monastic complex is a reflection, a yearning echo, of the original in Tibet's Dapchi Valley, whose spirit departed in 1959 when the then twenty-nine-year-old custodian of its spiritual wealth—a stash of teachings, initiations and practice disciplines—left for India. The eleventh Mindrolling throne holder, Trichen Jurme Kunzang Wangyal, lived for some years in Kalimpong. In 1972, when this complex on the outskirts of Dehradun was established, he moved in with his retinue of family, teachers and monks.

The Mindrolling lineage is part of a tradition in Tibetan Buddhism that is unheard of in non-Tantric Buddhism, where the prime holder of the lineage is not a celibate monk, but a yogi. He enters into marriage with a *sangyum,* 'secret consort', and what is essentially a dharma lineage is preserved and perpetuated through an unbroken bloodline and not by reincarnation. Like everything hereditary in patriarchy, this bloodline is male, passing from sons in one generation to another, almost as if it were encoded in the male XY genome. If there are no sons in any generation, the onus of producing them for the future falls on the daughters. Though at one level this non-celibate system could be considered inclusive and accepting of women, at another it could also foster a 'son anxiety' that devalues women.

When I walk into the orderly world of Mindrolling in July 2006, a whiff of impending change is in the air. Things are as if poised at tipping point, at the cusp between an end and a beginning. A new turn of the wheel is forecast, which is a continuity of the past as much as a break from it. The Mahasiddha of Mindrolling is not as robust as he once was, and has entered what will eventually prove to be the last phase of his life. He has no sons, and of his two daughters, one has ordained as a nun and the other is yet unmarried. The issue of succession looms over the monastic establishment like a cloud heavy with possibilities, threatening an immediate gender revolution as it readies and ripens. For once, the male religious hierarchy might find itself accepting and enthroning a woman dharma heir. And a small sliver of Sylvia Wetzel's fantasy of a 'women's dharma' might come alive in this day and age, right in our midst.

Is it my imagination, or has the Buddha-to-come on the giant stupa grown a softer countenance, a fuller silhouette, as I squint up at him-her in the afternoon sun?

Do we find our greatest fulfilment as human beings through individual effort and initiative? Or must we realize the interlinkages of past and present that overlap in us, the double-helixed call of continuity that echoes in us and directs our selves towards manifesting our destiny? Should we be only ourselves, or should we assume our place in the continuum of consciousness that links past with present with future? What exactly are our choices?

This is a dilemma that often surfaces in the process of 'finding' ourselves for many of us who live in cultures where tradition and its continuity hold sway and the individualism of modernity is a relatively new determinant of identity. Tradition relies on the young to ford its passage in every age, and the oldest living cultures are the ones that have managed to infuse each successive generation with deference, obedience and enthusiasm for its tradition(s). I think the truly successful cultures are not the ones that have merely survived, for survival can also mean slavish imitation of what has gone before, but the ones that have retained a dynamic elasticity that allows them to shift their shapes according to the imagination of each generation. Perhaps it is this quality that provides them with an underground stream of innovation that constantly freshens them and keeps them from stagnating, losing their relevance and eventually dying out.

In the past half-century, no other culture has been forced to confront its endangered continuity, its possibly imminent mortality, as urgently as that of Tibet. The high flatland of its birth, in whose thin air it learnt to breathe and in whose bosom it was nourished, was suddenly snatched away by the hand of history. With its motherland went its points of reference, its markers of identity, its roots and shoots, its perspectives and worldviews, much of what gave its traditions meaning. That the Tibetan culture has found ways of flourishing regardless is a story epic in proportion and telling, that must be examined for its relevance for exiled people everywhere. For aren't we all refugees in a sense, if not of war, famine and flood, then of spirit and heart? Don't we all suffer from loss of place and space, of a piece of land or sky, which could just as well be fragments of our psyches, unspoken bits of our selves?

What the Tibetans have not lost, what nobody has been able to exile them from, is that part of their culture that lives within them. Theirs is an elegy for a lost land *and* a ballad for a found self. As long as the roots that anchor us in ourselves and make us whole are well nourished and deeply grounded, the culture will live. In Tibetan culture, these roots are also purveyors of the dharma. In the mind of the Tibetan, culture ('Tibetanism') and religion (Buddhism) are one. For the modern Tibetan, the choice is not only between tradition and individualism, it is between uncovering one's roots and preserving and nourishing them, and giving oneself up to the flow of life and allowing it to wash one upon whichever shore its current flows towards.

Most second-generation diasporic Tibetans attempt to find some sort of balance between these two, perhaps in keeping with a cultural predilection towards the extremity-eschewing 'middle path' beloved to the Buddha. They are, for the most part, acutely conscious of the responsibilities of exile that have yoked them to the task of tending the fields of their unique dharma-culture and securing it from the preying influences of denigration, dissolution and desertification. The fact that they have to contend with an unprecedented intermingling of cultures brought on by an explosion in communication technology, a globalization not just of economies but of desires fattened on consumerist fantasies, in addition to the challenge of reseeding in alien soil much of what was uprooted, makes their task seem daunting, to say the least.

Does this make the process of questioning their culture even harder, then? For questions are potentially unsettling and carry the charge that can effect change. They can destabilize what has already been rendered fragile by the onslaught of unwelcome, forced change. Do young Tibetans feel protective of their culture because of this fragility, thus deferring their need to change things that don't fit in with their new worldview, or are they able to ask the necessary questions in a way that distinguishes between constructive and destructive change, with the understanding that the former is essential if their dharma and culture are to survive and remain relevant to their times?

In response, I am reminded of something the Dalai Lama has pointed out on more than one occasion, illustrating as much his unique individuality as an attitude that is fearless in the face of change because it is rooted in a deep understanding of the nature of reality. The Dalai Lama's interest in modern science is well known, as is the fact that he is one of the architects of a dialogue that brings perspectives from both science and Buddhism to bear upon topics of mutual interest. In this sense, he is a modern, renaissance mind who is able to sift his tradition and learning for that in it which pertains to the essence of truth, and use it like a microscope to focus on an issue which might range from the nature of the mind and universe to neuroplasticity to behavioural psychology. He is able to discard the outer form of the teachings while retaining their core insight, the part unbound by tradition or dogma and timeless in its ability to direct our minds towards an understanding.

In his relentless quest towards this kernel of truth in every bit of knowledge, the Dalai Lama is ever ready to change, to cast away that in his tradition which he finds cumbersome and unhelpful. For example, he has said that he doesn't subscribe any longer to the view expressed in Tibetan texts that the legendary Mount Meru holds up the centre of the earth, because he has travelled by airplanes and seen this to be untrue. In the same vein, he has asserted that he is willing to give up his belief in what appears to be the holy cow of Tibetan Buddhism—reincarnation—provided he is given conclusive proof of its non-existence. Until then, he says, he will continue to believe what tradition has taught him.

In his willingness to experiment and his openness to positive change, the Dalai Lama is actually embodying a key teaching of his tradition. In constantly pushing the circumference of his knowing, he is following the Buddha's constant exhortation to his followers to test everything they heard from him for themselves, in the laboratory of their own beings and minds, an attitude that is encapsulated in his precious last words, 'Be lamps unto yourselves'. Over the centuries, too much of Buddhism has veered away from this attitude that encourages the seeker to approach the path as a scientist of the self, ever ready to postulate, experiment, and *then* theorize and believe.

This precious quality of questioning has become overlaid with a need to coagulate a wisdom path into a religion with its set of automatically held beliefs, values and ethics. In a way, this may have served the purpose of preserving the dharma. But is it really worthwhile if the dharma is stripped of one of its most basic characteristics? The process of preserving spiritual paths must be dynamic enough to include intangible attributes that have to do with inner work and are therefore ungraspable by all but the devoted practitioner. Preservation of outward form without this quality of practice is like keeping the husk and discarding the grain.

There are many among the Tibetan diaspora who understand this and are working towards a preservation of the dharma that focuses as much on its spirit—its practice—as on its outer structures and traditions. The Dalai Lama's example is important because he advocates assimilation of new knowledge into the old, diligently seeking out and replacing that which has become unnecessary and possibly archaic, and moving towards a comprehensive model of knowing that integrates as many streams of thought as possible, not just the traditional texts and commentaries. His ecumenism and inclusiveness come from a relentless practice of the core truths of his spiritual heritage that provides the roots that anchor him to true knowing, as well as wings that help him soar in an ever moving search for a more complete understanding of reality.

Seeking out the 'middle path' between tradition and modernity, therefore, is not an apology for wishy-washiness or a front for not being able to make a definite choice. In its true sense, it is a philosophy of inclusion and integration, of being able to take into account the full spectrum of things rather than just a part, of being uninfluenced by an 'either/or' fragmentation of what is essentially an interconnected whole. When applied creatively to the issue of change and preservation vis-à-vis the dharma, and the culture that is its outer garb, the implications and outcomes can be fascinatingly and unusually fearless.

As the Dalai Lama's example shows, the ability to use dharma truths skilfully depends on the practitioner's own level of insight, and the stability and maturity of his or her practice. Today, Tibetan Buddhism has many practitioners in its extensive sangha in the East and the West, who are aware of the need for conscious, progressive change and are working towards it with the sensitivity and delicacy that the process requires, as if weaving a tapestry out of gossamer. A loving lightness that points to rather than hits at, that touches upon rather than roots out, that quietly rewrites rules rather than rabble-rouses, and that empowers from within rather than wages battles without, is perhaps the pace and quality of change that a wounded culture can handle best.

For instance, women of the dharma may not need to burn bras or misogynistic texts to make a statement about their emancipation. They have the option of a middle-path approach—educating themselves, taking any opportunity that comes their way to learn the dharma, practising with sincerity and dedication and then, from a primacy of inner knowing which nobody can deny or question, ushering in religious, hierarchical and social change. This may be more effective in the long run than extremist positions and extravagant symbolic gestures.

A braveheart who has taken this position, and steadily and quietly worked up a transformation within the baked earth bowl of tradition without shattering it, is Jetsun Khandro Rinpoche. The older daughter of the Mindrolling Trichen, she is possibly the only woman to be addressed by the honorific title 'Rinpoche'. She is also a rare woman tulku, for women are almost never 'checked' for signs of reincarnation. Feminine birth is considered inferior, so a master will obviously not choose to return as a woman. This might change soon, though, for the Dalai Lama recently indicated in a rather scandalous statement that *he* might be reborn as a woman, and a beautiful one at that!

At this time, Khandro Rinpoche has been teaching for more than two decades and has students all over the world. Wherever she goes, a reputation for strictness in dharma matters precedes her, so much so that she jokes that her students have nicknamed her 'Hitler'. I was not unaffected by these stories when I met her for the first time for an interview, at a guest house in Delhi, and I almost didn't recognize the gentle-voiced, quick-eyed, soft-cheeked nun as *the* Khandro Rinpoche. I suppose we are so conditioned by male models of power and strength that we often tend to equate power with physical stature, aggression and an overwhelming ego-personality.

Khandro Rinpoche subverts these patriarchal myths by exemplifying a power that originates from a complete lack of egoistic self-ness and competitive belligerence, that is compassionate, attuned to the other and never needs to raise its voice to be heard. That is, perhaps, a spiritual and feminine model of how deep and silent power can really be, of how we might have completely misunderstood power as an ability to control, rather than an ability to empathize and care.

In earlier writings I have described Ven. Khandro Rinpoche as a 'lioness of a woman' because of her fearlessness, swiftness of mind and clarity of thought. Her willingness to engage with uncomfortable questions regarding women in the dharma, Tibetan Buddhism, spiritual materialism and so on has brought me to her once more, for an 'inside view', as I deal with the vexatious issues of gender, exile and modernity and how they have impacted the ground realities of a living spiritual culture of our times.

—

At the appointed time, I am led through the manicured lawns of the Mindrolling complex by a soft-spoken young American woman, a student of Khandro Rinpoche. As we enter what is a family space in this monastery, I wonder whether this situation could count, in a superficial way, as a reversal of Siddhartha's journey. He moved out of his home in his quest for truth, and here the yogi returns to create a home in which he would play out part of his quest. Is this the Tantric element in Vajrayana, where reality is a dance of opposites held in rhythmic balance, and to truly know it, one must dance through the entire spectrum of human experience, the noise, the union, the dissolution, everything?

Khandro Rinpoche enters swiftly, and before I can bow in greeting, she has taken the ritual greeting scarf, the white *khata*, from my hands and placed it around my neck. She is already sitting down with a 'let's get on with it' air about her as I fumble to get my recording equipment in order. My mind takes a moment to remind me that part of the 'Hitlerian' lore about her is that she doesn't suffer fools. I look at her worriedly as I hand her the tiny microphone that I have at last managed to salvage from a tangle of wires. She seems as unruffled as a cloudless sky.

Sometimes it helps to begin with the obvious, the part that sticks out the most and is easy to discern in the dim light of a dawning conversation. Sylvia Wetzel's visualization fresh in my mind, I ask about the absence of female Buddhas, fully enlightened beings who began their journey as women.

Rinpoche's response draws from a variety of sources and traditions in Buddhism and is a patient, well-thought-out explanation of historical conditions, schools of thought and the ways in which these evolved. She must often be asked this, I think, as a teacher who has numerous women students, and as a roving ambassador who talks dharma to the world. Perhaps, also, it is a question that means much to her personally, as a woman on the path.

She speaks about Sutra and Tantra, the two lineages in Buddhism that Tibetans tend to place at an almost equal footing, though other Buddhist traditions may not. The Sutra lineage is what we now think of as 'original Buddhism', which originated in India during the Buddha's time and in which the Vinaya, or the code of monastic conduct, is dominant. This lineage evaluates spiritual attainment in terms of becoming an arahat, rather than a full Buddha, and many women did become arahats, as is evident from accounts in the *Therigatha*.

'In terms of different views among practitioners of Buddhism,' says Rinpoche, 'there is a certain category that sees the Buddha as the supreme enlightened being and all else are considered his followers. No one will say openly, "I got enlightened", or "He or she got enlightened".' So when enlightenment is out of the circumference of human possibility, neither men nor women have access to it, and there is no possibility of either male or female Buddhas. As Tenzin Palmo mentioned, if the prophesied next Buddha, Maitreya, will not appear for another 2,500 years, we might as well all relax!

Khandro Rinpoche credits the Tantric gene in Tibetan Buddhism with making it comparatively open to the possibility of enlightened women. 'Because of the influence of Tantra on Vajrayana Buddhism,' she says, 'you will find references to several women. I won't say a lot, but several women are said to be equal to Padmasambhava, the founder of Vajrayana Buddhism. In the iconography you have enlightened beings like Tara, Vajrayogini, Lion-Faced Dakini and so on. Yeshe Tsogyal and Mandarava—consorts of Padmasambhava—are said to have been at least equal to him. In the following centuries, you will find a number of remarkable women who could be said to have gained as much realization as any man did. Each tradition [within Tibet] has references to remarkable women who have achieved the same state of enlightenment.'

What about the contention that a woman could reach the penultimate stage of enlightenment but to go all the way she needed to change into the body of a man? This idea is also the source of a prayer with the infamous line, 'Let me not be born a woman', which so disheartened Tenzin Palmo that she vowed to work towards nirvana as a woman.

'That I absolutely disagree with,' exclaims Rinpoche, the flame of indignation leaping in her eyes. 'The biggest logic, I feel, is that when we talk about nirvana, we are talking about the exhaustion of the phenomenal world. Therefore to assume that ultimate nirvana has to have a solid basis of gender is entirely against the teachings of dharma, especially Madhyamika (the Tibetan 'Middle Way' school). Freedom from all extremes of establishing solidity can't be gender-based. Exhaustion is exhaustion of all concepts, no matter how good a concept might be. Ultimately, when you get nirvana, not just gender, you also have to stop being Buddhist.'

The metaphor of a vehicle, yana, has often been used for the dharma—that it is a means, a device, a boat to raft the mind across the turbulence of ignorance and unknowing. Once you reach the shore of understanding, the yana must be discarded; one does not carry the boat on one's shoulders once the destination has been reached. The goal of the spiritual quest is to make every possible effort to find that shore within the ground of one's self. The guru, the teachings, the path, the methods—all is yana. They are a means to an end, and are not to be confused with the end itself.

Khandro Rinpoche has expanded the metaphor of the vehicle to include all conceptual phenomena that are inherent to our experience of life. Those concepts that we are conditioned with are also a kind of vehicle with which we navigate samsara. Whether positive or negative, helpful or unhelpful, everything that can be classified as this or that, a viewpoint, condition or concept, must fall away at the moment of nirvana. The vessel of the dharma is also left behind, for it too is a conceptual, frame-worked methodology or philosophy that becomes untenable in the infinite horizon of the enlightened mind, which can no longer be hemmed in by anything. If the dharma, beneficial in all respects, is to be discarded, how can it be conceived that gender is the one thing that will still remain relevant?

The point is well made, and slam-dunks the issue rather decisively into the hoop of misogyny. If this Madhyamika perspective of ungendered nirvana has existed all this while, why did it not automatically overthrow the misogynistic interpretation of a 'men only' nirvana? In the history of Tibetan Buddhism, why aren't there more women masters and teachers? Once again, I am faced with the dilemma—is this because women didn't attain spiritual eminence, or is it simply because they were not known and therefore missed being recorded?

Rinpoche blames it on a patriarchal society that didn't educate its women and kept them yoked to gender roles, an aspect of which was a code of expected behaviour that required them to be submissive and docile. Women that did become known for their spiritual accomplishments were aberrations to the norm, encouraged by 'backgrounds that enabled circumstances that led to their education, or backing of family members or very good teachers who inspired them to be educated', points out Rinpoche.

The patriarchal attitude of devaluing women's accomplishments and not taking them into account also ensured that herstory very rarely made it to the pages of history. The actual number of distinguished women practitioners is probably far greater, according to Rinpoche, than it appears to be at first glance. This is true of many wisdom traditions, not just the Tibetan, so much so that one could postulate a phenomenon of what could be called the 'iceberg seeker'—a woman who walks the path within her being, silently growing in her practice. It all happens so subtly in the underground of her life that on the surface everything seems to remain the same, apart from the occasional peak of compassion or equanimity that blossoms forth spontaneously, a direct result of her secret liberation.

'I also see it as a very clever, skilful way, a woman's way of surviving in a rigid patriarchal society,' says Khandro Rinpoche of this phenomenon. 'There is a choice between do you want to teach authentic dharma, or do you want to make a big splash of it. And I think they were very wise in choosing to remain true to the dharma, and did not look to make a demonstration by having many students. So, yes, they did have an enormous amount of activities, but society in general ensured they maintained a low profile.'

Some 'iceberg seekers' did appear periodically in accounts and hagiographies, usually those of other people. They were referred to obliquely, in connection with the men they were related to or taught, and rarely as masters in their own right. 'Whatever little we have of women's biographies,' says Rinpoche, 'they will be just a few pages and in most cases they will be in reference to their brothers and monasteries and fathers. It will be an indirect reference to them. In certain lineages you will find a great master and an equally realized sister or wife or daughter, but the reference will be that she was also a great master equal to her brother or husband, and that's about it, even if her work has been just as great.' True to the metaphor of the iceberg, the actual extent of women's wisdom never got known in their lifetime, and rarely after, perhaps only when their bodies dissolved into beatific rainbows upon death, signs of the conscious passing of an accomplished practitioner.

Khandro Rinpoche mentions her father's aunt, Jetsun Tsewang Lhamo, as having been precisely this sort of 'iceberg seeker'. She was a teacher and had students, but while she was treated with love and respect, nobody paid much attention to her as a spiritual practitioner. According to Rinpoche, in whose family home she lived for many years, 'hardly anyone went to her to receive teachings'. The moment of realization came when she remained in unbroken samadhi for three days at the time of her death. 'That's when people said, "Yes, she's really a great master." That happens a lot in the case of women, maybe it happens with men also,' says Rinpoche. The difference, I suppose, is that male yogis may remain 'hidden' out of choice, while women do so to protect themselves and their practice from the insidious repression of patriarchy, or they are ignored because they are women and therefore not important enough in the patriarchal worldview.

Actually, Khandro Rinpoche's Mindrolling lineage could be considered a flowering of the women's way, for it was twice rescued from near disappearance by women who re-seeded and revived its distinctive set of teachings, and stabilized its then shaky structure before passing it on to new generations of male dharma heirs. Mindrolling's annals have recorded instances of herstory, where the 'icebergs' emerged from underwater and shepherded the lineage on its way. Which is why this is perhaps the only lineage of Tibet that has an acknowledged, recorded and celebrated line of women masters and practitioners who are given the title Jetsunma, the noble one, an honorific to rival Rinpoches, who are mostly male.

Incidentally, Khandro Rinpoche is both Jetsunma and Rinpoche—the former because of her place among the women practitioners of Mindrolling, the latter because she is recognized as the reincarnation of a yogini. Khandro Ugyen Tsomo, also called 'the Great Dakini of Tsurphu', was acknowledged as a great master and accorded the title 'Rinpoche' in her lifetime. Khandro Rinpoche was recognized at the age of two by the previous Gyalwa Karmapa, the sixteenth. An earlier Karmapa, the fifteenth, had formed a consort relationship with the Great Dakini who stayed on at his monastery in Tsurphu after he died, continued her practice and, in time, taught others. Even though Khandro Ugyen Tsomo's spiritual authority initially derived from her association with the fifteenth Karmapa, it endured and grew as she came into her own as a teacher and came to be called 'Rinpoche'.

Being unfamiliar with the Tibetan language, I ask Khandro Rinpoche whether there was anything in the title that implied a grammatical masculinity, as, for instance, in 'chairman'. 'Literally the title is gender neutral,' she explains. 'It means "precious jewel". It is often an honorific term used by students to refer to one's teacher. It is *not* a title conferred on a teacher but rather it is offered to a teacher by the student. Now it is almost as if a child can be given the title Rinpoche based on the fact that he or she is recognized as a tulku. The traditional way is to confer it on someone who manifests qualities of wisdom and understanding of the dharma. Out of devotion and gratitude, people joined their hands and said, "You are the wish-fulfilling jewel." It was a heartfelt expression of devotion that became the origin of the term Rinpoche. It could be given to a person who is not necessarily a recognized, enlightened reincarnation. The influence of society is such that the title has mainly been held by men, so when women are referred to as Rinpoche, it takes a long time for people to get used to it.'

I ask her whether she knows of any other women Rinpoches. There are many who could be called by this title because of the quality and calibre of work they are doing, she says, but by and large, people have been 'a little stingy' in referring to exemplary women masters as 'Rinpoche'. 'The previous Khandro Rinpoche was called Rinpoche,' she smiles. 'I think that was why there was a little less resistance in giving me that title!'

But who decides who gets to be a Rinpoche? It is the prerogative of that teacher's students, reasserts Khandro Rinpoche, just as it must be their initiative to record their teachers' stories and write their biographies. In both these, Tibetan women teachers seem to have lost out. Or perhaps they themselves resisted being recorded and en-titled. Says Rinpoche, 'In our society, and probably it is the way of eastern societies, women tend to be very humble and people do tend to be satisfied with the humility of women. Women don't say, "I need that title," and it is not felt particularly that they can be given that title.'

Almost as an aside, she mentions how she has also noticed that people find it easier to call somebody Rinpoche if they have a 'shaved head'. Does it mean it is easier for women to get that respect if they ordain, rather than practise in the secret, 'iceberg' mode? 'I don't know if it's easier. I think it is easier for those who have to say it to a woman.' She laughs, perhaps at the emptiness of such things, and their meaninglessness to one who is intently observing the shifting sands that swirl and obscure the clear light of true nature. Titles can at best be the paraphernalia of religion, and even if they act as external markers of attainment on the path, I suppose the seeker would look upon them as just so much dust, which can blind you if it gets into your eyes in the form of craving for recognition, to be dusted off if it lies upon the folds of your robes, to be left behind on the path as one walks on.

The only reason I probe this issue with Khandro Rinpoche is because of the lack of credible role models of feminine attainment, and because the title Rinpoche is a symbol of it, the need perhaps to have more women Rinpoches in the cause of constructive change. Another possibility of feminine role models has been suggested by Khandro Rinpoche—the remarkable Jetsunmas of Mindrolling, feminine offshoots of the bloodline who are the unacknowledged, un-enthroned co-heirs of this dharma lineage.

Like their 'throne-holder' brothers, the Jetsunmas grow up in a monastic environment surrounded by the sights, sounds and scriptures of the dharma, with fathers who are repositories of learning, and mothers who are yoginis in the sangyum tradition. In addition, they have as role models the original brave Jetsunmas who saved the tradition from withering away and infused it with new learning. Inspiration is a constant companion for the women of Mindrolling, in the stories of their illustrious ancestresses which, like the incense-laden air of a shrine room, are ever ready to waft in and stir their hearts and minds.

Mindrolling was established in 1676 by Chogyal Terdag Lingpa. Perhaps because of the brutal times he lived in where the possibility of invasion and ruin was a constant and terrifying reality, and perhaps also because he realized their equal potential as practitioners, Terdag Lingpa advocated dharma education for both men and women so that there could be as many repositories of the tradition as possible. He directed his descendants to continue the practice he had initiated by educating his own daughter, Mingyur Paldron, in exactly the same way as he did his two sons. Mingyur Paldron turned out to be something of a child prodigy, accomplishing many important practice disciplines when she was barely in her teens, and receiving teachings from the great masters of her time. It was just as well, for when she was sixteen, her father died and, three years after that, Mindrolling was attacked and razed to the ground by marauding Mongols, who also killed the lineage holder, Terdag Lingpa's eldest son.

Mingyur Paldron escaped to Sikkim where she became a Padmasambhava-like figure by establishing the dharma, teaching extensively and founding the Pema Yangtse monastery. A couple of years later, she returned to Tibet along with her surviving brother, and set about the task of reviving Mindrolling. This required not only rebuilding the monastic complex, but also regrouping the sangha and passing on the lineage's exclusive teachings to as many practitioners as she could. Because of Mingyur Paldron's key contribution in re-establishing the lineage, Khandro Rinpoche says, 'The Mindrolling we have now is not Terdag Lingpa's, but Mingyur Paldron's Mindrolling.'

She tells me of another time, in the nineteenth century, when the lineage of Dzogchen teachings that forms the core of the Nyingma wisdom tradition of which Mindrolling is a part, was about to become extinct. Dzogchen, literally 'the Great Perfection', is the path to a direct realization of our innate nature, characterized as pure, primordial, nondual awareness, *rigpa*—an all-knowing mirror that reflects everything it perceives but is unaffected by them, it is 'space that is aware'. A great Dzogchen master, Dudjom Rinpoche, describes it as the 'original face of emptiness which makes it pure from the beginning, all pervasive and all-penetrating'. A Buddha is one who is completely and perfectly aligned with this, our original nature. The path of Dzogchen requires the practitioner to open herself to experiencing every moment *as it is*, for that is the only way to access one's innate, natural consciousness.

Eminent twentieth-century master Dilgo Khyentse Rinpoche speaks of Dzogchen as establishing one in 'now-ness', with 'absolute simplicity and nakedness of mind'. In this way, 'seeing all things as naked, clear and free from obscurations, there is nothing to attain or realize,' he says. 'Everything is naturally perfect just as it is. All phenomena appear in their uniqueness as part of the continually changing pattern. These patterns are vibrant with meaning and significance at every moment; yet there is no significance to attach to such meanings beyond the moment in which they present themselves.' As the practitioner realizes this, gradually, the everyday practice of Dzogchen becomes increasingly non-conceptual, 'just everyday life itself'.

Dzogchen as a practice path is believed to have originated in the Buddhist kingdom of Uddiyana (or Oddiyana), geographically located in and around the Swat Valley, now in Pakistan. Uddiyana actually had a rather close approximation of the kind of women's dharma Sylvia Wetzel describes in the visualization that opens this chapter. Though a man (Garab Dorje) is credited with conveying Dzogchen to Tibet, it is quite possible that the path was experimented into being and nurtured by the yoginis of Uddiyana. And it was a woman, once again, who restored these precious teachings.

'At one time, the whole Dzogchen lineage of the Nyingmas came to a point where all the senior masters had died and younger ones were very young,' Khandro Rinpoche tells me. Because the teachings of Tibetan Buddhism are largely conveyed through a personal transmission process between teacher and student, if there are no living exponents, the teachings cannot survive. 'The continuity of the various precious teachings was very weak and they couldn't find anybody who had the authentic lineage,' she says. 'My great-grand-aunt, Jetsun Thrinley Chodron, was the only one who had that. Various Nyingma masters we have today have their Dzogchen lineage because they received it from Thrinley Chodron. She was considered a revivalist of the Dzogchen tradition. But she died at the age of twenty-nine. She managed to convey so many precious teachings in her short lifetime.'

So this must mean that in giving the teachings, no distinction is made between men and women? Though the women seem almost like stopgap arrangements to turn to in times of crises when no male dharma heir was around to save the day, largely ignored otherwise, for them to have come to the rescue in the competent way that they did, they must have learnt exactly what the men did.

'There shouldn't be [any distinctions]. But realistically speaking, it does become difficult,' says Khandro Rinpoche, her face creasing into laugh lines. Here's the gap between conventional and ultimate reality again, she seems to be thinking, the chasm between theory and practice into which so many good philosophies stumble and fall. Tibetan Buddhism, Advaita Vedanta and so many exalted wisdom traditions seem to end up falling short when it comes to issues of gender and equality at a lived, experiential level. 'In theory, there shouldn't be any difference. In practice, sometimes we find a lot of reluctance. People do have the tendency to treat women with... ummm... gentleness. I'll just use that word. Women are not thought to be capable of taking the teachings. Either out of reluctance, or great kindness, this happens.'

The words 'kindness' or 'gentleness' denote a patronizing, superior attitude on the part of some male teachers who think women will not, cannot, understand refined knowledge because either they have an undeveloped intellect—in Rinpoche's words, 'lesser potential for learning'—or because 'they lack courage or confidence or are not serious enough about what they are doing'. She is quick to point out that this 'gender-based profiling' is not something she has seen in 'the very highest level of teachers who are realized', and it 'usually happens in the middling level of teachers, when you relate to abbots, or geshes or acharyas and so on'.

Is this because realized masters have an understanding of the nature of reality and the emptiness of all conditioned phenomena of which gender is also one, and those that are scholars or pandits may not have this experiential knowledge? 'Yes,' she says. 'Probably it also has much to do with the fact that some of them allow the influence of their being ordained to restrict their interaction with women. There may be some valid reasons too, not always bad.' That which you don't know, you are more liable to fear or misunderstand. It is part of the growing understanding of the reasons for misogyny in religions that favour celibate orders, which is why I think the tradition of eminent yogis-with-sangyums, like Rinpoche's father, is a progressive trend on the whole as far as Buddhism is concerned.

A trace of the personal has crept into the conversation as Rinpoche speaks about discriminating teachers. I glimpse the possibility of this having been her experience as well, as she gives an example of the way women are sometimes treated. 'In a classroom, sometimes we may be the first ones to get the point. But the teacher will often repeat the point again and again, assuming everyone else has understood but the woman hasn't. Ultimately you have to say, "I understood!"'

Didn't being a tulku, and a daughter of a respected Rinpoche, inoculate her from experiences such as these? Surely if she, as a kind of 'dharma royalty', had to face this discrimination on account of her gender, the situation could only be worse for 'ordinary' women, as Tenzin Palmo discovered, receiving only crumbs when the whole feast was laid out before her.

'Sometimes being the daughter of the Mindrolling Trichen

helps, and sometimes it doesn't,' says Rinpoche candidly. 'My father was never the kind to use his position, he was never very active. He is a genuine Mahasiddha. The advantage my sister and I had is that he was always willing to teach if we were willing to learn. That has been the greatest blessing we have received. The difficulty was that a lot of people assumed we didn't have to learn. They thought, being his daughter, we got everything at home, which is not true. There are many aspects of Buddhism that you must learn from scholars and temples and rituals. And our father is not as available as people may think. You can't get the basics of all the different aspects of dharma, and have to approach many other teachers. There have been moments in our lives when people have been reluctant to give teachings, especially in philosophy. Then, there is always this thing of, "Why would you want to learn it anyway?"'

How did she deal with these layers of discrimination, some apparent, others subtle—the spiritual glass ceiling, condescension masquerading as concern, the mollycoddling of 'kindness and gentleness' which are really ropes of satin that tie women down by infantilizing them and keeping them out of areas designated as 'men only'?

'I'll give you an example,' says Khandro Rinpoche, clear-eyed still, not a trace in her voice of the emotion that often tends to coat memory. 'There was one Khenpo (a scholar with the equivalent of a doctorate) I really wanted to study with. And there was a group of tulkus who were receiving teachings. But he wouldn't teach me because he thought women were not capable of learning Mahayana. There was this point where he refused to teach the class if I attended.' Her carefree laughter dissipates the tension I feel as I listen to this, though nothing of the sort has stained her being even for the briefest moment. Am I watching a Dzogchen-aligned state of mind in action? Is this what it means to be fearlessly open to the challenge of every single moment, unmasked, uncovered, unclouded, naturally aware?

Did she go and argue with the Khenpo? 'No, no,' she shakes her head. 'I sat outside the window and took the lessons.' The simplicity of her solution could be a textbook example of what the Buddha called *upaya*, or skilful means. One cannot possibly change another's mindset, which has been shaped by who knows how many influences and layers of conditioning. Instead of setting up a 'him versus me' conflict or feeling sad and rejected, Rinpoche managed to fulfil her aim by improvising her response according to the situation.

I think of the question I brought in my heart, about women who are dharma-insiders, and their ability or the lack of it to interrogate tradition on issues of gender and repression. Rinpoche has shown me that interrogation need not be confrontational or aggressive, it can just as well be a non-violent non-cooperation with the misogynistic mindset. If somebody will not teach you because you are a woman, go and sit outside but make sure to listen in. In this way, you have fulfilled your aim without compromising your equanimity, your quality of consciousness, for that is the first casualty whenever one gets involved in a conflict, however righteous or justified it might be.

In fact, 'listening in' is a practical device women in patriarchy have long used to learn or do things that were unavailable to them because of gender taboos. In a climate like India's, with the need to keep doors and windows open for ventilation for several months in the year, one can almost visualize eager women at doors and outside windows, looking in, listening in as male relatives were taught scriptures, or reading and writing, or music and such. Hungry for knowledge and keen to absorb what they could, the quality of attention these eavesdroppers brought to the lesson must surely have been sharper and quicker, their sense of its preciousness greater than those for whom this learning occurred as a matter of course. Because of the iceberg phenomenon, most of these women remained anonymous, their minds unknown, their intellects unsung.

I remember asking a well-known exponent of the Dhrupad form of classical music, which also relies on the blood lineage system for its continuity, passing on from sons in one generation of the Dagar family to the next, about the women. He responded with stories of the numerous times he had been corrected on finer points of rendition as a child by the older women in his family. If women were never formally trained in Dhrupad, which incidentally can be considered a wisdom tradition in its own right, complete with a sophisticated philosophy of sound as well as a complete, yogic practice path, how did they know enough to discern an incorrectly intoned *swar*? Yes, my guess would be that they listened in, like Khandro Rinpoche, rendering the walls and ceilings of discrimination porous and pervious, and thereby irrelevant.

Khandro Rinpoche has said in the past that it isn't important to have many women teachers, only enough women who feel empowered to make their own choices. What about making positions of spiritual authority accessible to women so that they and others could get over notions of women's lack of ability to manage these? She sounds hopeful, saying that things *are* changing, in exile, with the destruction of so many aspects of culture and religion still in the foreground of memory. Education is being made available to all and, in her own experience with the monks at Mindrolling and the nuns at Samten Tse (her retreat centre named after Mingyur Paldron's nunnery in Tibet), 'their capabilities, qualities and understanding are the same'.

'In the next decade or so we are going to find a very interesting situation where I don't know how they are going to stop women from teaching and manifesting their qualities!' says Rinpoche excitedly. According to her, we are over 'that situation' of women being denied. What she is really concerned about is—what do women decide to do with the spiritual education they receive? 'How do you manifest what you have as qualities?' she questions. How do you practise? How do you become what you know? For the essence of the dharma is in the way the individual learns to use it as a tool to transform herself.

'The main thing is how you manifest your individual being according to the dharma. This is not about women in general, but about dharma practitioners. Dharma practitioners have a stage where they are studying and trying to understand and practise meditation. All of this has to culminate in a person who is steeped in the essence of dharma. The point of Buddhism is what kind of practitioner you become. And I am hoping women will realize that. They don't necessarily have to build or teach or do a lot, but keep the authenticity of dharma and become good practitioners. Women have the skill to do this. I think that's where we need to concentrate the most.'

For Rinpoche, identity and gender are secondary to the primary task of the practitioner, which is, quite simply, to practise. So while she is willing to take into account the ways in which these affect and condition our being, she also requires us to step away from them and focus on the work at hand—of transforming one from the ground up, inside out. To 'become a good practitioner', as she stresses, is also to consciously dissolve the ego-self, that idea of self that feeds off the lifeblood of a self-existing being that has a fixed identity, which includes a gender, a nationality, a worldview, a set of ideas and beliefs, a clearly defined past, present and future. A gendered perspective must also be dropped along the wayside, as one realizes that like everything else one bases one's identity on, it too is empty of any lasting substance. Khandro Rinpoche holds out this challenge to all women—are you going to be a woman, or are you going to be a good practitioner?

At times women cannot help being women, I think as I hear her say this, even if they would rather become good practitioners. Their lives are often entangled with others'; they are webbed within a network of relationships whose call they feel upon their conscience. They cannot just get up and go. It is an issue I have brought with every woman I have spoken to for this book, in the quest for a spirituality that takes into account women's needs and circumstances, instead of attempting to fit them into existing 'male' models of seeking and practising.

'I think women have an innate quality of spirituality that is very soft, and with or without [monastic] vows, I think they make excellent practitioners,' says Khandro Rinpoche. 'The problem seems to be, how important it is. A woman's life is so torn in responsibilities. Men also feel responsibilities but are able to find a way out by saying, "Oh, everyone has a life." They are able to find that freedom. Women have a basic kindness and they always interfere in order to care for others, take care of issues. They want to be there for people. So that kind of innate women's kindness tears them into so many directions that, ultimately, giving up everything and thinking of their own path is very difficult. They are very good, but are torn in so many directions that their individuality in coming forward one-pointedly, that takes time. Once they are able to cross that, there is really no problem at all.'

Can women be good practitioners even if they have not been able to 'cross' their roles as caregivers and nurturers? Is there some way of integrating the process of caring for others into dharma practice, of being able to love and nourish and work in the world without necessarily feeling torn between one and the other? I suppose what I am questioning is the suggestion of a compartmentalization of the spiritual that separates it from everything else. While I do get the need to make time in a busy day, to be able to sit in silence, to have a quality of consciousness that is not fragmented into a hundred things you need to take care of, surely with dedicated effort one can practise this in everyday life?

Khandro Rinpoche agrees with the basic premise that 'if women really connected with the dharma, it will become an integral part of their families, not just as a religion but as a way of living'. She recounts a question that was asked of an eminent Rinpoche, about monks and nuns giving up their vows. His response was, if you don't want to remain a monastic, it is fine to leave. But you take the dharma with you, which will shape and affect everything you do as a lay person—work, marriage, parenthood. 'I thought that was a very beautiful way of saying it,' says Khandro Rinpoche. 'Ultimately, what's the purpose of Buddhism? Not to increase the number of monks and nuns. It's very important, but the ultimate intention is to create good human beings.'

Apparently, the catch lies in what the goal of one's spiritual practice is. Is it to strive for enlightenment, or is it to live consciously according to dharmic principles? The latter, explains Rinpoche, is as integral a part of the dharma as the former, and she cites the development of a dharmic society in Tibet as a direct result of such an attitude. 'Society [in Tibet] in general is a kind society. It has deeply ingrained notions of karma, belief in virtuous action and abandoning non-virtuous action. Its history is of a barbarian, warring society, but the change occurred predominantly because the mothers were able to inspire children to walk the path of virtue. Though the education levels of women were not so strong, women in family are very strong. Even as refugees, I find that women do a tremendous amount of work in terms of ingraining in their children a sense of virtue and karma, and a sense of compassion.'

What about the path to enlightenment? 'That requires very dedicated work,' she says. 'It will ultimately require absolute renunciation.'

Historically, and 'herstorically', enlightenment has rarely been a mass goal of popular appeal. In every era, it has always been a determined few who strive towards it. A majority of the population at any given time is not looking for enlightenment. They would rather focus on sorting out their problems, quelling their suffering, ensuring peace and happiness for themselves and their loved ones, all goals that are perfectly harmonious with the spirit and practice of the dharma. The spiritual can never be oriented only towards fulfilling a minority's exclusive quest; it *must* be wide enough to address the aspirations of all those who come to it. The Buddha's dharma is not only a renunciate's path; in fact, the Buddha envisioned it as permeating every aspect of life which is why his sangha not only included the laity, it also envisaged a social role for the monastics.

The earliest settlements of monastics, during the Buddha's time, were usually right at the periphery of towns, and not far away into forests as was customary among other renunciates of the time. The Buddha never wished for his sangha to exist in isolation. A Buddhist *bhikkhu* is not a 'monk' in a Christian, or even in an Indian *sramana* sense. The Buddha probably saw him as a 'sharesman'—one who received a share. His begging for alms was symbolic of his renunciation of possessions and of his reliance on common wealth. In that sense, the bhikkhu was very much a part of society and often had a symbiotic relationship with patron householders, with whom he shared his dharma knowledge and offered a spiritual perspective on worldly matters. This integration of sangha and society appears to have been a first in India where, for as long as anybody could remember, spiritual seekers had wandered out of society. The Buddha led them right back in, giving the sangha an integral vision that was really another articulation of his middle-path approach, which took into account both social responsibility and spiritual seeking.

In the same spirit, I would like to think that samsara and nirvana, worldly quests for happiness and ultra-worldly quests for enlightenment, are not mutually exclusive, that I could seek one without removing myself from the latter. A separation which actually might not be possible and the very idea of it may be an illusion just as the ego-self is, or the solidity of one's existence is. So, for women who carry the responsibility of relationships, divesting themselves of these to pursue a solo journey towards an imagined enlightenment might actually be unhelpful and set the stage for a damaging internal conflict.

In her own work as a teacher, I ask Khandro Rinpoche whether she is able to provide a model of practice for women that is sensitive to, and weaves together, different aspects of their lives.

'Basically, what we do is to provide different levels of practice,' she says. 'You have to understand that if a person is able to take even 5 per cent of what is required of you, generally you do concentrate on that 5 per cent so it develops into 10 and further. But the process has to be according to the potential of the person. Buddhism can't be taught generally. It is very individual. It has to be particular to each individual's potential. In the case of women, in teaching I try not to let any gender idea come to my mind. I don't think, I am a woman teaching, nor do I think that I am teaching women.'

So does gender not enter her mental space at all? 'I have been thinking about this whole issue,' she says. 'I have grown up in a monastery and the only three women there were my mother, my sister and me. I was thinking the other day, have I been brainwashed into assuming I am a monk?' She laughs at the thought, and suddenly everything seems infused with lightness, not of mind but of heart, of touch. Rinpoche has a way of releasing a moment from the prison of perspectives into the clear blue sky of infinity, reminding me that all debate must at some point cease, and the mind allowed its natural ease.

—

Khandro Rinpoche attended a convent school in India where she received a Western education, as did I. She was drawn to science, not unusual for the rational Buddhist mind, and had ambitions to study medicine until she discovered the horrors of dissecting animals. When the time came to make a choice, 'I had become active in my father's work at the monastery, and had begun relating to nuns and their issues. Meditation and teachings of Buddhist philosophy also seemed natural to me. By the time I was eighteen or nineteen, it became quite clear what I felt connected with.'

Listening to her, I am deeply aware of the fusion of the old and the new, of tradition and transformation, which has been such a huge part of her life experience. She *is* continuity in the midst of change, turning the wheel even as she is being turned upon it, like pliable clay, being formed anew. The language of modernity comes easily to her as she articulates ancient realizations in the idiom of today, the timeless truths glinting bright and clear in the laser beam a new century has cast upon them. Feminism is part of that questioning new light, and the dharma has had to bear its scrutiny and engage with its questions. As a questioner of tradition herself, does Khandro Rinpoche feel any kinship, any alignment with feminism?

'Western feminists have done a lot of good work,' she says. 'Without their actually raising the issue, the changes we have today wouldn't have taken place. However, the little bit of difference that occurs is that while it is good to raise the issues, respect can't be demanded. That's the main point on which I differ with some feminists. They demand respect which, even if you get, is not *actual* respect,' she stresses.

In her own life, she has had the experience of being respected because of who her father was. She has worked hard to convert that 'automatic' respect into something she deserves because of who *she* is, because of her work, her qualities. 'One kind of respect is where you respect your teacher, say, the Mindrolling Trichen, and so you respect the daughters of His Holiness, and you respect the dogs of His Holiness,' she says with her characteristic witty directness. 'In general my sister and I may get a lot of respect, but in terms of earning the respect beyond the name of Mindrolling, that has to be dependent on our own hard work and understanding. That is very difficult.'

Women must earn their respect fair and square, she asserts, something I feel she might be particularly sensitive to because of her own life experiences. Today she has an independent identity as a dharma teacher, and a lot of people outside the Tibetan community, including myself, come to know of Mindrolling through our acquaintance with her, rather than the other way round. As a supporter of women's right to equality, she would rather that women work hard, keep their dignity and not expect to get what they haven't made an effort for just because of their gender.

It is a view that is often challenged, she tells me. 'Although Eastern women have been blamed for being laidback or humble or not confident, I think there is absolute grace in really practising humility and selflessness. Sometimes I have been told that this humility and selflessness backfired and created a situation where women were treated as second-class citizens. I agree with that. But to *demand* equal rights, at least in the case of spirituality, doesn't seem appropriate. I think that's why there has to be a toning down of demanding. I have talked to women who are strong feminists in spirituality about raising issues about empowerment and education. There are certain things you shouldn't demand because if you are taking care of the grassroots level, the outcome is going to be indisputable. To demand the fruit without having worked on the roots doesn't seem to be accurate.'

There are other, perhaps more cosmetic changes that feminism demands, which Rinpoche doesn't agree with either. In *yab-yum* (Tantric union) depictions, for instance, where the female figure is shown with her back towards us, seated in the lap of the male deity and encircling his waist with her legs, feminists suggest a rotation and increase in size so that the female deity becomes prominent. There are also demands to reconfigure 'lineage trees', which trace the history of a dharma lineage, to include more women, and so on. These may be valid at one level but they miss the point, the real meaning of empowerment, according to Rinpoche.

'I disagree with all this. A lineage tree can't be changed because the lineage has happened that way. It is the given unbroken lineage and you can't, out of partiality, put someone who has not worked for that lineage. Then, for the artist who is working with Vajradhara (the male Tantric deity) who has to be shown in union, you have to have the Vajradhara's face visible, so you either have the woman's face to the side or you can shorten her. Those are artistic issues that are addressed by artists. Ultimately, every icon is a method to be used to allow your mind to exhaust concepts. Now if you are using an icon to increase a concept, then you have missed the point completely.'

The feminist perspective often does examine the dharma in the same way it does, say, sociology or history or linguistics, or any other stream of knowledge. The dharma is not just a philosophy, or even a religion. A distinction must be made, because the dharma is a precise tool, a specific path that aims at an 'exhaustion', to use Rinpoche's term. The Buddha's dharma is geared towards a particular end result, and that is to successively drop each conditioned thought and attitude, every reactive impulse to grasp or repulse, each mental concept, each emotional wave, in order to discover the basic ground of being, which is unfettered awareness. The very term for this objective, nirvana, means 'extinguishment because of the lack of fuel', the fuel being the 'concepts' Rinpoche refers to. Buddha Sakyamuni actually used the metaphor of fire to describe nirvana—just as the fire goes out when its fuel is exhausted, so is one liberated when one stops clinging to form, feeling, perception, thought processes and consciousness, elements that make up one's ego-personality.

The choice, thus, *is* between being a 'good practitioner' and being a woman. For a practitioner would prioritize the progressive movement towards exhaustion of the fuel provided by the self, which includes gender, rather than strengthen it using tools of the dharma, whether it is iconic representations or scriptural sources. In fact, Rinpoche is cautious about ways in which the dharma might be misused even with the best of intentions. The dharma has undoubtedly benefited from its increasing contact with the world outside sequestered, cloistered spaces, but it has also become vulnerable to new infections that this contact might bring.

Here, Rinpoche alerts one to the possibility of veering away from the true aim of the path and allowing it to become another arena in which to play out the drama of identity and gender. She urges similar carefulness with branding Buddhism as a method of psychoanalysis, an idea that has become quite popular these days. 'I don't feel it right to connect psychoanalysis with Buddhism,' she says, 'simply because it opens Buddhist teachings up to misuse, knowingly or unknowingly. Buddhism emphasizes becoming better, vast, free. The misuse can happen if people use the teachings to understand themselves and then become self-absorbed, rather than becoming more open and available to others. If we take Buddhism as a way to understand better there is no harm, but its true essence should always be kept in mind.'

In this sense, Khandro Rinpoche is a protector and a 'holder' of the dharma and it does not seem to conflict at all with that part of her that is an interrogator, a bringer of change. She ensures that the teachings and their transmission remain authentic and true, and that the knowledge is understood in as direct a way as possible without having to pass through unnecessary lenses and prisms that might have a distorting effect. Part of her authoritarian reputation actually seems to come from this insistence that students drive themselves to study and practise in as 'original', true-to-tradition way as they can, and not allow themselves the indulgence of letting some things slide (I would imagine this might be the 100,000 prostrations) because at first glance they do not seem necessary.

In everything about her, a state of being is becoming apparent, that attempts to find the ground of truth that lies beneath appearances and contexts and circumstances, and which can best be approached by letting go of the tendency to choose and react. To know without judgement, without the discursive mind that forces us to choose, is true knowing, one that keeps its fist unclenched and the being uncoiled. It is also the Dzogchen practice of experiencing without the 'reference points' that we have fixed based on past memory and impressions.

To try and assign long-term values to anything is being unreal, which is what extreme positions essentially are. Khandro Rinpoche seems to be able to hold each issue up to the light of this moment and examine its different facets, the perspectives involved, without pronouncing judgements. Her perception of misogyny in the dharma, therefore, has the quality of 'telling it like it is', it is neither frustrated nor is it unquestioning. She is pro-women, but does not automatically agree with everything feminist activists might take issue with, and is more interested in shifting our gaze within, and realizing dharma-truths in our lives. She is also willing to take what could be an unpopular position, for instance, because of their hardships women are more likely to progress on the spiritual path than men.

'You can always use what is apparently an unfortunate situation to your advantage. In the Mahayana teachings, you have to keep one slogan in mind—All adverse circumstances have to be transformed to the path of *bodhi* (knowing). And women have so many opportunities to do that.' Which is probably why the great eighth-century yogini Yeshe Tsogyal, the 'mother of Vajrayana' and an almost-equal consort of Padmasambhava, said, 'The best life to attain enlightenment is that of a woman.'

'This could be seen in two contexts,' says Khandro Rinpoche. 'If you live the life of a woman in a patriarchal society, you have the best possibilities of not having any attachments. As a woman, if you can struggle through life, I think you will make a very good practitioner. Also, there's a certain innate gentle kindness and a precise wakeful quality in women. Women are sharp and intuitive. That's why *Prajna Paramita* is feminine. At a mundane level, it means intuition. At a pure level, it is intrinsic awareness. If you use your mundane intuition and work with it, it highlights your intrinsic awareness. These make a woman's lifetime a great one to lead to exhaustion (nirvana).'

Like Tenzin Palmo, Khandro Rinpoche recognizes that there is something about a feminine heart that resonates more readily with the unstruck note beneath the noise of the world that nourishes it and holds it together. And yet, if this silent, intuitive melody is not consciously understood and worked with, it can degenerate into an internal cacophony of emotionality, which can ignite an unruly, destructive energy and be the single largest roadblock on the path for women.

'If the intuition and intrinsic awareness [in a woman], goes wrong,' says Khandro Rinpoche, 'it becomes dissipated and scattered. The main thing is the incisiveness—you are very sharp and because of that you know so many things—that can make for heightened neurosis.'

Women do have to make an extra effort with emotionality, and doesn't this make Vajrayana, that works with transforming the energy of emotionality, the ideal path for them? 'Vajrayana requires both the method and the *prajna*. Only prajna heightens the neurosis. Only method, which is the masculine aspect, may be a very dull state rather than being precise and aware. So you require both. That's why the union of method and prajna is emphasized in Tantra. In the case of women, stability in meditation is very important. If women don't meditate, their inner quality never gets tamed.'

Actually, emotional wavering and vacillating, what she refers to as indecisiveness, is another pitfall on the path for women, according to Rinpoche, because it keeps one from following the dharma with single-pointed determination and dedication. Which is why, perhaps, she herself is so clear and precise. Not many 'ummms', no ifs and buts; she is quick to see the point and respond.

But indecisiveness may not be only a woman's thing, as she discovered during a conversation with another, male Rinpoche. 'I was talking about women in general,' she says, 'and was saying that the main problem we have with nuns, but also in general with laywomen, is the age-old women's tendency to be indecisive and always changing their minds. As dharma practitioners, determination is very important. He said that actually, women are more decisive than men because you have no idea how indecisive men can be!'

One of the lessons I have learned on this journey is to steer clear of generalizations regarding what is a male issue or quality, and what is a feminine one. Even motherhood, that essentially feminine of all things, cannot be called a women's quality only. Certainly it is so biologically. But in terms of the qualities of a mother, her soothing love, her careful nurture, her healing caress, her reassuring heartbeat, her unconditional forgiveness—how many times has one felt these in men, especially realized gurus who become so warm and motherly in caring for their students? *Prajna Paramita* too is the wisdom womb of all creation, and not just the feminine part of it. She may be feminine in character, but she dwells everywhere equally, ready to be discovered by the dedicated seeker.

I am now at what is turning out to be *the* question to ask Buddhist women. I cannot keep myself from inwardly cringing as I ask this, for we have talked about so much and it seems to be a step backwards to bring this up now. But if anybody would give me an honest answer, it is the truth-speaking Khandro Rinpoche. And so, I ask. What do you think of the statement attributed to the Buddha, in which he says the sangha would diminish with the induction of women?

'I agree,' she says calmly, without batting an eyelid.

I bat mine several times. This is certainly not what I expected. '*You agree?*' The italics quiver in my voice as I inadvertently repeat her words.

'I agree,' she says once more, smiling at my confusion, which makes me suspect that she might be kidding me. Her explanation, though, soon disabuses me of any imagined notions of levity. 'What the Buddha meant was that the induction of nuns would dissipate the concentration into two areas—men and women. Whenever such a situation comes, you will find that the energy of what you are trying to create decreases. This is not only in the context of men and women. If you take a monastery and concentrate only on that, you can make it run very well. But growth happens and you create a second branch of this monastery. Your concentration is immediately broken into two.' In her own life, she says if she were to stay only at one place and teach, she could perhaps achieve a lot more. By travelling, her energy is divided and distributed among so many. More people do benefit, but 'your concentration has split into too many parts'.

So it was really a question of preserving one's energy and working for fewer people? But the Buddha taught tirelessly till the moment he died. He walked from one village to another, endured physical hardship and took a break only when the monsoon rains made it impossible to tour on foot, all to ensure that the dharma reached as many people as possible. Could he really have been so annoyed about women entering the sangha as to attribute its future end to them, only because he thought it might dissipate his concentration?

'If you run monasteries and nunneries, you will understand what the Buddha meant,' says Rinpoche patiently. 'This is my perspective. The essence of the monastic order is keeping the vows—don't kill, don't steal, don't lie, don't take intoxicants and, most importantly, do not indulge in any kind of sexual activity. Those are the five basic principles. If any structure is kept, it's like a Camelot. If you keep to the original, it's easy to maintain. When change is brought in, Camelot doesn't exist. If you have only monks, you can concentrate on the monastic order's authenticity. When it becomes co-ed, keeping the vows becomes difficult. One of the biggest obstacles for a monk or a nun is keeping their celibacy vows. I'd like to believe that anyone who becomes a monk or a nun has no more desire left. But that's not true. Where your situation and environment has changed, where you do have objects that increase desire, that's an obstacle.'

But isn't working with desire a part of dharma practice and training? Surely a path that attempts to train the mind towards achieving greater stillness and equanimity could also be used to deal with the desire brought on by the presence of the opposite sex?

'Theoretically that's correct,' Rinpoche agrees. 'Many people are able to do it, many can't. Anyone who has been working in the discipline area with monks and nuns will find that age is also not a barrier—young or old, it doesn't make a difference. We live in this world that is called a desire realm. There is so much desire, and not just sexual, but material as well. You sometimes think, I have done so much practice and I have understanding and I really have selflessness and renunciation. Then suddenly something happens, and thirty years of understanding dissolves in that one moment. That happens to many people, especially in today's society where you have internet, telephones, mobiles and TV. Everywhere you look, it is the material world. Some of the monks and nuns are young people and are surrounded by all of this. They also get a lot of respect from people—they are told how nice and good they are, how beautiful and peaceful they are. It twists your mind in a certain way. And situations evolve. That's a very big obstacle.'

Again, Rinpoche has managed to align herself with that which is real, rather than judge on the basis of what should be, or can be. It is easy to jump to conclusions based on one's reference points, I discover, and so much more difficult to keep an 'open fist' attitude at all times. Her compassion for those who find their practice challenged by the 'desire realm' is palpable, possibly stemming from her ability to see and feel without the barrier of conditioning that forces the ocean of the mind to run into narrow gullies and channels.

What about her own experiences with the 'desire realm'? Was it ever an issue with her? With a different master, I would not ask this question out of respect for their personal space. Khandro Rinpoche doesn't seem to divide her self into tight boxes; she doesn't seem to have a 'public' face that is different from her 'personal' one. She has brought a quality of nondualistic perception to everything we have discussed, and it emboldens me to venture into a space that is intimate. It is a question I ask on behalf of all spiritual seekers who are grappling with a gamut of desires which are not just sexual, as Rinpoche has pointed out.

'In my case, you see, the responsibilities fell at a very young age,' she says, without a flicker in her being which remains open, fearless, direct. 'I was barely out of school when situations arose where I had to take on responsibilities. I was talking to an old friend of mine, and she was asking me, how did this happen because it wasn't really planned in this way. Since 1987, things have just sort of evolved at such a speed that I didn't really have the time to sit back and think.'

Or get tempted by desires?

'Jokingly, I sometimes say that I have been on guard about somebody else making a mistake so much that it's helped actually,' she laughs. 'You know sometimes it helps when you are concerned about someone else breaking their vows, and I've always been known to be very strict. That's helped. There's never been much of an issue.'

The Dalai Lama has spoken about desire in his own context as a young person, and how he was able to work with the mind and create a watchfulness that would remind him of his vows as a monk whenever desire arose, even in sleep. 'That kind of situation, I think, happens for many people,' says Khandro Rinpoche. 'Every human being goes through that. You see a movie and think, what a nice movie star that is. At those levels, yes, certainly. But something that would make you think, "I should give back my vows," I don't think that's happened. His Holiness has to be rightly understood because he is talking about how easy it is for the mind to waver. In that case, it wavers every time you see a new model of mobile phone!'

I think of all the young monks I have seen carrying mobiles and playing with them, one of them recently,on what appeared to be solo 'chanting duty' in the grand stupa of Mindrolling. It also reminds me of how I love getting mail and will compulsively break the flow of writing to check for new e-mail. Desire does acquire many forms in our lives and takes our energy away from a restful, aware state of being towards grasping, agitation, anxiety. Somewhat like the old allegorical story of Mara, described as a demon but probably symbolic of the tendency of the mind to 'waver', who tries to lure the Buddha away from his final, nirvanic meditation by appearing to him as a beautiful woman. And Mara fails because the Buddha refuses to allow his mind to splinter into hankering or even its opposite, rejection, both of which would fragment focus, and keeps it open and ungrasping, single-pointedly fixed on the task at hand.

If he did it, perhaps so can we?

—

'Khandro', which is Ven. Khandro Rinpoche's reincarnational title, literally means 'sky dancer' or 'sky goer', and it is the Tibetan term for the Dakini principle. The Dakini is one of the most tantalizing figures in Vajrayana. In her different forms, she is the ethereal beauty that populates the margins of *thangkas* and *mandalas*, who appears as a woman, a cloud, an animal, or one's own innate wisdom, at crucial points in the spiritual journey. The Dakini is a deity, visualized and invoked, as well as a 'spiritual midwife' who is said to enable a practitioner's sadhana shift from a purely intellectual pursuit to a more experiential way of understanding.

The Dakini principle is dynamic and direct and is thought to inspire and guide one towards true realization unfettered by punditry when she assumes the form of a teacher. The Dakini principle has thus come to be expressed in real women throughout the history of Buddhism in Tibet, such as Yeshe Tsogyal and Khandro Urgyen Tsomo (the Great Dakini of Tsurphu), whose reincarnation I am currently conversing with.

Of late, dakinis have received much attention from dharma women activists who are keen to populate the pantheon of Tibetan Buddhism with female deities and role models. Dakinis also seem to fulfil a need for the exotic and the esoteric for some, and they have been romanticized in a way that reminds one of Shambhala, which might have been indicative of a spiritual state or practice, but was turned into a mysterious fantasy of a 'lost kingdom' populated by perfect creatures.

Quite understandably, then, Khandro Rinpoche is impatient with the kind of press dakinis have been getting recently. 'I think the term has become commercialized,' she says. 'It has happened through the ages and is not just a Western influence. Many religions have been misused for personal gains, including Buddhism. You like a woman and you say, "You are like a dakini." And how many women have spun when they heard that. I have a real complaint against that!' she laughs. Clearly, women who behave like fools in love are not in favour with Rinpoche, who would rather they did something useful with themselves, like practise, for instance, instead of swooning to some fantasy of dakini-hood.

She is also critical of attempts to emphasize the gender of dakinis and hold them up as icons for living women. 'Bodhisattvas or dakinis have been given a certain iconographic gender. But Buddhism is so much a non-theistic religion that you have to understand that ultimately, you are going to have to go beyond the personification and refer to the essence. The essence is gender-free. If you need the reference, if a mind that is lesser in understanding needs the reference, then the reference is given in the form of icons. But you have to let it go. In Vajrayana Buddhism you always find two phases—the creation and the completion. Everything is created from emptiness, you visualize and do the mantras and the practice, and it ends again with dissolution into emptiness. The dominant factor is, it begins gender-free and ends gender-free. What you are doing in the interim is a reference that you require at this moment to stabilize your meditation. The practitioner has to know not to get attached to the gender of the wisdom beings.'

From emptiness to emptiness. Like the sand mandala, created with elaborate magnificence and hard work and then effaced. Could we do the same with our gender, creating its experience out of the void that is our true nature, and allowing it to merge back into nothingness when its functionality is no longer required? Could we obliterate the need for all reference points in this way and create the mandala of our lives each day, each moment, anew?

Khandro Rinpoche might be the anti-dakini, the non-khandro, in many ways, but she has some consonance with the ideal whose name she bears in terms of her role as teacher. Today, she is known globally for her facility with interpreting the dharma in a modern idiom, while keeping its essence intact. She is committed to helping her students realize their innate potential, and is not averse to pushing them out of their comfort zone towards a more intense practice. Says Mary Pat Brynner, the administrator of Khandro Rinpoche's annual Baltimore retreat in the US, 'She expects us all to believe that we can be enlightened in a lifetime and she works with people toward that goal. So I suppose some might call it "tough". But in a lot of ways it's really stronger encouragement and higher expectations of our abilities to stay on the path and be committed to it.'*

---

* From 'Khandro Rinpoche's Tough Love', by Trish Deitch Rohrer, *Shambhala Sun*, July 2004.

I share with Rinpoche the fact that most women gurus I have met are recast as mothers in their students' minds because of their role in nurturing their spiritual lives. She laughs out loud at the possibility of anybody thinking of her as a 'Mataji'. 'I don't think they really see me as a mother! Even in Tibetan Buddhism we have had exceptionally great masters who have been like mothers. But I don't consider myself that. Probably it has something to do with having been brought up in a monastic situation with monks. I see in myself a much more regimental, disciplined teacher, and though I don't think of myself as very strict, commonly I am regarded as a strict teacher. People say, unless you are serious about doing it correctly, don't go to her. I find this quite funny but also think that if by being straight and precise I can help people in their practice, then that is fine.'

You'd rather be strict than motherly, I say. 'Yes, because ultimately it is about training people to practise properly. I don't think people should practise because they love me or feel good about being near me. I think they should practise because they find value in the teachings. The moment they get attached to the teacher, they have gone in the wrong direction.'

Eastern wisdom traditions emphasize a substantive difference between a guru and a teacher—a guru not just imparts knowledge, he or she commits to 'taking the student across the ocean of samsara' by providing the boat of dharma and true understanding. The bond between a guru and student is deep and intuitive, like a magnified mother–child relationship but, crucially, without the clinging. The guru is thought to teach in numerous direct and indirect ways, always steadily working towards clarifying the student's understanding and thus enabling shifts in consciousness. No matter how many lifetimes it might take, the guru is said to never abandon a student he or she has taken on, and will reincarnate, if needed, for their benefit.

Would Rinpoche see herself as a guru, then, or a teacher? Or both?

Neither, it seems.

'I believe that guru devotion is very important because that is the essence of Vajrayana Buddhism. I personally don't encourage any student to see me as the guru—it is something I have always spoken about. I don't think that in my life the responsibility I need or can have is the responsibility of being a guru. We should, in our generation, the younger people teaching dharma today, have this sense of being a spiritual friend and guide people on the path of practice. But being a guru is a very, very high responsibility. The people we are and the amount of understanding we have, we don't have the quality of being a guru.'

A spiritual friend is what is called a *kalyana mitra* in Buddhism, one who is a friend on the path, a co-walker almost. This is a crucial insight into the way Khandro Rinpoche sees herself and the relationship she seeks with those that come to her. She makes no promises of lifetimes of guidance, nor does she rivet herself to her students and take on all their issues as a guru would. 'I always say, I can teach you dharma and show you where you can go, but ultimately you have to find your own guru. Guru principle is very precious, a very profound relationship that you establish. You can't say, "Are you my guru?" If you are asking that question, then you are not ready to find one. Someone can't say, "I am your guru" or "I am not your guru". The guru–shishya relationship is beyond expression and the need to question and answer. It has to be an unquestionable, unhesitating sense of feeling that doesn't have to be exchanged through dialogue or conversation. It is a profound, intrinsic connection that you build that requires no room for confirmation or denial.'

Rinpoche says she doesn't consider anybody her student and that whatever she knows of the dharma, she shares with others. Ultimately, they must practise on their own to really understand its essence. It is a moment of epiphany—she really sees herself as a seeker too, I think, not as somebody who has 'arrived' and can therefore help others arrive. Perhaps there *is* no arrival in this path of the open fist, where life refreshes itself in each moment, and where memory of the past, a definite present or a planned future are all illusions, like sculptures of smoke. Where does one go, then, where can one go? Who seeks what? In the mandala of the open, sky-like being, nothing comes nothing goes. Everything is here, perfect.

In this, as in so much else, Khandro Rinpoche has been inspired by her father's attitude, which is one of immense humility. 'When I studied with Rinpoche, he said that a teacher must always think that his shoulder is a footrest of the student. He has to allow each student to use his shoulder as a stepping stone to a higher level. The moment a teacher says, you have to sit lower than me, he is not fulfilling his responsibility. I would like to believe that as much as possible I have taken this seriously—allowing students to use what they can and go forward.'

This ideal actually subverts the dominant and perhaps flawed perception that exists of a guru who requires *seva* to be rendered unto him or her; here, the guru is the one who offers his or her being and knowledge in the service of students. The guru's position has been misunderstood, and misused as well by unscrupulous individuals, and this has created a bubble of negativity in the minds of many regarding what must be one of the most sacred relationships in the human bandwidth. Though she may not want to be slotted as a guru, Khandro Rinpoche and others like her are attempting to dispel some of these false notions through their own conduct and integrity in the way they deal with their students. This is one of the reasons why she is resistant to the idea of 'fan-clubs' forming around spiritual teachers and the dependency that arises as a result of the 'feel-good' factor that nearness to a guru brings the student.

'You can't get stuck with one person because there is a danger, especially in today's world, of spiritual materialism, of teachers creating fan clubs,' she says vehemently. 'That is the downfall of the teacher, spirituality and the student. I absolutely resist this. My whole philosophy has been that I teach as much as I can, whatever I know. But after that, I don't stay with the students. I don't socialize with them, I don't keep in touch with them, I don't write to them or call. So that there is no emotional bonding that can make them lose track if they get attached to the person and the feel-good aspect of it. The connection has to be with the truth of the dharma and absolute freedom. When they hear the teachings and go back and practise, it is their freedom what they do after that. I like to keep it that way.'

This is her way of diffusing the scourge of 'spiritual materialism' that uses new media like television and the internet to advertise itself, and has led to the creation of a category of 'spiritual executives' for whom this is another business option that plays off a genuine need people have for a panacea for their problems. Khandro Rinpoche denounces this trend, saying that the biggest problem spirituality faces today is that of commercialization. When I ask her for a definition of spiritual materialism, she says, 'When teachers don't practise their teachings, or when they try to take advantage of what they are teaching. Basically, it is dealing with spirituality as if it were a material thing. From the student's perspective, spiritual materialism comes when you listen to the teachings but pick only those you like. You listen but don't use your intelligence. And if you do it because it is fashionable.'

Does she think this could have been a problem that began with Buddhism's journey to the West? Where for some time there was a danger of it becoming another one of the therapies and feel-good pills that lined the shelves of the spiritual marketplace? 'I am not so worried about the West because the West has begun to learn the dharma well,' she says. 'Whenever there is good learning and understanding and learned people, spiritual materialism or any other problem becomes weaker. What I am worried about is spiritual materialism in the East. There is a fascination with fame, popularity and somehow people have begun to associate being busy with being successful. That's very dangerous. When renunciates become "executive renunciates", there is a problem. Spirituality then becomes worldly. You can't teach someone to go beyond the world by being worldly yourself!'

It is dusk as I step out of the monastery. My imaginary feminine Buddha-to-come appears curvy and confident on the forehead of the giant stupa at Mindrolling. I don't know yet that a year from this moment, the Mahasiddha of Mindrolling will pass into *parinirvana* (ultimate extinguishment) and, in the absence of a male heir, Khandro Rinpoche's activities, as well as her name, will expand to include her connection with Mindrolling. That when I actually sit down to write this chapter, she will be newly referred to as 'Her Eminence Mindrolling Jetsun Khandro Rinpoche', merging the 'Rinpoche' and 'Jetsunma' aspects of her being, placing her in an even more prominent place of authority in the stuffy patriarchal world of Tibetan Buddhism.

During our conversation, I had asked her about the requisite male dharma heir to bridge between the old and the new. 'If I was born the son, it would have been easier,' she admitted. Certain 'people' had complained when she decided to ordain as a nun, which wasn't required for her to fulfil her duties as a reincarnate. But she wanted to, she said defiantly, because of the work she could accomplish on behalf of nuns in both the Kagyu and the Mindrolling lineages.

Even if Khandro Rinpoche's current eminence at Mindrolling is a kind of a keeping-the-seat-warm endeavour, it will do much to expand the horizon of possibilities available to all women in the dharma. The wheel of change has begun to turn. The exact shape and direction of that change will become apparent in the years and decades to come.

We are back to where we began this book. Somewhere in the shadow of the mighty Himalayas, not far away from the Ganga. I set my bag of questions beside me, stretch out my dusty feet and look out into the horizon where earth becomes sky, mountain becomes cloud, time touches eternity.

With a teacher, a spiritual friend, like Khandro Rinpoche, I think I might learn to look past my gender, that which conditions so much of the path, but which is ultimately also a conditioned construct to confront and, ultimately, to let go. It can be used, certainly, as a means to an end; it may even give me some unique tools. But then, the boat has to be left behind on the shore. The pot must crack, allowing its waters to merge in the larger ocean. As much as gender can be refined and honed and used skilfully in the stages of the spiritual journey, it must cease to matter at some point, releasing the mind of its particular conditioning.

From a dusty twilight, the deep blue-black night blossoms out, embracing the horizon into a secret enchantment. Why do I feel that this approaching night is feminine? Why do I think she will tell me tales of Kali, of Tara, of the khandros of Tibet, of the dakinis of earth and sky? Clearly, the pot won't crack tonight. For I still feel like a woman, with a foot on the path, sincere and determined to walk on, looking for women who went before me, whose lotus feet have imprinted this sacred ground, somewhere.

Will I find more stories of silent revolutions of the spirit? Will there be more rebels and freespirits, more songs of sadhvis and seers, more diamond-edged wisdom to gather?

Where will the Ganga of my seeking flow next?

Bibliography

Alexander, Ram, *Death Must Die*, Indica Books, Varanasi, 2000

Allione, Tsultrim, *Women of Wisdom*, Snow Lion Publications, New York, 2000

Swami Amritaswarupananda Puri, *Mata Amritanandamayi: A Biography*, Mata Amritanandamayi Math, Amritapuri

Brown, C. MacKenzie, *The Triumph of the Goddess: The Canonical Models and Theological Issues of the Devi-Bhagavata Purana*, State University of New York Press, New York, 1991

Swami Chidananda Saraswati, *Peace*, Parmarth Niketan Ashram, Rishikesh, 2000

Coburn, Thomas P., *Encountering the Goddess: A Translation of the Devi-Mahatmya and a Study of its Interpretation*, State University of New York Press, New York, 1991

Cornell, Judith, *Amma: Healing the Heart of the World*, William Morrow & Company, New York, 2001

Deitch Rohrer, Trish, 'Khandro Rinpoche's Tough Love',

Shambhala Sun, Nova Scotia, Canada, 2004

Frug, Mary Joe, 'A Postmodern Feminist Legal Manifesto (An Unfinished Draft)', *Harvard Law Review*, Vol. 105, No. 5., March, 1992

Gatwood, Lynn, *Devi and the Spouse Goddess: Women, Sexuality and Marriages in India,* Manohar, New Delhi, 1985

Gupta, Mahendranath, *The Gospel of Sri Ramakrishna*, Sri Ramakrishna Math, Chennai, 2005

Hecker, Hellmuth, translated by Ayya Khema, *Buddhist Women at the Time of the Buddha,* Buddhist Publication Society, Kandy, 1982

Hesse, Hermann, *Siddhartha,* Bantam Books, US, 1951

ed. Jane Hirshfield, *Women in Praise of the Sacred: 43 Centuries of Spiritual Poetry,* HarperCollins, New York, 1994

Hirshman, Mitu, 'Negotiating the "Modern": Sri Sarada Devi and Feminism', *Eternal Mother,* Sri Sarada Math, Kolkata, 2004

de Kalbermatten, Gregoire, *The Third Advent,* Penguin, New Delhi, 2004

Krishna, Gopi, *Kundalini: Evolutionary Energy in Man,* Robinson & Watkins, London, 1971

Lowenkopf, Anne, 'The Mother Goddess', *Living Wisdom: Vedanta in the West*, edited by Pravrajika Vrajaprana, Vedanta Press, California, 1994

Mackenzie, Vicki, *Cave in the Snow,* Bloomsbury, London, 1998

Milarepa, *Sixty Songs of Milarepa,* translated by Garma C.C. Chang, introduced by Bhikkhu Khantipalo, Buddhist Publication Society, Kandy, 1966

Pechilis, Karen, *The Graceful Guru: Hindu Female Gurus in India and the United States,* Oxford University Press, New York, 2004

Pravrajika Vedantaprana, 'Sarada Shodashi', *Eternal Mother,* Sri Sarada Math, Kolkata, 2004

Swami Saradeshananda, translated by J.N. Dey, *The Mother as I saw Her,* Sri Ramakrishna Math, Madras, 1982

Spivak, Gayatri, 'Empowering Women?', *Environment* Vol. XXXVII. i, 1995

Srivastava, C.P., *A Life of Truth in Politics*, Oxford University Press, New Delhi, 1995

Swami Tapasyananda, *Sri Sarada Devi, The Holy Mother*, Sri Ramakrishna Math, Madras, 1958

Therigatha: Verses of the Elder Nuns, translation from http://www.accesstoinsight.org/tipitaka/kn/thig/index.html accessed on 01-04-2010

Tsomo, Karma Lekshe, 'Mahaprajapati's Legacy', *Buddhist Women Across Cultures*, Sri Satguru Publications, Delhi, 2000

Walters, John, *Mind Unshaken: A Modern Approach to Buddhism*, Rider and Company, London, 1971

Wetzel, Sylvia, *Heart of the Lotus: Women and Buddhism*, translated from the German *Das Herz des Lotos. Frauen und Buddhismus* by Jane Anhold, from http://www.sylvia-wetzel.de/english/ImagineYouAreMale.htm. as accessed on 01-04-2010

Acknowledgements

I owe the greatest debt of gratitude to the spiritual gurus, teachers, aspirants and seekers who spent time with me, spoke with me, and patiently answered my questions, a lot of which were deeply personal to their lives and spiritual quests. Even though all of them could not be individually featured in the book due to paucity of space, they contributed significantly to the development of the core ideas that make up this book.

I am grateful to those who helped me gain access to the women I interviewed and, in some instances, contacted me with ideas of women I could meet when they heard that I was working on this book. Without these gracious facilitators, too many to name, there would have been no conversations and, consequently, no book.

A big thank you to Rajiv Mehrotra and Dr Meenakshi Gopinath who, through the WISCOMP (Women in Security, Conflict Management and Peace) initiative of the Foundation for Universal Responsibility of His Holiness the Dalai Lama, provided crucial support in the form of a grant, which enabled me to engage full time in my research. They also gave sustained encouragement to my efforts through the years it took me to research and write this book, for which I am very grateful.

A special thanks to Dr Kavita A. Sharma, Director, India International Centre, New Delhi, and a spiritual seeker, for her ready acceptance of my request to contribute a foreword, and for writing one that captures the spirit of this book. I am honoured to have Dr Sharma's insightful words open the book.

At HarperCollins India, I am very grateful to Karthika V.K., who believed in the book strongly enough to publish it. Thanks also to Neelini Sarkar for editing the manuscript, and to Shuka Jain for creating a beautiful cover.

And most importantly, two people who were as indispensable to my work on this book as they are to my life, who contributed ideas, engaged me in discussions that refreshed my perspective, and supported and nourished me throughout. They are my dear mother, Champa Chopra, and my beloved husband, Shakti Maira, who apart from his invaluable advice and critique, offered an exquisite painting from his 'Ganga as Grace' series for the cover. I cannot express adequately in words the deep gratitude I feel towards them.